HERMAN MELVILLE

The Tragedy of Mind

HERMAN MELVILLE

The Tragedy of Mind

William Ellery Sedgwick

NEW YORK

RUSSELL & RUSSELL · INC

1962

THIS BOOK IS DEDICATED

TO THE MEMORY OF

NATHALIE SEDGWICK COLBY

FOREWORD

This book was found on my husband's desk at the time of his death two years ago. He had entirely completed it, but the manuscript needed a certain amount of cutting and editing which I knew he would have done before turning it over to the publisher. This editing I have completed with the advice of Theodore Spencer, who has been unfailingly helpful throughout. I am also indebted to John H. Finley, Jr. and F. O. Mathiessen for reading the manuscript and making suggestions.

Students of Melville will notice that certain of Melville's works, especially *Benito Cereno,* are not here discussed. But since my husband intended the book to be a study of Melville from a particular point of view, rather than an exhaustive treatment, and since I never heard him mention these works in connection with it, he obviously did not consider them relevant to his purpose.

The quotations, which are mostly from Melville's works, are very numerous and form an integral part of the flow of the book. It seemed to me that page references would be interrupting and unnecessary, and I have therefore left them out. The quotations, however, have all been carefully checked.

Sarah Cabot Sedgwick

May 9, 1944

CONTENTS

HERMAN MELVILLE

The Tragedy of Mind

CHAPTER ONE

Introductory

I T WILL DO very well to begin this study of the works of Herman Melville by quoting from a letter of his to Nathaniel Hawthorne, written when Melville was bringing *Moby Dick* to its overwhelming conclusion and when his name was known around in virtue of his first five books, *Typee, Omoo, Mardi, Redburn,* and *White Jacket,* published in that order. It is not, however, because of the date of the letter that I refer to it here, but on account of a quality it shows, which, if comprehended rightly, will lead as directly as possible to the fountain-head of the peculiar force and character of Melville's works. In this letter Melville wrote, "All Fame is patronage. Let me be infamous: there is no patronage in *that.* What reputation H. M. has is horrible. Think of it! To go down to posterity is bad enough, any way; but to go down as a 'man who lived among cannibals!'—" why, what is to be made of that? Melville, as it happened, had lived among cannibals, a fact that might be arresting about any man. But the mention of it by Melville about himself strikes with a various meaning which leads off in many directions. For one thing, the thought occurs that Melville was having a little fun at Hawthorne's expense; for what, in all truth, were cannibals of flesh and blood to a man who knew, like Melville and not quite like Hawthorne, that a man can be visited at his own fire-side by thoughts that eat his heart alive?

That this presentiment anyway was in Melville's mind is borne out by what follows. For he suddenly animadverts on Solomon, whose *Ecclesiastes* he called in *Moby Dick* "the truest of all books" and "the fine hammered steel of woe." In the letter to Hawthorne he adds, "I read Solomon more and more, and every time see deeper and deeper and unspeakable meanings in him." Then follow some words on his own development which I shall come to later, and after these Melville goes on to say that in reading some of Goethe's sayings, so worshipped by Goethe's votaries, he has come across this, *"Live in the all."* That is to say, as Melville explains, suppose one's separate identity is wretched; very well; just get out of yourself and expand and feel the tinglings of the universal life that is in the flowers, the planets and the fixed stars. "What nonsense! Here is a fellow with a raging toothache. 'My dear boy,' Goethe says to him, 'you are sorely afflicted with that tooth; but you must *live in the all,* and then you will be happy!' As with all great genius, there is an immense deal of flummery in Goethe. . . ." Melville finishes the letter almost at once after this and signs it, but adds, between two postscripts, that there is some truth to this "all feeling," and Hawthorne, he imagines, must have felt it "lying on the grass on a warm summer's day. Your legs seem to send out shoots into the earth. Your hair feels like leaves upon your head. This is the *all* feeling. But what plays the mischief with the truth is that men will insist upon the universal application of a temporary feeling or opinion."

Whatever else one might go on to say about it, this letter is the expression of a high-spirited personality. What waywardness is here, one might add, to turn from savages to Solomon and from the sere wisdom of *Ecclesiastes* to the exuberant mysticism of Goethe's votaries, and all this in the shortest compass, and then to stop cosmic mysticism in its tracks by presenting the particular physical fact of a toothache at it. Yet waywardness is not the word for these abrupt transitions, these steep ascents and declivities of thought. For they are not wilful; that is to say, they are not wilfully of the mind but of a deeper and more inward nature. The quality that deserves our closest attention here I cannot do better for the moment than call an amazing ductibility. At the end of the letter Melville reflects on the mysterious ebbs and flows of human consciousness.

But the entire letter shows the ductibility which is of consciousness itself and which all the mental reflections upon it cannot show by themselves.

This quality which is so deeply present in all Melville's characteristic writings often gives them an air of chaos when viewed at close range. But this air of chaos disappears when they are seen from a point of vantage which commands a comprehensive view of them. In this respect they are like the earth's surface. Seen close to, at this point or that, it presents a wayward variety of features, an inconclusive stringing out of different altitudes and configurations. But apprehending it from a proper vantage point, the mind becomes alive to the slow even curve that at all points and in all directions completes the great globe of the whole earth.

The only means of commanding a sufficiently comprehensive view of Melville's works at the outset of this study is to see them in the perspective of such final questions as, What is truth? What is the nature of human life? How are we as human beings to accommodate ourselves to the external creation in which we find ourselves? Only in the perspective of these final questions can we frame the interest of Melville's works as a whole, to which, as I see it, every interesting detail leads in one surprising way or another.

I recognise that there is great danger in such an initial view. For these questions, thus baldly put, are what we have come to expect from the earnest, naive bore, who is not the least of our social problems. We all know his kind and most of us, because they flatter our vanity, have made pets of one or two such, and like to have them around, and are even inconsiderate enough to want our friends to like them with us. They are rather soothing, the truth is, and not only to our vanity. Their boringness comes over us at times like a pleasant after-dinner sleepiness. And yet, for all this, we fear their entrance into the conversation much as we might fear the misconduct of our dog, who is not yet house-broken, when he visits with us in the library of an acquaintance. We fear their insistences that will take the ground right out from under the feet of the conversation and close all the doors to those tentative explorations which are the delight of social intercourse. "What *is* life?" or "What *is* truth?" the earnest bore will ask, and we know the game is up and, losing ourselves in picking invisible lint from our sleeves or slapping the dust from our shoes with furious attention, we think desperately of an excuse to get him out of the house and back to his home as quickly and with as little pain as possible.

Unfortunately, the bore's mistake is deep-seated. It is not that the questions he asks should not press themselves upon us and even intimate themselves in the conversation we enjoy. But the bore, in the very act of asking these final questions about life, drops the only thread we can have to the answers. He drops the realities of living so that his questions are ghostly externalizations, hanging in a void and looking with anxious scrutiny just nowhere. Or, to put it another way, he is determined to put a bead on life and, in consequence, sees only the slightest fraction of his mark. With but one or two facets to his nature at best, the perspective in which he sees things is as simple and smooth as the shape of an egg, and as innocent of a sense of implications as an egg appears to be. He cannot leave it to the sideways drift of the meaning of things or their somehow circling implications to reveal, if not the truth about life, what at any rate is truthful to it.

Nevertheless, I think I am justified in raising in connection with Herman Melville just such final questions as the earnest bore will ask when the first pause in a conversation offers. Moreover, in going on to say that Melville raises them himself I do not feel called upon to argue wherein Melville and the bore differ from each other. That would hardly make a promising beginning for this discussion, and I would be putting myself under the most unnecessary handicap. It so happens that Melville was earnest and, as it may well seem to some people, that he was naive. He was certainly a most immoderate and importunate seeker of the truth. But—and here we take leave of all that blights in the nature of a bore, as also all that soothes— his was a drastic and many-sided personality. That Melville had lived among the cannibals in the South Seas may stand for one facet of his personality; his active nature and his gift for rendering it which made such an impression on the Hawthornes one evening in their parlor in Lenox. The story is that Melville told impromptu about a fight he had seen between some savages and described how one huge savage among them attacked his enemies fiercely with a heavy club. Melville gone home, and Mr. and Mrs. Hawthorne left to themselves, she asked where the club was "with which Mr. Melville was laying about him so?" Hawthorne thought he had taken it away with him, while Mrs. Hawthorne was quite certain he had left it somewhere. There had been no club. Melville's realistic account had produced the illusion of one flying around in his hands.

To be put beside this is another impression, diametrically opposite it will seem, which five or six years later Hawthorne wrote down in his journal after Melville had made a short visit at his house outside Liverpool: "He stayed with us from Tuesday till Thursday; and, on the intervening day, we took a pretty long walk together, and sat down in a hollow among the sandhills, (sheltering ourselves from the high, cool wind) and smoked a cigar. Melville, as he always does, began to reason of Providence and futurity, and of everything that lies beyond human ken, and informed me that he had 'pretty much made up his mind to be annihilated'; but still he does not seem to rest in that anticipation and, I think, will never rest until he gets hold of a definite belief. It is strange how he persists—and has persisted ever since I knew him, and probably long before—in wandering to and fro over these deserts, as dismal and monotonous as the sandhills amid which we were sitting. He can neither believe, nor be comfortable in his unbelief; and he is too honest and courageous not to try to do one or the other."

This was five years after *Moby Dick* was finished and Melville was on his way to the Holy Land, to make a pilgrimage there. Had "pretty much made up his mind to be annihilated," his own words which Hawthorne quotes, have a characteristic fascination of diverse implications, but there is not time to pursue them. What is salient in Hawthorne's impression is Melville's intellectual energy, driven by an exigency of the human mind not to rest until it has fixed itself on finality and is in possession of the ultimate truth; and, as emphatic as his speculative energy, a religious capacity that he felt like a thirst in his vitals. He would not rest in a religious faith which discounted his intellectual findings. On the other hand, he would not rest in an attitude of skepticism, by which, as he believed, a man demeaned his human nature. Accordingly, his mind was forever tacking as if against a powerful headwind, now in the direction of religious feeling and now in that of religious disbelief; and on either tack his mind was taut to a passion of sincerity.

Melville projecting himself in adventurous action and gulping down vivid sensuous impressions in the remote Pacific; Melville as actively pursuing the dictates of his intellectual nature, over deserts of thought, as Hawthorne has it;—here one might agree was an extraordinary spread of life, yet at the same time questioning if Melville was not the kind of man who only comes to life in lonely extremities of being. The best retort comes in the form of impressions picked up anywhere from Melville's own letters: They show him, not isolated from the daily world, but soaked in the details of common life. For example, he wrote after a dinner in Pittsfield with two litterateurs of the day, "We cracked the Champagne, & our first glass (all round the table) was Mr. Duyckinck & Mr. Mathews. But the cigars!—The oriental looking box! and the Antilles smell of them! and the four different thrones & dominations of bundles, all harmonizing together like the Iroquois." And one or two impressions of Melville on his farm in the Berkshires will complete the decisive outlines of his personality. "Do you know how I pass my time?—I rise at eight—thereabouts—and go to my barn—say good morning to the horse and give him his breakfast. (It goes to my heart to give him a cold one, but it can't be helped.) Then, pay a visit to my cow—cut up a pumpkin or two for her, and stand by to see her eat it—for it's a pleasant sight to see a cow move her jaws—she does it so mildly and with such a sanctity." "It has been a most glowing and Byzantine day—the heavens reflect the hues of the October apples in the orchard—nay, the heavens themselves looking so ripe and ruddy, that it must be harvest-home with the angels. . . ."

Mere scope of experience and personality as I have been indicating it is not, however, of final importance. For—as has become a commonplace of characterization—there are some rare people who can "see a world in a grain of sand and a heaven in a wild flower," and without some of this intensity a personality, even a many-sided one, will have little effect. It will be departmented and inert. This kind of intensity is the possession, or self-possession, of one's free consciousness to bestow on any object. Free, I call it, because the inner life of consciousness is kept free from the external order of things, and, therefore, there is a free exchange between all the facets of personality, regardless of the character of the object in question. Melville, of course, in addition to extraordinary scope, was gifted with this intensity of being. The most disparate things and considerations associated freely in his mind, like Solomon and cannibals, Byzantium and his own apple tree, by way of heaven; cows and sanctity. Opposites like these came together and by their association took on new dimensions of meaning and gained a greater currency for expression in all directions. Whatever the object of his attention, that object he informed with the freedom of his own consciousness. Hence that ductibility I have noticed; hence too those mutations and permutations, like deep sea-changes, between near and far, the familiar and the sublime, the abstract and the concrete, which invigorate so many of his pages.

I began by calling the characteristic in question intensity. Yet it is of a very passive aspect. Perhaps to call it feminine would be to give the fullest view of it in a word. So strongly passive is it that it becomes absorptive; and in Melville it sometimes reminds one of a similar side to Walt Whitman. Was it an aspect of character that they both came by from the Dutch inheritance which they shared? At any rate, this trait among others in Melville was caught to the life in a description by Mrs. Hawthorne, so perceptive that it should endear her to everyone interested in the author of *Moby Dick.* She was not sure, Mrs. Hawthorne wrote, that he was not a very great man; a man "with life to his fingertips!"—when talking, "full of gesture and force," losing himself in his subject. "Once in a while his animation gives place to a singularly quiet expression . . . an indrawn, dim look. . . . It is a strange, lazy glance, but with a power in it quite unique. It does not seem to penetrate through you, but to take you into itself."

As the anecdote about his story in the Hawthornes' parlor will testify, Melville could mould his being in the form of an action. He could also mould his being in the form of a thought, so that his most imponderable thoughts could take on the same power of illusion as such tangible objects of description as a club in the hands of an angry savage or a boat hook levelled at an enemy in his own. This is borne out briefly in a letter in which a reference to a friend's having gone mad takes on the full measure and weight of Melville's realizations. "Poor Hoffman," he wrote, "This going mad of a friend or acquaintance comes straight home to every man who feels his soul in him,—which but few men do. For in all of us lodges the same fuel to light the same fire. And he who has never felt, momentarily, what madness is has but a mouthful of brains."

What goes on in those words deserves the closest attention. The apprehension of a particular fact runs to a generalization about the nature of life and the perilous stuff of which it is compacted. The main generalization sprouts others. And it and its offshoots all spring up in obedience to the mind's need to see things comprehensively— with a view, it may be, to finality. But what more has to be noticed at once is that the generalization, while running out, does not run away from the realities of living. It does not take off into a region of impalpable abstractions where the mind goes naked and alone. In Melville's hands it takes on a concrete image in virtue of which, as by a contrary force to the mind's instinctive impulse to get a bird's-eye view of things, it is pressed upon life and gets lodged in the innermost folds of sensation. Melville's sensuous being has been poured into the action of the mind. "In all of us lodges the same fuel to light the same fire"—what immediacy to our sentient lives is here! And from this form, as it happens, some three years afterwards it passed into the tragic exclamation in *Pierre,* the book that came right after *Moby Dick:* "Ah, muskets the gods have made to carry infinite combustions, and yet made them of clay." And here, again, there is the same ambidexterity, the same equal availability for the intake of our senses and for our intellectual comprehension of things.

And so it is with Melville's works as a whole. His mind has its commanding place in them. Importunate, he was forever precipitating himself against the ultimate truth of creation; reasoning, as Hawthorne said, "Of Providence and futurity, and of everything that lies beyond human ken";—very much like the intellectuals among Milton's fallen angels who

> *reason'd high*
> *Of providence, foreknowledge, will and fate,*
> *Fix'd fate, free will, foreknowledge absolute. . . .*

To Melville, as to the angels, the ultimate truth presented itself in the form of the age-old questions of Christian theology. Like them, too, he "found no end, in wand'ring mazes lost." If it be urged that these questions were antiquated and could lead nowhere, and that the mind that occupied itself with them could only find itself in a void, the objection is to be brushed aside as trivial. For, to go no further, not the forms in which the truth seemed to present itself, but his mind's urge out of its own deepest and universal nature to get at the truth was the source of vital interest.

Yet that is not half the truth about Melville that I must insist on here. "What is truth?" "What is the nature of life and creation?" These are generalizations which Melville fairly shouts; and at times it is as if he had creation by its mysterious axis and were trying to

hold it up for an answer. Asking these final questions, he did not
divorce himself from the realities of life. Nor did he find himself
like Shelley, "pinnacled dim in the intense inane." He did not raise
these questions but that, as if by the same inclusive stress of his
being, his varied experience of life pressed itself home to his
senses. It is as if the questions and their only possible answers were
flashed out simultaneously. Does he ask what is the truth about
life? At the same instant, as it seems, a broad picture of the world
and many men and many conditions of life spreads itself out before
him. And if we would think of this as a conscious process, then I
might say that while he also tried to put a bead on life, he knew
very well that there was nothing less to this than levelling at the
whole round horizon. For Melville the question was as broad as it
was high, and as concrete as it was abstract.

Nor is this all. The question was as deep as it was broad and
high. For if we can distinguish here between coil and recoil, then
the recoil to his objective questions was not fundamentally a display
of his varied knowledge of the world, although that followed quickly
enough; but it was a realization of the inward reality of life. His
questions, contrary to being an evasion of this, were the means of
realizing it.

Moreover, his varied knowledge and experience of life took on
different aspects under all the different pressures to which it was
subject. It stands in its own objective and literal character in a
story. It assumes the aspect of data with reference to the ultimate
truth. And it becomes the terms in which Melville's realization of
the inward reality of life is set forth. Is it then, one might ask, that
the facts of Melville's experience become symbols? I must answer
that they are certainly put under a pressure in the direction of symbolism. But as symbols they are not like the signs in algebra with
fixed quantities. They share in the nature of the thing they symbolize. If this thing, this inward reality I speak of, is something
more than an abstraction, it is nothing else than consciousness.
Therefore Melville's characteristic symbols have an almost endless

capacity for taking different turns and weights of meaning, according to the endless flux and—across the flux—the ebb and flow, the contractions and dilations, of consciousness.

As if by a reciprocity that balanced on an exigency of his being, while Melville's experience was impressed into the service of his truth-seeking, giving it substance and reality, his experience took on new life, out of the inward realization, which to his objective questioning was as recoil to coil, as systole to diastole. And there is, I believe, still another effect of his importunate truth-seeking on Melville's materials than this general vitalization.

In connection with fiction, if we think of consciousness at all apart from particular acts and motivations, we are likely to think of it as a stream that meanders along, reflecting this and that as chance directs. We think of it as passive, as conditioned by a thousand and one accidents and accidental coincidences. If we think of it as more than passive, then we have in mind that it is responsive, malleable, informing; not lumpish and intractible. Melville's consciousness, as I have been at pains to point out, was richly responsive and malleable. It could mould its entire substance to the form of an action or a thought. Yet it was gifted with a more positive form of exertion. It combined a masculine force with its rich, feminine receptivity. It could impress as well as be impressed, imparting a quality of its own, a timbre, a resonance, a capacity to cohere. Lending itself to the centrifugence of things, it opposed a centripetence of its own. It maintained an independent principle of equilibrium, which shows elusively in a sense of bourne, and in a deep inward revelation of regular alternations and revolutions, like day and night, the ebb and flow of the tide, and the seasons of the year. Captain Ahab and Moby Dick, for instance, pursue each other round and round on the horizon of their ultimate significance. Lending itself to the tangential variety of impressions on all sides, when it came to Melville's deepest creations and most vital symbols, his consciousness impressed itself on them, moulding them to its own realizations of itself.

It was not quite that his consciousness pulled itself up by its bootstraps. More accurately, it was because he did not feel himself in the perspective of things so much as he saw things in the greater perspective of himself; which is to say, he subordinated all things in his mind to his preoccupation with the ultimate truth that lies beyond all things. Reasoning "on all things beyond human ken," as Hawthorne put it, he was brought to realize, as few other men have, a great many things within human ken, and even to realize, in the manner I have just described, what it is that kens. Reasoning high like Milton's angels, instead of like them becoming "in wand'ring mazes lost," he brought himself home to reality and, in the midst of this, brought himself home to himself.

But to look back a moment; the sense of the interdependence of ultimate truth and inward realization, of each being a fulcrum to the other, was fundamental in Melville; it was more a law of his mind than an axiom that he consciously entertained. It is figured in his books in single characters and pairs of intimately related characters, the one outward looking, the other more inward looking. And crossing this is another fundamental stress of Melville's thinking, the sense that outward truth and inward reality are opposite extremes and that a means of balance is necessary to reconcile the one to the other and serve as a transit between them. He was inclined to identify the means of balance with outward reality—with things as we all see them in the same common daylight—and it followed from this that he felt instinctively that the effective use of a fact as symbol, having both outward and inward reference, depended on the preservation of its objective reality. Here, I think, we just glimpse the secret of why it is that we see things in Melville's books in a wonderful manifold perspective, at the same time that they present such an appearance of matter-of-fact reality. But these are ultimate considerations about Melville which would be better left for adequate illustration when the time comes.

2

It will seem at first sight a far cry from Melville's first book, *Typee,* so largely a straightforward story of adventure, to *Moby Dick* with all its coils and different levels of meaning. For that matter, while Melville was at work on *Moby Dick,* it appeared to him that he had left *Typee* way behind him. "To go down to posterity is bad enough, any way; but to go down as a 'man who lived among the cannibals'!" So he seems to dismiss his first book; adding, it will be remembered, that he was reading Solomon and finding "deeper and deeper and unspeakable meanings in him." From *Typee* to *Moby Dick* it seemed at the moment all the way from cannibals to Solomon. Yet the two books were not completely sundered, as another look at Melville's letter to Hawthorne and a glance at *Moby Dick* will amply show. "My development," Melville wrote, "has been all within a few years past. . . . Until I was twenty-five, I had no development at all. From my twenty-fifth year I date my life. Three weeks have scarcely passed, at any time between then and now, that I have not unfolded within myself."

As it happens, Melville was twenty-five when he wrote *Typee;* some six years later, when he wrote this letter, he was finishing *Moby Dick.* In the earlier book, to be sure, there is nothing intimated of the acrid wisdom of *Ecclesiastes* which was a presiding influence over *Moby Dick.* In *Moby Dick,* however, we have Solomon and cannibals cheek by jowl. Queequeg, a happy-go-lucky cannibal, with a pleasant sort of healthy animal sagacity, is perhaps the one lovable character in the whole book. He has an important place in the story. He also embodies the wisdom of Solomon, "There is nothing better for a man, than that he should eat and drink, and that he should make his soul enjoy good in his labour. . . . He that observeth the wind shall not sow; and he that regardeth the clouds shall not reap . . . of making many books

there is no end; and much study is a weariness to the flesh." It was
also from a different response to Queequeg and his like in temperament that Melville was moved to write that not the man who
"throughout a care-free lifetime swears by Rabelais as passing wise,
and therefore jolly;—not that man is fitted to sit down on tomb-
stones, and break the green damp mould with unfathomably
wondrous Solomon."

Thus we come to see that in the six years of growth and development between *Typee* and *Moby Dick*, it was not that Melville had
passed on from cannibals to Solomon—there had been no such
break. Rather, in the unfolding within himself of which he wrote
to Hawthorne, his consciousness had come to comprehend them
both, so that they no longer stood as opposite poles in a meaningless external relationship but had assumed the capacities toward
one another of an organic relationship. It is what I have spoken
of before. The one has helped to a fuller realization of the other.
Each is a hammer to the other's nail to drive it home.*

Moreover, it is plain that the ductibility that I began by men-
tioning was not for a moment only, or for the few moments it took
Melville to dash off a letter. It went on for years. It went on from

* It is the opinion of the author of the most extensive work on Melville to
appear recently that the subjective element in his works is of little account;—
is, for that matter, and always has been, a decided liability to his reputation,
and constitutes a real setback to the intrinsic value of his books. Melville's
popularity, writes Mr. Charles Roberts Anderson, "was not based upon the
overwrought satire of *Mardi*, the sailor metaphysics of *Moby Dick*, or the
philosophico-nonsensical ambiguities of *Pierre*. And the popular judgment
seems today to be a sound one. The survival value of Melville's reputation lies
in the fact he was the literary discoverer of the South Seas. *Typee, Omoo,
White Jacket* and *Moby Dick* (as a romance of the sea and not as "a hideous
and intolerable allegory") have been all along his most popular books; and, as
literature, they are beyond question his best." With Mr. Anderson's opinion, in
so far as it is a critical judgment, I disagree emphatically, and I shall take a
wholly opposite point of view in this study. Moreover, it appears to me incredible that any critic could suppose that without the subjective element in
his works Melville could have assumed his full stature in literature. It is not
Melville's recapitulation of his novel experience, but his resourceful use of it
to body forth his inward sense of being, that makes him the great and
fascinating writer he is.

the year he was twenty-five till the end of his life, so that between *Typee* and posthumous *Billy Budd* one feels a continuous flow in common references with the same special implications.

I shall consider Melville's books as the record, in their innermost recesses, of that unfolding. It is, as I must see it, an unfolding of inward vision, a vision not so much of life as of what it is to be alive, and alive as a complete human being and not a mere two-thirds or three-quarters of one. How much there was, as one might say, to implement that vision I have indicated by the range of Melville's diverse capacities and the interaction between them. These capacities, or different facets of his personality, were like so many lookouts from which he looked around; but closer still, the result of the interaction between them was the warm, plastic substance of his being which poured itself into all the realizations and divinations of his mind. In *Moby Dick* and elsewhere his seeing partook of the substance of his being, and from here I might take a step further and say that the different elements and modes of his being are the salient features which his books have in common. In his narrative drive, for instance, there is the weight of his physical energy; in his vivid word paintings and in his rich and rounded cadences there is the plastic fullness of his instinctive and sensuous nature in repose; and there is the insistent tenor of a man's spiritual and intellectual nature—sometimes on the surface only, in the form of a comment or simple innuendo, sometimes going deeper and giving a new range of meaning to the facts of the story; and sometimes diving to the bottom and driving the whole book before it to its own ends. It is the presence of these elements, in different proportions to be sure, but all always commingling as in a common being, that stamps what is best as also what is most characteristic in Melville's writings.

But to return from the means and resources of Melville's inward vision to the vision itself: it comes full circle or full globe in *Moby Dick*. Yet it shows itself in different stages of progress in Melville's books before *Moby Dick*, and always it has the same absorbing

interest. How in the course of Melville's development from book
to book it expands and deepens and rounds itself out is the story
which I am about to tell. The story begins with *Typee* and although
it reaches a certain high point in *Moby Dick,* it does not end there.
"Lord, when shall we be done growing?" wrote Melville to Hawthorne, just when he was feeling *Moby Dick* off his chest at last;
"As long as we have anything more to do, we have done nothing. So,
now, let us add *Moby Dick* to our blessing, and step from that.
Leviathan is not the biggest fish;—I have heard of Krackens." He
went on—to write *Pierre*.

An integral part of the story as I see it, and quite as interesting
as the rest, is the way Melville's inward vision requisitioned all his
varied experiences of life—stretching all the way from genteel best
parlours in up-state New York to sailors' dives in Liverpool, and
from the smelly horror of these to the blue and green earthly paradise of Tahiti,—and how without abating a particle of its reality, or
attenuating it in the slightest degree, his inward vision built itself
into all that solid substance.

The story I am about to tell will have the aspect of an unfolding panorama. Yet if rightly told it should come home with more
force than a slowly lengthening "landscape in the soul," as Melville once referred to a book of Hawthorne's. For Melville did not
stand passive like a pitcher into which his growth as a human being
was slowly poured. In *Moby Dick,* his seeing is hardly to be distinguished from his being. In like manner, in his other books, his
growth is consciously, even wilfully assumed. It becomes an action.
The unfolding within Melville takes on the character of a drama
in which his identity—or soul—is the protagonist. The drama is
familiar enough to us all, and it can be exhibited under the span
of an entire life-time or compressed to the duration of a single day.
Passing from the ruddy, solid-seeming world of very young manhood, the protagonist comes to feel himself assailed and ambushed
by one shattering realization after another of the true nature of
things. Instead of solid, stubborn familiarity, ambiguous strangeness

is all around him. More terrible, he feels this same strangeness inside himself. Hamlet recoils upon his realization of the foul truth of human nature, sprung upon him by his mother's conduct, and he shudders with loathing at the thing he is and that by his common human nature he cannot help but be;—while always, in the outer mysteriousness of things, crouch the terrors of the ultimate truth which may spring upon him in that sleep of death; and which need not, and do not wait till then to spring upon their prey. The horror of the casualness of life is all too palpable and close at hand. Why, as King Lear cries over the body of Cordelia, "Why should a dog, a horse, a rat, have life, and thou no breath at all?" Against such realizations how keep one's equilibrium, how hold fast to one's identity, how cherish and care to preserve one's common humanity?

> Ay, look; high heaven and earth ail from the prime foundation;
> All thoughts to rive the heart are here, and all are vain:
> Horror and scorn and hate and indignation—
> Oh why did I awake? when shall I sleep again?

In another letter, also to Hawthorne, Melville remarked, "There is a certain tragic phase of humanity. . . . We mean the tragedies of human thought in its own unbiassed, native, and profounder workings." That, it seems to me, is one side of the drama of human growth. The other side, the necessary counterpoise to it, Melville unwittingly added in speaking of what he called "the usable truth." "By usable truth, we mean the apprehension of the absolute condition of present things as they strike the eye of the man who fears them not, though they do their worst to him,—a man who, like Russia or the British Empire, declares himself a sovereign nature (in himself) amid the powers of heaven, hell, and earth." The drama of human growth revolves on these two realizations about life; and, rearranging Melville's words to put it as concisely as possible, the dramatic stress lies in the effort to preserve one's equilibrium, "one's sovereign nature in himself," in the teeth of the "unbiassed, native, and profounder workings" of the human mind,—which are nothing less than the tragic necessities the human mind is under, out of its own deepest nature, to apprehend "the absolute condition of present things," regardless of the desolation that this invariably brings.

This is the tragedy of Hamlet and the tragedy of King Lear. It is crucial in the tragedy of Captain Ahab, the one character in American literature whom one would dare name beside Hamlet and Lear. And we can assume it was the tragic drama of Shakespeare himself, as it is the tragic drama of Herman Melville that takes place in his books.

This drama of human growth is much more to the fore and directly before us in Melville's books from first to last than in Shakespeare's plays. It begins with *Typee* and closes with *Billy Budd,* written in the last year of Melville's life, and which stands to *Moby Dick* and *Pierre* in much the same relation in which *The Tempest,* say, stands to Shakespeare's greatest tragedies. A tragic drama I have called it, and I cannot but regard it as that. But I must insist that I do not use the word tragic with reference to Melville's private or domestic life. That will be no concern of mine. The drama in which I am to show Melville as the protagonist has nothing peculiar to him except a particular accentuation and the terms in which it is set forth. It is of the universal nature of human life, and of Herman Melville simply because he had such a deep stake in human life. It is of the substance of the tragedies of Hamlet and King Lear. But to the extent that we have ventured or been forced to let our minds bring the truth home to our hearts, we have all of us shared in it. A "certain tragic phase of humanity . . . the tragedies of human thought," so Melville referred to it. More roundly, as I believe and as I shall undertake to show, it is the tragedy of mind—a tragedy which has been since man first began to reflect among the carnivores, and will be so long as there is any distinction worth making between his race and the termites.

CHAPTER TWO

Typee

THE STORY of *Typee* is so familiar that it needs only the briefest repetition here. It is based, as everyone knows who knows anything about Herman Melville, on his experiences in the course of a long and diversified voyage into the Pacific which began on board a whaler out of New Bedford early in January, 1841, and ended more than three and a half years later, when as a member of the crew of a United States man-of-war Melville sailed into Boston harbor and was honorably discharged. Skipping the voyage out around Cape Horn, *Typee* begins at the point where his ship, the *Dolly* as Melville calls her, turned away from a usual cruising ground of whalers and pointed to Nukaheva, in the group of islands in the South Seas known as the Marquesas. In the harbor of Nukaheva, Melville deserted and with a single companion from the crew, Toby, made his way to the valley of Typee.

According to the story as Melville wrote it, he and Toby struggled desperately to get beyond the mountains to where they would be safe from pursuit. They meant to take refuge among the Happars, a tribe of the island of Nukaheva who enjoyed a reputation for kindness to white strangers. Unluckily, as it turned out, they followed the wrong trail and descended into the valley of Typee, the inhabitants of which were reputed to be cannibals of a particularly virulent stripe, and as their reluctant guests Toby and Melville were pressed to stay. To make matters worse, Melville had hurt his leg in the descent from the steep mountains and the use of it caused him severe pain. In the course of time, Toby was allowed to make his way to the harbor as best he could on the excuse of getting medical assistance for Melville. He never came back. Melville remained alone among the Typees, until, at the end of four months, he made a perilous escape in a little boat sent to fetch him from a whaler that was in need of sailors to man her.

Melville's escape is the high point of the yarn he spins in his first book. As his rescuers rowed to the beach, the Typees, suspecting something was up, gathered around. Melville suddenly broke from his guards and waded to the boat, which put about as soon as he reached her and started for the open sea. The savages, running to a point, plunged into the water and swam out to head her off. One, with a tomahawk in his teeth, almost reached the boat and was on the point of grabbing one of the oars. Melville, whose hands were free, seized a boat hook. "Even at the moment," he wrote, "I felt horror at the act I was about to commit; but it was no time for pity or compunction, and with a true aim and exerting all my strength, I dashed the boat hook at him." The savage sank under the blow and when he reappeared he was helpless. "Never," Melville wrote, "shall I forget the ferocious expression of his countenance."

The passage shows that here already Melville was in command of his great gift for describing action. We are made to feel an excitement that almost hurts in this final scene of *Typee* and the issue of it. Nevertheless, as soon as the excitement subsides and the book as a whole comes back to mind, we cannot help feeling that the narrative climax is deeply at odds with a great part of the book, and that the excitement it gives us grates on the feelings which the rest of the book has stirred up. For the natives of Typee, as Melville has described them at length, are hardly the kind of people from whom a man would have to fly for his life, or, for that matter, a man would care to take leave of under any circumstances whatever.

The little, far out-of-the-way world of Typee, which we have shared vicariously, is a world of almost visionary loveliness, luxurious peace and unbroken joy. At his first sight of the valley, Melville tells us that, had a glimpse of the gardens of Paradise been revealed to him, he could scarcely have been more ravished with the sight. "I looked straight down into the bosom of a valley, which swept away in long wavy undulations to the blue waters in the distance. Midway toward the sea, and peering here and there amidst the foliage, might be seen palmetto-thatched houses of its inhabitants, glittering in the sun that had bleached them to a dazzling whiteness. . . . On either side it appeared hemmed in by steep green acclivities, which, uniting near the spot where I lay, formed an abrupt and semicircular termination of grassy cliffs and precipices hundreds of feet in height, over which flowed numberless small cascades. But the crowning beauty of the prospect was its universal verdure." With this for the outline, there follow many passages that complete the lovely picture: "Birds—bright and beautiful birds—fly over the valley of Typee. You see them perched aloft among the immovable boughs of the majestic bread-fruit trees, or gently swaying on the elastic branches of the Omoo; skimming over the palmetto thatching of the bamboo huts; passing like spirits on the wing through the shadows of the grove, and sometimes descending into the bosom of the valley in gleaming flights. . . . Their plumage is purple and azure, crimson and white, black and gold. . . . They go sailing through the air in starry throngs."

And of this green paradise the Typees are the worthy denizens. Their physical appearance by itself would seem a goodly enough heritage from nature: "In beauty of form they surpassed anything I had ever seen. Not a single instance of natural deformity was observable. . . . The men, in almost every instance, are of lofty stature, scarcely ever less than six feet in height. . . ." Except for here and there a scar from a wound received in battle, "every individual appeared free from those blemishes which sometimes mar the effect of an otherwise perfect form."

Mixing harmoniously with the moulded elegance of the men is the volatile charm and beauty of the women. Their type is best seen in the lovely maiden Fayaway, whom Melville describes at length, remarking afterwards, "Though in my eyes, at least, Fayaway was indisputably the loveliest female I saw in Typee, yet the description I have given of her will in some measure apply to nearly all the youthful portion of her sex in the valley. Judge ye then, reader, what beautiful creatures they must have been." With Fayaway, Melville tells us, he lived on terms of enchanting intimacy, such terms of intimacy as were to shock some of his readers in faraway nineteenth-century America. "Her free pliant figure was the very perfection of female grace and beauty. Her complexion was a rich and mantling olive. . . . The face of this girl was a rounded oval, and each feature as perfectly formed as the heart or imagination of man could desire. Her full lips, when parted with a smile, disclosed teeth of a dazzling whiteness; and when her rosy mouth opened with a burst of merriment, they looked like the milk-white seeds of the 'arta,' a fruit of the valley. . . . Fayaway—I must avow the fact—for the most part clung to the primitive and summer garb of Eden. But how becoming the costume!"

Fayaway's little vanities which she shared with the companions of her sex were gay and ever so ingratiating: "Flora was their jeweler. Sometimes they wore necklaces of small carnation flowers . . . or displayed in their ears a single white bud . . . the delicate petals folded together in a beautiful sphere, and looking like a drop of the purest pearl." They crowned their heads with chaplets like strawberry coronals, or put on bracelets and anklets of intertwined leaves and blossoms. "Indeed, the maidens of the island were passionately fond of flowers and never wearied of decorating their persons with them; a lovely trait in their character. . . ." Yes, surely.

A blessed people, these natives of Typee appear to be; beautiful girls and young men with magnificent bodies, living in an environment of green valley and blue sky and distant blue sea; nowhere at all, as Melville adds, the concerns and anxieties which we think of as inseparable from middle age, nor any of the usual disappointments and deformities of old age. Physical beauty is not unsupported by moral well-being but is linked—a point I shall return to—to beauties of sincere feeling and spontaneous affections. Yet from this world and from this people Melville tells us he had to fly for his life, and he did not hesitate to practice deception and make use of physical violence in order to effect his escape.

2

What accounts for the paradox that is forced upon us here? I do not think we can easily convince ourselves that it lies in the facts themselves which Melville undertook to report. Was it then that he was divided between his instinct for exciting climax while he told a story and his romantic love of the exotic, showing in lavish and exaggerated descriptions? That is partly the case. Yet the paradox that glares so on the surface of the book reaches up from far below the level on which artistic intentions can be discriminated. It reached out of realizations that grew upon Melville as he wrote *Typee* and which were to impel him to his later books.

Melville swore to the literal truth of *Typee*. According to common report, the book was accepted for publication in London only after Melville had vouched for its entire veracity. Afterwards he was irritated by the incredulity of many of its readers. Nevertheless, it seems certain that as a yarn of personal adventure, *Typee* does not always stick to the literal truth.

A recent biographer of Melville during his years of vagabondage in the Pacific has tracked his devious wanderings and outlined the literal truth about them.* He shows that Melville's sojourn in the valley of Typee was closer to four weeks in duration than the four months that Melville said and he casts doubts on the circumstances of his escape as Melville recounted it. He proves that Melville borrowed from the accounts of other travellers to fill out his picture of the natives and that he exaggerated their reputation for ferocity. He also exaggerated the good traits of their character: "Following a long and ample tradition, both literary and philosophical, Melville

* C. R. Anderson, *Melville in the South Seas* (New York, 1935).

consistently adopts a romantic attitude in his account of the Noble Savages he found in Typee Valley."

As ethnology I am willing to leave the book to others. As to its literal autobiographical truth, I am concerned with it only incidentally. What I am concerned with is a third aspect of the truth of *Typee*—its truth to Melville's mind at the time he wrote it and, beyond this, its truth to the experience of universal human nature. It is under this aspect that we can best account for the paradox in the book which forces itself on our attention.

When Melville wrote *Typee* he was twenty-five, just the age when, as he wrote to Hawthorne some years later, he began to unfold within himself. While he was writing it the impressions received in the course of his travels began to work in his mind and take on new overtones of meaning precisely because his mind was coming to a sense of itself. Certain observations generally connected with Typee had made a deep impression on his mind. But this is not as interesting, in my opinion, as the indisputable fact that while he was writing his mind was impressing itself on this body of observations. Being intelligent and curious, he naturally supplemented his own observations of Polynesian life with whatever reading on the subject he could get at. That does not alter the case. From my point of view it is immaterial in what proportions Melville drew (a) from his own observations, (b) from his reading, (c) from his imagination. In the book as we have it his reading and his observations have fused into a single substance which was cast in the image of his mind just when he had arrived at a self-conscious view of life.

In *Typee* there are two perspectives. There is the perspective of the story proper, or of the events at the time they happened; and there is the broader perspective of the book as a whole, in which the events of the story and their circumstances are seen at a distance of four years across all the light and shadow of Melville's experience in the interim. Accordingly Melville wrote, "I will frankly declare, that after passing a few weeks in this valley of the Marquesas, I formed a higher estimate of human nature than I had ever before entertained. But alas! since then I have been one of a crew of a man-of-war, and the pent-up wickedness of five hundred men has nearly overturned all my previous theories." It was a year after he quitted Typee that he enlisted on the man-of-war, the *United States,* which was to return him to America after fourteen long months of the rigors of life in the navy. His experiences on board the *United States* and his repugnance at the severities and the brutalities of naval life are on record in his book *White Jacket* (1850). In this book, too, his thoughts reaching out beyond his immediate subject matter, he reflected not once but many times on this "man-of-war world" of ours, where, under professions of adoration of the Prince of Peace, the great civilized nations behave like a pack of armed ruffians. This insight into the civilized world, which so plumes itself on its superiority and lords it over the weaker members of the race, was a present influence in Melville's mind when he wrote his first book. In the murky moral obliquities of the civilization to which he had come home, the island valley of Typee shone brighter and brighter in the distance of four crowded years and across thousands of miles of sanitary ocean.

As well known as the story of Melville's captivity among the Typees in his first book is his indictment there of civilization. It need not be rehearsed at length, but something of the tone and temper of it may be recalled. It will be objected, Melville wrote, that these unprincipled islanders are cannibals: "Very true; and a rather bad trait in their character, it must be allowed. But they are such only when they seek to gratify the passion of revenge upon their enemies," and, he asks, does this eating of human flesh exceed the barbarity of some forms of capital punishment in the civilized nations? "The fiend-like skill we display in the invention of all manner of death-dealing engines, the vindictiveness with which we carry on our wars, and the misery and desolation that follow in their train, are enough of themselves to distinguish the white civilized man as the most ferocious animal on the face of the earth." The term "savage" is too often misapplied—"and indeed when I consider the vices, cruelties, and enormities of every kind that spring up in the tainted atmosphere of feverish civilization, I am inclined to think that so far as the relative wickedness of the parties is concerned, four or five Marquesan islanders sent to the United States as missionaries might be quite as useful as an equal number of Americans dispatched to the islands in a similar capacity."

Of course it will be insisted by critics of a certain stamp that in this contrast between civilized and savage life Melville is still following "a long and ample tradition, both literary and philosophical," namely, the exaltation of the Noble Savage at the expense of his civilized opposite. True as this may be, it is not the whole truth nor the most interesting part of it. If there is a literary convention here there is the pressure of personal responses to animate it. In Melville's exaltation of the savage in *Typee* we come on the first of many instances in which Melville instinctively took the side of the underdog. Besides, in his idealization of the savage of Typee there are certain traits peculiar to him which are worth considering.

In view of his deep-seated and life-long preoccupation with religion, it is significant of more than his aversion for professional missionaries that he should have viewed the irreligion of the Typees with such sympathetic amusement. "They are sunk in religious sloth, and require a spiritual revival. A long prosperity of bread-fruit and cocoa-nuts has rendered them remiss in the performance of their higher obligations. The wood-rot malady is spreading among the idols—the temples themselves need re-thatching—the tattooed clergy are altogether too light-hearted and lazy—and their flocks are going astray." Elsewhere, Melville, dissenting from other "scientific voyagers," lets out the truth about the islanders, that "they are a community of lusty savages, who are leading a merry, idle, innocent life. . . . For my own part, I am free to confess my almost entire inability to gratify any curiosity that may be felt with regard to the theology of the valley. I doubt whether the inhabitants themselves could do so. They are either too lazy or too sensible to worry themselves about abstract points of religious belief."

Melville was delighting in the light-hearted hedonism of these savages. Their life of luxurious sleeping, healthy appetite and undisguised impulses touched a very sympathetic chord in him. Yet partly out of fidelity to the facts and partly under the stress of another trait in Melville's character, the colors of hedonism in his painting of Typee are softened by a gentle radiance of spiritual well-being. He insisted that truth and justice were the mainstay of the Typees' social and political life. They approximated a lovely ideal of democracy; and the individual among them was remarkable for his freedom from arrogance and social pretentiousness, and for his kindliness and generosity: "They deal more kindly with each other, and are more humane, than many who study essays on virtue and benevolence, and who repeat every night that beautiful prayer breathed first by the lips of the divine and gentle Jesus."

Melville's delight in sensuous life and his love of goodness, of goodness as it is set forth in the *New Testament*, contend in his idealization of the Typees. Yet the joyous sensual life and the simple, spontaneous virtue which he pictures have something very deep in common. They unite in standing apart, both of them, from the complications of intellectual reflections and from the anxieties of moral and spiritual self-consciousness. They stand together in the sunlight and freedom outside the "shades of the prison-house" that begin to close about a man's maturity.

It appears more and more that the picture painted of Typee valley was not at last view an adoption and adaptation to himself of an external literary ideal. It has far too much warmth and flowing fulness to have been that at bottom. It came from within, out of personal recollections, and out of recollections far more integral in Melville's consciousness than the literal facts about an outlandish people he had chanced to visit. What Melville is finally expressing in *Typee* is an inward and universal phase of human experience, obtaining in individuals and peoples alike;—the phase in which life lies along the easy slopes of spontaneous, instinctive being, in which human consciousness is a simple and happy undertaking of rudimentary sensations and simple sensuous impressions; in which physical health and good animal spirits have a large preponderance; in which the impulses and affections of the human heart suffer no disguise nor any distortion; the phase, finally, in which as yet no painful cleavage is felt dividing a happy animality from the gentlest and most guileless impulses of the heart.

As we feel our way into the book, it comes over us more and more that we have all been to Typee, and that under one set or another of associations and images, it lies in all our minds. It is an embodiment of the world as we have all felt it in the glow and rapture of youthful love, whatever the object of that love. To one person it is one thing, to another something else. As one poet looks back on it, it is the "blue, remembered hills" of his boyhood, the "land of lost content"; while to another poet it stands under a wholly different train of associations:—

> *Thou wast that all to me, love,*
> *For which my soul did pine—*
> *A green isle in the sea, love,*
> *A fountain and a shrine. . . .*

In this light Melville looked back on Typee valley. Perhaps he had been in love with Fayaway; perhaps she was his first love. But the literal truth about it is not important. Somewhere, sometime or at different times, Melville had experienced the first just-ensanguined raptures of young love, and from an association of actual circumstances, or by a transfer in his imagination, that rapture gives his picture of Typee its warmth and incandescence.

The phase of his life which he identified with Typee is not present in the book, but it is recollected there. It is a recollection not remembered in tranquillity, but amidst all the stresses of a consciousness which has expanded far beyond the simplicities of sensuous, instinctive being. Yet in his imagination he returns to the

Typee phase of life and embraces it. Furthermore, by this identification of a phase of his inward experience with an island people of the South Seas whom he had undertaken to describe, he did not sacrifice the objective reality of his picture. The objective reality of *Typee* held itself intact. While being the occasion for emotions that sprang from deeply felt personal recollections, it clarified them by drawing them forth and embodying them anew in concrete forms, at the same time that it invigorated itself on them. By this identification, simply, a dimension of being was added to Melville's picture. And far from detracting from the objective truth of the picture, it extended it, adding to the truth about a particular people a universal truth about human consciousness.

The labored antithesis, then, which Melville drew between savage life and civilization goes deeper than differences of place and lies between youth and maturity, between the carefree vagabondage of mostly sensuous being and the rigors of intellectual and spiritual self-consciousness. And how lovely by contrast, how infinitely lovely and ingratiating, is the former! "In the secluded abode of happiness"—the green valley that so rejoiced him— Melville writes, "All was mirth, fun, and high good humor. Blue devils, hypochondria, and doleful dumps went and hid themselves among the nooks and crannies of the rocks"; and again, "One peculiarity that fixed my admiration was the perpetual hilarity reigning through the whole extent of the vale. There seemed to be no cares, griefs, troubles, or vexations in all Typee. The hours tripped along as gayly as the laughing couples down a country dance." What has such a child of the sun as a native of Typee, "what has he to desire at the hands of civilization? She may 'cultivate his mind,'—may 'elevate his thoughts,'—these I believe are the established phrases—but will he be happier?" "When I looked around the verdant recess in which I was buried, and gazed up to the summits of the lofty eminence that hemmed me in, I was well disposed to think that I was in the 'Happy Valley,' and that beyond those heights there was naught but a world of care and anxiety."

Praise it and delight in it as one will, nevertheless one cannot reënter into full possession of the "Happy Valley." One cannot stay long. There are intimations of the mind that will not be shut out; thoughts, they may seem, of a "dry brain in a dry season." It is forced upon us to know that Typee is not the human thing itself, and a man cannot duck his human destiny. For all its loveliness it is wanting in the elements of man's intellectual and spiritual consciousness. Its fawn-like impulses of affection, although they are ever so engaging, do not amount to the ties through which the heart fulfills itself. Fayaway showed more human than the rest: "I was almost led to believe that her mind was swayed by gentle impulses hardly to be anticipated from one in her condition." When news went around that a boat was coming for him and Melville begged to be taken to the beach, only one native in the whole crowd, an old man, could understand the human necessity he was under to escape.

It is a necessity of our human life that we should sojourn in Typee, and that we should open to it with all the pores of our sensuous being and that we should cherish it for the refreshment which it alone can give. Lovely, easy-lying, green valley! surrounded as it is by the veiled heights and the appalling ocean vastnesses of man's completer consciousness, it will grow lovelier and more and more desirable the further it is left behind. But it is a dark necessity of our being human that a time comes when we must escape from it for our lives.

Yet, after all, it is not so much that a man leaves Typee behind him as that he passes on to other aspects of life while Typee remains one element among others in his consciousness. The man in whom this element does not persist, or in whom it has been reduced to a few scraps of memory, is very much the poorer. He has lost a range of impressionability, as also a source within himself at which to bathe his whole emotional being. And of all men it is the artist, of course, who counts most on the survival of this element as a living principle. It remained strong in Melville, and I believe it might be pointed out that, because of the compact, objectified expression of it in his first book, it was all the more viable and re-sourceful in representing itself in the later ones, showing in his vivid visualization of things and in adding to such effects as meet the eye a bodily sense of textures and of the heft of things and of the tug-of-war play of elemental forces.

There is a deep-flowing continuity between *Typee* and *Moby Dick,* as also between *Typee* and the books which preceded and followed *Moby Dick.* This is to be observed in the way that facts written down as such in *Typee* keep recurring in its successors in strange contexts and with a new figurative or symbolic accentuation. For instance, a whaler is mentioned in *Typee* which had been many years at sea and was thought lost, but which turned up in a harbor in the South Seas, her hull all encased in barnacles and "three pet sharks" in her wake. The description of this ship is repeated in the much more elaborate description of the *Pequod* in *Moby Dick;* and the three pet sharks reappear with a new sinister connotation in the wake of Melville's canoe in *Mardi.* Again, at the very beginning of *Typee,* Melville is expressing how parched he felt after months spent out of sight of land: "Oh! for a refreshing glimpse of one blade of grass—for a snuff at the fragrance of a handful of the loamy earth! Is there nothing fresh around us? Is there no green thing to be seen?" At once we are reminded of the many references in *Moby Dick* to farms and fields in summer time, connoting growth and nourishment—April butter, for instance, and smells of meadows at hay-making—which make up an imagery of life in contrast to the salt, bleached imagery of the sea.

The significance which Melville attached in his first book to the island valley of Typee continued to unfold the further it dropped behind him in point of fact and as the perspective in which he looked back at it continued to open and to fill in with further realizations of life. The meaning of Typee varied as Melville re-flected on it under the various pressures of his human make-up. Now it wore the complexion of joyous bodily living identified with Rabelais; now it wore the colors of the heart's deeper affections; and yet again it wore the subtilized colors of the soul. Still, for all this variation, the meaning that Typee had for Melville remained within recognizable limits. Whether Rabelaisian or spiritualized, and spiritualized, as we shall see it in some instances, in the likeness of Ralph Waldo Emerson, it was never out of reach of the idea of natural goodness, and always in Melville's dramatic view of life and his dramatic experience of what it is to be a human being it had for Melville the relish of salvation in it.

The outwardness or extroversion of the senses grew to include the outwardness of human ties and affections and, beyond that, the outwardness of religious faith. Thus, I believe, the significance of Typee was reëmbodied in Lucy, the good angel of *Pierre*, which is the most desperate and the least outward and objective of all Melville's books. Thus, too, the meaning of Typee grew into the symbolic significance of the land in *Moby Dick*, as opposed to the sea—the land being the sphere not only of sensuous and affectionate being, but also that in which men share together in worship and practical pursuits. Against this common continent of man stands the sea—"a foe to man, who is an alien to it." "The first boat we have read of floated on an ocean, that with Portuguese vengeance had whelmed the whole world without leaving so much as a widow. That same ocean rolls now . . ." and "however baby man may brag of his science and skill, and however much, in a flattering future, that science and skill may augment; yet forever and forever, to the crack of doom, the sea will insult and murder him, and pulverise the stateliest, stiffest frigate he can make. . . ."

While taking its place in this comprehensive and impersonal view of man, Typee retained its place in the perspective of the individual's consciousness, lying there a green island valley of sensuous and instinctive being against the arduous heights and ocean vastnesses of man's tremendous intellectual and spiritual nature. Its significance of outwardness, beginning with the outwardness of the senses and reaching to love and faith, is flashed against its terrible opposite in the words, almost the most im-

pressive in all *Moby Dick*, "Though in many of its aspects this
visible world seemed formed in love, the invisible spheres were
formed in fright." It retained its place in the perspective of the
individual's consciousness. That is to say, it retained its place in
Melville's personal spiritual drama as representing his vital need, in
the teeth of opposite needs almost as vital, to hold on to and to
find his way back to those resources of life which he included
under the significance of Typee. In that great act of being which
was his life, which we are to see reflected in his books, so long as
he might keep touch with Typee and might repair thither to re-
fresh his sensuous and affectionate and spiritual nature, then no
matter how far he might press into the invisible spheres of man's
thought and consciousness it would be well with him. In the last
view to take here of the meaning Typee came to have for Melville
it appears under its original image, although, a point of no importance, the name is different: "Consider them both," wrote
Melville, "the sea and the land; and do you not find a strange
analogy to something in yourself? For as this appalling ocean sur-
rounds the verdant land, so in the soul of man there lies one insular
Tahiti, full of peace and joy, but encompassed by all the horrors of
the half-known life. God keep thee! Push not off from that isle,
thou canst never return."

3

Melville was nothing if not individualistic. Bodily as well as
intellectually and spiritually he travelled a wide eccentric orbit.
True as this was, there was much that he had in common with
such Americans of his time as Emerson, Thoreau, Hawthorne,
Whitman and Poe. For they were each and all of them individualistic and eccentric, some of them almost as much so as he. Going off
in their separate directions, they were in accord in that they were
all facing off at tangents to American orthodoxy and respectability.
Melville and these others were at odds with America. That is, they

were at odds with their nineteenth-century America of the industrial revolution which was spreading its rigor mortis of standardization and gentility over the face of the land.

In a larger view of things, however, it was not they but the solid mass of their respectable compatriots who were at odds with the main American movement and experience. Looking back to the seventeenth and eighteenth centuries one sees that a dominant impulse in American history was to break away from authority and to step free of the shackles of traditional society. That impulse was embodied in the Puritan and the pioneer alike. In the nineteenth century, all the way from the Atlantic seaboard almost up to the frontier, it was opposed by a growing dead weight of conventionalism and gentility. Nevertheless it persisted. It existed chiefly beyond the frontier and it signalized itself in some of the most moving events and greatest creations in American literature and literary history. For example, there is Leatherstocking, to whose spirit Cooper was never so loyal as at the end of *The Pioneers.* Civilization and society in the person of Judge Temple would persuade the old hunter to stay the remainder of his days where he had been all his life. True, these lands have become the judge's vast domain which he is parcelling out to hundreds of tenant farmers. No matter: the old hunter may feel himself as much at home as of old. But Leatherstocking will not accept the judge's kindness. Between the impulse which he represents and the circumspections and circumventions and circumscriptions impersonated by Judge Temple there is no reconciliation. Old as he is, he leaves his familiar hunting grounds and presses alone into the western wilderness where he dies. So, too, at the end of *Huckleberry Finn,* Mark Twain was true to the impulse which created the hero of his finest book. Huck will not be fooled a second time by Tom Sawyer's slick salesmanship that would persuade him that he can be free—free as it was in his soul to understand freedom—and remain a respectable member of society with good prospects of amassing a reputable fortune. This time Huck will not submit; he will not be tamed: "I reckon I got to light out . . . because Aunt Sally says she's going to adopt me and sivilize me and I can't stand it. I been there before."

"I am a free companion." "I confront peace, security, and all the settled laws, to unsettle them. . . ." Walt Whitman's revolt against the restraints of society and his vagabondage was the same as Huck's but on a cosmic scale. And how close, by the way, to Melville's response to the graceful insouciance of the Typees was Walt's response to the animals, "so placid and self-contain'd":

They do not lie awake in the dark and weep for their sins,
They do not make me sick discussing their duty to God,
Not one is dissatisfied, not one is demented with the mania of
* owning things,*

. . . . .

Not one is respectable or industrious over the whole earth.

Emerson experienced the conflict between society and solitude, as he called it—the restraints of the one and the freedom of the other. His heart chose solitude. Thoreau turned his back more boldly on society. "They who know of no purer sources of truth," he wrote, "who have traced up its stream no higher, stand, and wisely stand, by the Bible and the Constitution, and drink at it there with reverence and humility; but they who behold where it comes trickling into this lake or that pool, gird up their loins once more, and continue their pilgrimage toward its fountainhead." It is as if the long process of revolt which originated in England in the seventeenth century and was carried forward by successive generations of Puritans and pioneers, which dissented from the Church of England and broke away from the British government, came to a climax when Thoreau turned his back on civilization and went to live alone at Walden Pond. There was nothing closer dramatically and spiritually to Thoreau's action than Melville's, in giving up the respectable occupations of clerk and schoolteacher to sail off in the crew of a disreputable whaler and find an earthly paradise among the cannibals of Typee.

NOTE

In his next book, *Omoo,* Melville went on with the story of his life from the point of his departure from Typee. But the internal drama of *Typee,* which supplies the first act of the drama of Melville's experience of what it is to be a human being, is not resumed in *Omoo.* It is only resumed in *Mardi,* his third book. In spite of the external continuity between them, *Omoo* is entirely different in internal atmosphere from its predecessor. Without the poetry of *Typee,* it has far more humor. It is the least moody of all Melville's books. There is a heartiness about it that suits well with its broad realism, which is the broad *genre* realism of the eighteenth century. In *Omoo,* I would add, there is what serves as an explanatory footnote to the allegory of Melville's escape from Typee. The ship which effected his rescue touches presently at a small island where lives a white man who has gone native; "a renegado," Melville calls him, "from Christendom and humanity." "Some of us gazed upon this man with a feeling akin to horror," which intensified when it got known that he had voluntarily submitted to having his face tattooed. Worse, "far worse than Cain's," says Melville of these marks of a man's abdication from his human nature. For all its charm and its ingratiating ways Typee is sub-human. A man cannot reside there but at the price of undevelopment.

CHAPTER THREE

Mardi

"The World of Mind"

"WE ARE OFF!" *Mardi* begins precipitately and presses forward on a gigantic scale in a style which often sounds like a regimental band. Sound passes into sight in humming colors and in a sort of cosmic imagery, like the imagery of Christopher Marlowe: "But now, a bright mustering is seen among the myriad white Tartar tents in the Orient; like lines of spears defiling upon some upland plain, the sunbeams thwart the sky. And see! amid the blaze of banners . . . day's mounted Sultan, Xerxes-like, moves on, the Dawn his standard, East and West his cymbals."

The world of *Typee* is the world of natural facts in which the law of gravity is paramount. *Mardi*, although a commentary on the world of natural facts, is not of it. In *Mardi* we are in a world in which the sense of metaphor takes precedence over the law of gravity. There are passages in it of almost incredible beauty and only inferior to the best passages in *Moby Dick* because—such is the distillation of the sense of metaphor—they are less substantial and more fantastic. This world we *see* in *Mardi* is a reflection of the islands of the South Seas. Lovely enough these would seem to be from all accounts, but in this reflection it is as if they had been shaken from their foundations and had turned extravagant and wildly beautiful beyond the limits of even tropical nature. For that matter, the whole book has the air of being off on a drunk. It is a piece of *libertinage* in which Melville's sensuous delight, his speculative mind, his imagination at its most fantastic, his curiosity

and his wayward mysticism all disport themselves with wilful pro-
fusion.

Nevertheless, the book holds to its serious purpose and avails itself of every device of thought that offers to hunt out the truth
of creation. It is called *Mardi* after an undiscovered archipelago in
the Pacific which stands for the world, its different islands representing the different nations. Of all the metaphors which the book
offers to apply to itself the most commanding is this, that Melville
here sets out from the island innocence and the simple, unreflecting
life of Typee valley to embark on the great ocean of man's consciousness, with all its depths and reaches in man's instinctive, spiritual
and intellectual natures. I say embarks in the present tense de-
liberately. For we shall miss the force of *Mardi* if we take the
metaphor to stand for experience seen in retrospect only. That is
not the way Melville wrote autobiography. The experience of his
unfolding and expanding consciousness went on while he was
writing, which he as much as confesses to toward the end of the
book. "I've chartless voyaged," he wrote. "And though essaying but
a sportive sail, I was driven from my course by a blast resistless."
To these words he added what is also substantially true about
Mardi: "But this new world here sought is stranger far than his,
who stretched his vans from Palos. It is the world of mind; wherein
the wanderer may gaze round, with more of wonder than Balboa's
band roving through the golden Aztec glades." Coming upon it
from Typee it was, this world of mind, a new world indeed; and
as he wrote *Mardi* it unfolded and dissolved around him like a
stormy sunset—a vast kaleidoscopic wonder of beauty and terror.

Mardi has for its theme the human mind's quest for truth. Its
story is as exciting as any ever told, and Melville in the character
he assumes is impatient to get on with it. The whaler he is aboard
is slow and dull. The crew, including a half-score of Polynesians,
are good fellows all. "Nevertheless, they were not precisely to my
mind," for there was not one to talk "sentiment or philosophy" or
to page "a quotation from Burton on Blue Devils." Melville, or Taji,

as he will call himself, has imaginings which make him restless. He determines to desert. With an old salt called Jarl he makes off one night in the ship's boat and when morning breaks he is safely out of sight. Then follow days of drifting westward over a beautiful and benignant ocean—westward into those almost final waters of the middle Pacific where, according to a later story, Captain Ahab came face to face at last with the White Whale.

From a derelict brigantine which they encounter they pick up a new companion, an islander called Samoa. Then after more drifting they sight a large canoe in which are eight men, an old priest and his seven sons. There is a tent in the canoe which conceals a beautiful maiden, Yillah, who is being taken to a remote island to be sacrificed. Taji boards the canoe determined to rescue the maiden. In the scuffle that follows he stabs the old man and kills him, and then the two craft drift apart. Yillah is surrendered to Taji. His soul thrills with passionate joy at possessing her. He has seen the old priest's body sink below the water. Alas! That was not the last he was to see of him. Though "he had sunk in the deep, his ghost sunk not in the waters of my soul. However in exultations its surface foamed up, at bottom guilt brooded."

In time the wanderers land on the island of Odo in the archipelago of Mardi. Here the hero announces himself as a returning demi-god and is received as such by King Media, himself a demi-god, who calls on him and entertains him royally. Taji and Yillah live together in a secluded bower in Odo, where day by day Yillah becomes more strangely beautiful. "Often I thought that Paradise had overtaken me on earth, and that Yillah was verily an angel, and hence the mysteries that hallowed her." Then, suddenly on a day Yillah vanishes, leaving no trace behind.

Taji is struck with an irremediable and speechless grief. He asks Media's permission to leave Odo and seek Yillah to the ends of the earth (that is, Mardi). Media consents. What is more he will accompany Taji and bring in his equipage his royal philosopher, Babbalanja, and old Mohi and youthful Yoomy, respectively his historiographer and his poet laureate; all of whom take an intense interest in Taji's quest. A lovely morning hangs above them when they start off—"the new-born clouds all dappled with gold, and streaked with violet; the sun in high spirits."

Among other things, the book becomes a vast panoramic satire in the manner of Rabelais and Swift. Mardi is the world, as I have said; its islands stand for the different nations, as Dominora for Great Britain, Franko for France, Vivenza for the United States; or they stand for different institutions, as Maramma for Roman Catholicism, Serenia for primitive Christianity; or they stand for different types of men and manners. The travellers expatiate at length on the peculiarities and customs of the countries they touch at. Wherever they land they are received as becomes a king and his friends. There is a great deal of feasting and drinking and smoking. Among themselves or with their hosts on shore there is endless talk that shuttles back and forth between fanciful persiflage, broad Rabelaisian jesting and the most importunate discourse on the nature of things, usually under the topics of fate and free will, the problem of evil and the immortality of the soul.

There is in *Mardi* a satirical representation of many lands. However, in a sense esoteric to Melville, *Mardi* is a book of the sea. That is, its sphere is the world of thought and consciousness. (A quest for truth I have called it. As such it looks two ways: outwardly at the objective truth about creation and inwardly at the realities of being, its twofold vision dividing generally between Taji and Babbalanja.) Its satirical aspect is secondary. It cannot pause over particulars of time and place and for such opacities, the deserving objects of satire, as England and the United States in the nineteenth century. The truth it looks for through the eyes of Taji and Babbalanja is as universal as the nature of life. Accordingly, the book's most truthful *mis-en-scène* is the sea, than which there is no better image of timelessness.

Yillah is sea-born. Her symbolical significance varies between different points of view. According to the superficial satirical aspect, she is truth in the sense of a standard of righteousness by which nations and institutions are judged. Beyond this she is identified with truth in the absolute sense, the truth about creation and human destiny. Nonetheless, she belongs mostly to the subjective aspect of the book and is primarily an ideal of being—an ideal unity of being, I should say, in which all the elements of man's nature share harmoniously; his sensuous being and his spiritual on one hand, his spiritual and his intellectual propensities on the other. It is primarily as this ideal that Yillah is identified with the sea (man's consciousness) and that Taji pursues her. For him she is sea-born. When lost, he puts out to sea to find her and, to anticipate, when he last catches sight of her he sees her darkly under the water, being swept oceanward, whither he plunges after her. The whole book is an image of the ideal significance of Yillah to Taji.

Of all the characters in *Mardi* only Babbalanja emerges with a human personality. King Media counts for the cynicism, the light-hearted hedonism and affable indifference which set off the philosopher's earnestness. Mohi and Yoomy are bare types, the one a crabbed antiquarian, the other a poet hinting vaguely at Shelley when Shelley was his most egregiously poetic. In the long discussions in which they all knock their heads together, Babbalanja does most of the talking. Taji is mostly silent. Yet his presence is felt. After all, he unites all the others in his determination.

Taji is an aspect of Melville. He is Melville on the side of his will and idealism. He is a projection of Melville's radical protestantism, which was no less exorbitant than Job's, who said of his Creator: "Though he slay me, yet will I trust in him: but I will maintain mine own ways before him." Taji also represents what I have called Melville's humanism, his Promethean loyalty to the right and dignity of human nature. Babbalanja is another not altogether different profile of Melville. He, too, represents Melville's protestant humanism. Babbalanja is mainly the vehicle for Melville's impassioned speculative thinking. With him the emphasis is on mind, with Taji it is on will. The two supplement each other, yet there is a structural and philosophical antithesis between them. *Mardi,* I have said, looks outwardly and inwardly; Babbalanja being identified with its outward and Taji with its inward action. Both join in the pursuit of Yillah. Each has his separate story. But the story of one, as we shall see, is contingent on the story of the other. In other words, there is a continual interaction between objective truth and inward reality, between knowledge and being.

The book abounds in high spirits. It acknowledges no restrictions on the mind of man to grasp truth. Appallingly vast as the universe is, the mind is strong and free to encompass it and probe its very secret. At the same time, the eye of faith shines brightly. Under the vastness and welter of creation it sees a unity of divine love and purpose. God is, and He is sufficient to His great design. "There are more wonders than the wonders rejected, and more sights unrevealed than you and I ever dreamt of. Moles and bats alone should be skeptics; and the only infidelity is for a live man to vote himself dead." All life is from God and love is the law of life: "the thrones and principalities in the zodiac; the shades that roam throughout space; the nations and families, flocks and folds of the earth; one and all, brothers in essence. . . . All things form but one whole; the universe is a Judea, and God Jehovah its head. Then no more let us start with affright. In a theocracy, what is to fear?" This is the view of creation in the eye of faith. This is the view of creation that *Mardi* takes initially, and this is the view which admits of a hope of Yillah. From it as premise the corollary follows of a possible inward harmony of life.

Will this view of creation stand before the inquisitions of the mind? Will it stand up before such investigations and speculations as Babbalanja is driven by the exigencies of his human intellect to press home? In the struggle that is represented here there is the epitome of the conflicting views of two successive phases of human thought and, I would add, between the dominant views of two successive generations in America in the nineteenth century. Against the view of order, harmony, divine love and purpose, whether Christian or transcendentalist, another is set up, nowhere better expressed than by Henry Adams in his *Education*, of the universe as "a void of shapeless energies, with resistless mass, colliding, crushing, wasting, and destroying what these same energies had created and labored from eternity to perfect."

Melville's faith was not chicken-hearted, to give way easily. "But let us hold fast to all we have"; he wrote, "and stop all leaks in our faith; lest an opening of but a hand's breadth, should sink our seventy-fours. . . . Panoplied in all the armor of St. Paul . . . let us fight the Turks inch by inch, and yield them naught but our corpse." None the less, the strain of the conflict begins to tell. Even the passages of faith have ambiguities which seem to belie it. The exultation becomes too insistent. The book grows more and more sombre, till the colors in the foreground show with a rueful brightness, like flower beds when a gathering thunder storm darkens the afternoon.

Love, we read, is the law of life, and hate is wrong; "as well hate a seraph as a shark. Both were made by the same hand." But, Melville adds, "of all sharks save me from the ghastly White Shark. . . . This ghost of a fish is not often encountered. . . . Timon-like, he always swims by himself," stealing along "like a spirit in the water, with horrific serenity of aspect. . . ." On the next page, when he has told how sharks will attack a whale and kill it, he exclaims: "Oh, believe me, God's creatures fighting, fin for fin, a thousand miles from land, and with the round horizon for an arena, is no ignoble subject for a masterpiece." Although occasioning not a ripple here, I wonder if this observation was not a hidden reef to Melville's ship of faith, piercing it so as, if not to sink it, at least to impair its buoyancy. For this observation was to reappear, crossed with a scene from *Omoo*, in the wonderful chapter in *Moby Dick* called "Midnight, Forecastle"—and to reappear there as nothing less than the presentiment of the whole earth as an arena in which men like sharks display the brazen savagery of nature under the indifferent eye of a spectator God. In *Mardi* the observation leads to a view of the importunate universal facts of sin and suffering and, beyond this, to a consideration of the Creator's ambiguities in his creation. His purposes are unintelligible, so everlastingly alien is He to men. He has no passions, no purposes, no ends; "He lives content; all ends are compassed in him; he has no past, no future; he is the everlasting now; which is an everlasting calm; and things that are,—have been,—will be. This gloom's enough." Babbalanja's meaning here has been anticipated on another occasion. "How still!" he cried. "This calm is like unto [God's] everlasting serenity, and like unto man's last despair."

Babbalanja is caught up in the conflict of faith against reason. As Hawthorne said of Melville, he can neither believe nor be comfortable in his unbelief. Yet this is only one aspect of his tragedy. His eye penetrates all illusions and disguises. Evil is not to be laid to the dereliction of a few individuals in a theocracy; "For evil is the chronic malady of the universe; and checked in one place, breaks forth in another." It is vain of the citizens of Vivenza (the United States) to suppose they can escape the bondage of the past. Real progress there is none; what passes for it is but the expression of man's cheap ingenuity. "How vain to say that progress is the test of truth. . . . Truth and Merit have other symbols than success." History shows a meaningless repetition, says Babbalanja, refusing to assent to the optimism of Vivenza: "Nothing changes, though much be new-fashioned. . . . In the books of the past we learn naught but of the present; in those of the present, the past. All Mardi's history—beginning, middle, and finis—was written out in capitals in the first page penned." In the individual as in history there is but a purposeless going round and round; "Men fight and make up; repent and go at it; feast and starve; laugh and weep; pray and curse." "Thus with the wisest of you all"; Media says to Babbalanja, "you are ever unfixed. Do you show a tropical calm without? then be sure a thousand contrary currents whirl and eddy within." "Have you that, then, of which you speak, Babbalanja?" Media asks another time, "Are you content, there where you stand?" "My lord, you drive me home. I am not content. . . . I am in darkness, and no broad blaze comes down to flood me. . . . For the more we learn, the more we unlearn . . . and take away more than we add."

To the mind that questions and speculates the boundlessness of the universe becomes oppressive—like a dungeon! Says Babbalanja: "There is no place but the universe; no limit but the limitless; no bottom but the bottomless." He is driven by a noble necessity to seek out the truth—to assume his full intellectual stature. Preoccupation with ultimate truth is of the very essence of what it is to be human. And yet! Has his cup any lees in it? King Media enquires. "Plenty, my lord; we philosophers come to the lees very soon." Not his faith only, but his tranquillity of spirit, his sensuous joy of life and his self-respect are all tormented under the inquisitions of his mind. "Of all simpletons, the simplest!" he cries out about himself. "Oh! that I were another sort of fool than I am, that I might restore my good opinion of myself. Continually I stand in the pillory, am broken on the wheel, and dragged asunder by wild horses. . . . All round me, my fellowmen are new-grafting their vines, and dwelling in flourishing arbors; while I am forever pruning mine, till it is become but a stump. Yet in this pruning will I persist; I will not add, I will diminish; I will train myself down to the standard of what is unchangeably true."

Completely human as he is, Babbalanja is aware of a consciousness within himself which is other than the life of his senses. Call it what one will—his soul or his spiritual consciousness—in any case it lies at the core of the human mystery. Very well, as King Media would say, why worry about it? It happens that King Media is a demi-god and therefore above human compulsions. He has never been sad or troubled in all his life. He frowns when Babbalanja, as so often, discourses on religion. It is a subject, he says, which all gay, sensible people "who desired to live and be merry, invariably banished from their social discourse." He protests, "Why, Babbalanja, I almost pity you. You are too warm, too warm. Why fever your soul with these things? To no use you mortals wax earnest. No thanks, but curses, will you get for your earnestness. You yourself you harm most. Why not take creeds as they come? It is not so hard to be persuaded; never mind about believing.' 'True, my lord; not very hard; no act is required; only passiveness. Stand still and receive. Faith is to the thoughtless, doubts to the thinker.' 'Then, why think at all?' " the king parries. The answer lies deep in Babbalanja's humanity; so deep that he cannot articulate it on demand.

Babbalanja's apologia is a noble defense of the mind of man. Elsewhere he delivers himself to Yoomy, saying that gods and demigods have no need to discourse of things perfectly understood by them, and by themselves ordained. "But you and I, Yoomy, are men, and not gods; hence it is for us, and not for them, to take these things for our themes." Man's reason is a noble faculty, and is it to be used "but for a paw, to help us to our bodily needs, as the brutes use their instinct? Is not reason subtle as quicksilver — live as lightning—a neighing charger to advance, but a snail to recede? Can we starve that noble instinct in us, and hope that it will survive?" For Babbalanja it is inhuman not to think and hardly less so to confine one's thinking to the objects of external science. That is to overlook the mysteries within and their implications in thought and conduct,—all that Doctor Johnson once referred to as the great and frequent business of the human mind. For Babbalanja it is not enough to face these mysteries with the mental simplicity which it takes to enjoy the birds and the flowers. The mind of man is bound by the necessities of its nature to be concerned about the deepest compulsions of human consciousness and to follow up the tortuous ascent of their implications to those bare metaphysical heights where in the face of things all aspects familiar to man's sentient being are appallingly lost sight of. Babbalanja defends the grounds of theology in speculative thought proceeding from given premises. He defends the reasoning as distinguished from the intuitive intellect. On the other hand he will not submit to any dogmatic system, for that would be to surrender the free intuitive use of his mind.

He will have both, the reasoning and the intuitive, since both are of the dignity and complement of what it is to be human. To such a one as King Media, who would prefer the charming insouciance of the natives of Typee, or who in contrast to men points to the engaging objectivity of the animals—to such a one Babbalanja would reply as he did to one Nulli in Vivenza, who defended slavery because it assured the slaves their happiness; are they not fed, clothed, and cared for? They have "no thoughts, no cares." "And are their souls, then, blown out as candles?" cried Babbalanja. "Thoughts and cares are life, and liberty, and immortality."

Babbalanja's humanism is heroic action. His pursuit of truth is the form which his Promethean loyalty to human nature takes. And what is the outcome for him? Man's reason is "live as lightning" yet its flashes only serve to expose a more massive and colossal darkness. Looking at man in the individual and the aggregate, wherein does he find any stability, any symmetry or coherence? "In the old footprints, up and down, you mortals go, eternally travelling your sierras." Our mortal lives have an end; but that end is no good. His human burden is almost more than Babbalanja can bear. He envies a moose who swims by; "Hail! mighty brute!—thou feelest not these things: never canst *thou* be damned . . . and thy life hath not the consciousness of death." His own soul he calls "that scorched thing." "Life is wearisome to all: the same dull round." Yet death is "life's last despair." "Hard to live; hard to die; intolerable suspense!" Anon, lifting his bowed head, Babbalanja speaks again. "Yillah still eludes us. And in all this tour of Mardi how little have we found to fill the heart with peace: how much to slaughter all our yearnings." Harassed, Babbalanja sometimes envies a simple condition of existence in which the individual is not burdened by the questioning and speculative mind which seems only to torment itself and the nature to which it is joined. "Sick with the spectacle of the madness of men, and broken with spontaneous doubts, I sometimes see but two things . . . to believe:—that I myself exist, and that I can most happily, or least miserably exist, by the practice of righteousness. All else is in the clouds." But Babbalanja cannot rest on these simple intuitions. As he confesses immediately, "Yet, alas! too often do I swing from these moorings." "I may have come to the Penultimate, but where, sweet Yoomy, is the Ultimate?" His mind will not be satisfied save with the Ultimate. Yet, as he must acknowledge fondly, "The last wisdom is dumb." Nevertheless, if his mind cannot grasp the final truth, it can at any rate be truthful. To borrow from Melville's metaphor in *Moby Dick,* it can refuse the lying half-truths of the land and keep "the open independence of [its] sea." So Babbalanja: " 'Ah! my lord, think not that in aught I've said this night I would assert any wisdom of my own. I but fight against the armed and crested Lies of [the world], that like a host assail me. I am stuck full of darts; but, tearing them out from me, gasping, I discharge them whence they come.' "

"So saying, Babbalanja slowly drooped, and fell reclining; then lay motionless as the marble Gladiator, that for centuries has been dying."

2

Far spent, the travellers arrive at Serenia, an ultimate sort of land. Serenia is Christianity, but Christianity without dogma and without ecclesiastical establishment. It is Christianity immediately inspired by the New Testament. True, the Serenians call Alma (Jesus) Master. They believe, however, that the law—namely Truth, justice and love—was not bequeathed by Alma. "Alma but opens unto us our own hearts." In spite of the lowering aspect of the book at this point, Melville never wrote with such radiant and tender gravity as in his account of Serenia. An old man greets the travellers when they land, calling them brothers.

" 'Call ye us brothers, whom ere now ye never saw?'

" 'Even so,' said the old man . . . 'Thus Alma, the Master, hath commanded . . .'

" 'Do ye then claim to live what your master hath spoken? Are your precepts practices?'

" 'Nothing do we claim: we but earnestly endeavor.'

" 'Tell me not of your endeavors, but of your life. What hope for the fatherless among ye?'

" 'Adopted as a son.'

" 'Of one poor, and naked?'

" 'Clothed, and he wants for naught.'

" 'If ungrateful, he smite you?'

" 'Still we feed and clothe him.'

" 'If yet an ingrate?'

' 'Long, he cannot be; for love is a fervent fire.' "

In the perspective of Melville himself, Serenia is Typee, but Typee spiritualized. And although the inspiration here is from the New Testament, its outward delineation assumes a likeness to Emerson. The profile is unmistakable. There is a simplicity and freedom to Serenia that Babbalanja has sometimes longed for. Its life is not burdened by the reasoning intellect. It lies on the level of instinctive, spontaneous existence and shows a happy unity of perception and action. True, the instincts which guide the Serenians are the instincts whose infallibility Emerson preached, not those that prompted Fayaway's graceful and affectionate behavior. Typee lay under the "organic law" of physical life. Serenia, on the contrary, lies under "the law of mind." Yet the similarity is unmistakable.

Babbalanja is profoundly stirred by what the old man says: "My soul sets back like ocean streams, that sudden change their flow." The old man continues; he repeats Alma's words, "In *me* is that heart of mild content, which in vain ye seek in rank and title. I am Love; love ye then me." "Alma is for all; for high and low. . . . He lays the lashings of the soul's wild aspirations after things unseen." Babbalanja is struck like Paul on his way to Damascus. "Oh, Alma, Alma!" he cries, "prince divine! in *thee*, at last, I find repose. . . . Gone, gone! are all distracting doubts. . . . I see with other eyes:— Are these my hands? What wild, wild dreams were mine;—I have been mad. Some things there are we must not think of. Beyond one obvious mark, all human lore is vain. . . . All I have said ere this,

that wars with Alma's precepts, I here recant." That night an angel
visits him in a dream and questions him: "This have I learned, oh
spirit!—In things mysterious, to seek no more; but rest content, with
knowing naught but Love." In the morning he announces to his
comrades that his voyage is ended: "Not because what we sought
is found; but that I now possess all which may be had of what I
sought in Mardi. Here, I tarry to grow wiser still. . . . Taji! for
Yillah thou wilt hunt in vain; she is a phantom that but mocks
thee. . . . Wise counsel take. Within our hearts is all we seek. . . .
Once more: Taji! be sure thy Yillah never will be found; or found,
will not avail thee. Yet search, if so thou wilt . . . and when all is
seen, return, and find thy Yillah here."

Taji is intransigent. All the others promise to cherish Alma's
doctrine and return in due time to Serenia. King Media himself
undertakes to dissuade Taji from further pursuit: "thy Yillah is behind thee, not before. Deep she dwells in blue Serenia's groves."
Taji is "fixed as fate." "Then sweet Yillah called me from the sea,
—still must I on!" Suddenly the corpse of the old priest rises and
strikes against his prow. "Then, then! my heart grew hard, like
flint. . . . I prayed not, but blasphemed."

Taji will not make a renunciation corresponding to Babbalanja's
renunciation of the ultimate. He will not accept a marked-down
Yillah, a Yillah of mild content. His Yillah expresses the fullness and
joy of human life. He has possessed her once, at the moment of
his life corresponding to life in Typee valley,—that is, when he was
just on the threshold of spiritual self-consciousness. Now, when he
has grown mature, shall he not possess her more deeply than
before?

Yillah, I must repeat, is a symbol of sensuous delight. "Was not
Yillah my shore and my grove . . . my soft shady vine, and my
arbor?" She is also a symbol of spiritual joy in harmony with
sensuous delight; "of all things desirable and delightful, the full
plumed sheaf, and my own right arm the band." Her adven
signalizes Taji's soul's coming of age, without which his rapture

in the blood had been less than it was. However, it is to be remembered that in the act of possessing himself of Yillah he sinned. Acting wilfully and violently he caused the murder of the old man. Instantaneously, with the joy that flooded his soul, guilt sank deep into his consciousness. From that moment to the last we see of him Taji is pursued by three dark forms from the ill-fated canoe. Together they represent guilt, remorse and a mortal need of expiation and atonement or, more generally, his need to submit his will, which he refuses to do. They have, of course, these spectres, especial reference to Taji's murder of the old priest. They also refer generally to that burden which is inseparable from a man's spiritual self-consciousness, which has gone by the names of the knowledge of good and evil and the sense of sin, regardless of any particular sinful act, and which, under whatever name, was so charmingly absent in Typee.

While Taji pursues Yillah, then, he is himself pursued by the spectres of his spiritual self-consciousness. He is also followed by another set of pursuers, the seductive emissaries of Queen Hautia, of Flozella, who, significantly, always appear just before or just after these spectres. Yoomy translates their sign language for Taji. "Sad your path . . . but merry Hautia's." "Taji . . . fly to me! I will dance away your gloom, and drown it in inebriation." Queen Hautia stands for spiritual death—from pride, as her name suggests, and, according to her conduct, from sensuality. Afflicted as he is in mind and spirit, Taji is peculiarly vulnerable to her attack. Queen Hautia, of course, would have no influence in Typee, for in Typee there are no cares to urge a man to bestial oblivion. It has to be added that neither the spectral figures nor Hautia's emissaries can enter Serenia. But Taji has left Typee behind him and has refused to take sanctuary in Serenia.

On the other hand, the idea of Hautia is hateful to him. "Dire presentiments, like poisoned arrows," assail him. Yillah was all beauty and innocence; Hautia his soul abhorred: Yillah he sought; Hautia sought him. "Nevertheless, in some mysterious way seemed

Hautia and Yillah connected." At last he consents to visit Hautia. The reefs around Flozella are strewn with wrecks. She advances to greet him "with gliding, artful steps:—the very snares of love!" Taji thinks of the mysterious tie between Yillah and Hautia: "Then two wild currents met, and dashed me into foam." In her bower Hautia offers Taji a cup: "Quaff! Every drop drowns a thought!" Has Hautia ensnared Yillah, he asks; has she murdered her? Remain with her in Flozella, Hautia bids him, "where thou wilt soon learn to love the living, not the dead." Sweet music plays and dissolves his woes. "Strange languors made me droop; once more within my inmost vault, side by side, the Past and Yillah lay:—two bodies tranced." Recovering himself, Taji spurns Hautia, "Oh vipress, I could slay thee!" "Go, go,—and slay thyself," she answers, "I may not make thee mine;—go,—dead to dead!—There is another cavern in the hill."

"Swift I fled along the valley side; passed Hautia's cave of pearls; and gained a twilight arch; within, a lake transparent shone. Conflicting currents met, and wrestled; and one dark arch led to channels, seaward tending.

"Round and round, a gleaming form slow circled in the deepest eddies:—white, and vaguely Yillah."

3

The allegory here will need little further explanation. Yillah was connected with Hautia in as much as she represented joy of the flesh. The Yillah sought by Taji, however, included both sensuous and spiritual delight. That Yillah proved to be a phantom. At the end of his long pursuit he fails to recover that fullness and joy of life which he had experienced briefly in his flowery retreat on the island of Odo. Instead, he is confronted by the stark antithesis, Serenia or Hautia? Spirit or Flesh? A man must choose one or the other. Human life cannot show a full, harmonious whole. When pushed at all, it betrays a tragic dualism. As Babbalanja has said, man is a cunning compound, "seamless as the vestment without

joint, warp or woof—yet divided as by a river, spirit from flesh;
growing both ways, like a tree . . . I give thee up, oh man! thou
art twain—yet indivisible; all things—yet a poor unit at best."

Phantom though Yillah be, Taji will still pursue her. "Nay, mad-
man! Serenia is our haven. Through yonder strait, for thee, perdi-
tion lies." "Nay," cries another of his companions, "commit not the
last, last crime." Renounce, he would say, even as Babbalanja renounced. Submit to the law of life by which it lives. But Taji is still
intransigent. And the result? He has brought death on others; his
oldest companions, Jarl and Samoa, have been killed by the
avengers' arrows intended for him. He has turned his back on the
color and warmth of sensual life (Hautia) and also put himself
outside the pale of the spiritual universe (Serenia): therefore he
is, as he says, "twice dead." So dead he has no ghost. "I am his
spirit's phantom's phantom." Nothing remains for him but to accept
the blind play of the material universe, which he does. "Now I am
my own soul's emperor; and my first act is abdication." Turning his
prow into the racing tide which seizes him like a hand omnipotent,
"Hail! realm of shades!" he cries.

Mardi is a heroic effort, and not for its length only. That some of
its conclusions are the commonplaces of literature and others the
commonplaces of Christian piety, or nineteenth-century skepticism,
is not important here. To the imaginative writer it is true, as the
poet Keats said: axioms "are not axioms until they are proved upon
our pulses." In *Mardi* Melville proved his propositions on his pulse.
A heroic undertaking, I call it; for out of *Mardi* there took shape for
Herman Melville that apprehension of life which was his tragic
vision. Compelled by his experience in *Mardi*, this vision had an
organic capacity for further growth and self-expression. First
glimpsed in *Mardi*, it was to reappear with tremendous force, because substantially embodied, in *Moby Dick*. After *Moby Dick*, it
was to appear once more in *Pierre*.

Man walks in a terrifying antiquity of his race and of creation
which dwarfs his mind and dumbfounds his spirit. His life is

enacted against a background as vast as it is incalculable and mysterious. Human life is noble. "To live at all is a high vocation," Melville wrote in *Mardi*. The proposition lies so deep that it is not subject to reasonable conjecture. Over against it, and not quite outweighing it, is the recognition that neither in the aggregate, nor in the individual, does man show coherence or symmetry or power. He is a mass of self-contradictions, of grandeur and infamy, of good and evil. Is he, as Hamlet says one second, "the beauty of the world! the paragon of animals!" or, as he says the next, "the quintessence of dust?" Is he, as Montaigne said before Hamlet, "the Scrutator without knowledge, the magistrate without jurisdiction; and when all is done, the vice of the play?" Babbalanja repeats the burden of the mystery: "Do our dreams come from below, and not from the skies? Are we angels, or dogs? Oh, man, man, man! Thou art harder to solve than the Integral Calculus—yet plain as a primer."

An English critic who writes about tragedy is, very sensibly, reluctant to make positive statements defining it. This, however, he does say:—it is of the essence of tragedy that it is true to life and that it shows life to be serious and to matter. In tragedy, the writer adds, "is embodied the eternal contradiction between man's weakness and his courage, his stupidity and his magnificence, his frailty and his strength." * If we allow these statements to stand, then clearly Melville's tragic vision had much in common with those of other tragic writers. And I believe that some other comparisons along these lines can be made with illuminating results, in a way to profit our understanding of Herman Melville.

With Melville, as with Aeschylus, Sophocles and Shakespeare, tragedy is identified with men and women of heroic proportions; that is, with individuals whose human stature in one respect or another makes them tower above their fellow beings. These exceptional persons are seen to be beset by dangers. The dangers are from without and from within. According to the Greek view,

* F. L. Lucas, *Tragedy in Relation to Aristotle's "Poetics,"* Harcourt, Brace and Co., 1928, p. 57.

primarily, but not exclusively, the dangers are from without. Put in the simplest language, the gods are jealous of their prerogatives of knowledge and freedom of action. For a man to presume to know and act beyond the limits laid on mortals is to be guilty of pride and presumption, what the Greeks called *hubris*, a transgression which, with obvious reservations on their part, the gods invariably punish. Melville's version of *hubris* is apparent in Babbalanja up to a point, and in Taji to the bitter end. To Melville, who was nothing if not drastic, mortal greatness is *ipso facto* guilty of *hubris* and is punished by the gods or in the ineluctable nature of things. In *Moby Dick*, before introducing his great hero, he lays it down that the man "formed for noble tragedies" is characterized by "a half-wilful over-ruling morbidness at the bottom of his nature." And he adds, "For all men tragically great are made so through a certain morbidness. Be sure of this, O young ambition, all mortal greatness is but disease." He distinguishes between mortal, or human, greatness and this other greatness, of those who make up "this choice hidden handful of the Divine Inert, who say, with Jesus, 'Thy will, not mine, be done.'" These are not examples of mortal greatness and their end is not tragic, as Babbalanja proved at last. All mortal greatness is "tragically great."

This association of greatness and disease touches the view of greatness, beset by dangers from within, also supremely embodied by Shakespeare and to which the Greeks were not strangers. The more really endowed a man is with the attributes of human nature, the more likely he is to fall into the pitfalls that lie concealed in this common human nature. By his own gifts he is victimized. Thus, it was her great capacity to love as a mistress and a mother, quite as much as her disregard of the divine statutes and her presumption in taking justice into her own hands, that, according to Aeschylus, ensnared Clytemnestra. It was the heroic resolution of Œdipus, exercised at the time on behalf of justice and patriotism, that blinded his eyes to the fallibility he shared with his inferiors, so as to render it fatal to him. It was the noble simplicity of Othello, inseparable from his kind of strength, that blindfolded him with such tragic consequences. It was the passionate and generous self-abandon of Lear, hastening his spiritual regeneration, that misled him fatally in the first place. From Hamlet most of all we get the impression of a fatal superabundance of human endowments. If not universal, it is at any rate common in tragedy. To come closer in time to Melville and ourselves, it is to be found in Tchekov. Here, too, though diffused throughout the plays rather than attaching to a single character, is the tragic impression that the more there is of human nature, the more ripe and full-flavored it is, just so much the more does it stand in imminent danger from self-destruction.

In *Mardi*, Babbalanja is tragic, until his self-renunciation in Serenia, because he is infinitely human. Although he is forever speculating on the ultimate truth under the topics of fate and free will, the problem of evil and the individual's responsibility, he is no pale intellectual. His thinking is of his heart; it is bloodwarm. Has he knowledge of things, it is because, as he says, "Woe it is, that reveals these things. He knows himself . . . who knows adversity. To scale great heights we must come out of the lowermost depths. The way to heaven is through hell. We need fiery baptisms in the fierce flames of our bosoms." Taji destroys himself because he insists on the full expression of his manifold nature. To look ahead, if Captain Ahab's human stature had been less than it was, had he been less gifted in heart or mind, he would never have been caught and maimed in the self-conflicts of his human nature. Precisely the same remark applies to Melville's youthful hero in *Pierre*.

Melville's heroes, then, are exceptional human beings who, therefore, suffer tragic ends. This is the fact which Melville envisages along with other writers of tragedy. In Melville's case, however, the fact is felt to have a generalization behind it. In the tragedy of mind it is assumed that knowledge, or the pursuit of truth and being, are, if not wholly related, at any rate interdependent. Half-men see half the truth. The more man a man is, the more he knows, and vice versa. The relationship here is that of form and substance. The pursuit of truth is the form under which what it is to be human expresses itself. A heroic action—on it depends not alone the safety of a Thebes or a Venice, a Britain or a Denmark, but the vindication of the noblest aspirations of our race.

For the assumption of the interdependence of being and knowledge, far from composing and unifying experience, acts like a lever to uncover layer after layer of painful stress and self-conflict and ambiguity. In *Mardi* it is represented in the contingency of Babbalanja's and Taji's stories. The tragic forces to which it gives head, however, are not so much projected and dramatized in *Mardi* as they are felt within the book as exertion on Melville's part. Two years later, when, incidentally, Melville had matured his conception of what he describes in his letter to Hawthorne as the "usable truth," he suggested very concisely the dramatic and tragic possibilities that the assumption brings into action. "By usable truth," he wrote, it will be remembered, "we mean the apprehension of the absolute condition of present things as they strike the eye of the man who fears them not, though they do their worst to him,— the man who, like Russia or the British Empire, declares himself a sovereign nature (in himself) amid the powers of heaven, hell, and earth. He may perish; but so long as he exists he insists upon treating with all Powers upon an equal basis." To this Melville added, "If any of those Powers choose to withhold certain secrets, let them; . . . that does not make me tributary."

The tragedy of mind is a version of the great universal drama of being, in which the mind plays the crucial role, a role fairly shrouded in ambiguities. Between the mind and the heart of man there is a fatal conflict, of which the heart is invariably the innocent victim. At first sight, the mind appears to be the villain of the piece—a veritable Iago, practicing on the simple candor and generosity of the nature with which it is joined. Yet a closer examination of these tragedies will show that this is not the case. Melville's view of the dilemma was less romantic and more complicated, if not more realistic. Again writing to Hawthorne, who subscribed to the simple, romantic view and had dramatized it in his story *Ethan Brand*, which Melville was fresh from reading, Melville took exception to it. "It is," he wrote, "a frightful poetical creed, that the cultivation of the brain eats out the heart. But it's my *prose* opinion that in most cases, in those who have fine brains and work them well, the heart extends down to hams. And though you smoke them with the fire of tribulation, yet, like veritable hams, the head only gives the richer and better flavor." To set beside this is the description in *Moby Dick* of mortal greatness "formed for noble tragedies," in which "a globular brain" is modified by "a ponderous heart."

In Melville's view of life, a great man combines a great heart with a great mind. Both are integral parts of his greatness. The trouble begins, as Melville also perceived, in that their respective exigencies lead them in opposite directions. The human heart has its roots in the earth. It fulfills itself in the loving acceptance of men and women as they are within the limits of our common human nature. The heart, as Melville thought of it, is a great democrat. It embraces its kind, whether of high or low degree, whether Greek or Barbarian, wise or unwise. The mind is constituted quite differently. The mind is no democrat to embrace the commonplaces of the actual and the possible. It is a fiery autocrat and spurns these commonplaces. It insists on striving for the ultimate truth, which is to say that it proposes a noble, impossible ideal for the nature in which it shares. Far from being a villain, like Iago, the mind is like Prometheus. But the dualism of human nature is such that where it would glorify it brings ruin. At the centre of the destruction which it wreaks is the death of the heart, which, like Antaeus, is shorn of strength and life itself when lifted above its mother earth. Herein lies the mainspring and conclusion of the tragedy of mind. The great man, the fairest possible semblance of humanity, is impelled to achieve a noble and impossible ideal, and in the very effort to achieve this ideal destroys the fairest semblance of humanity. He brings death within and without. Thus it was with Taji, whose two oldest companions were killed by the avengers' arrows intended for him. Captain Ahab,

already maimed, dies cut off from the crew of his ship, who were also
the victims of the heroic, indeed the superhuman, exertion of his
humanity. Pierre, like Hamlet, royally endowed with the attributes
of human nature, is determined to shoulder all the claims of human
nature. And, like Taji, he brings death on the only two persons
who cling to him and dies himself at his own hands.

Mardi is the first of Melville's tragedies. Its tragic force, as I have
hinted, is less projected or dramatized in the story it tells than it is
felt in its innermost recesses, that is, in a heroic undertaking on
Melville's part. His Calvinist's importunity to confront the truth
directly is identified with Babbalanja, who, not content to have arrived at the penultimate truth, cried out for the ultimate. There is
this fierce preoccupation in *Mardi*. And there is another preoccupation just as forceful. If the first represented Melville's Calvinism, the
second represented his no less idealistic revolt against Calvinism. I
speak of Melville's preoccupation with being. Melville, identified
with Taji, would be satisfied with nothing less than the expression of
his whole human nature. He would not shirk his spiritual nature by
resorting to materialistic negations. He would not abate his speculative mind by hiding ostrich-wise for the sake of an easy faith or
worldly peace of mind. He would not deny his physical nature as a
short-cut around truth to salvation. Quite apart from the allegory
in *Mardi*, the book is an insistent image of the full human life. In
other words, it is an image of Yillah's significance to Taji. It has
the preoccupation with truth which alone can satisfy man's spiritual
and his intellectual nature. The world of *Mardi* is "the world of
mind." Not only does it contemplate this world; but its allegory
is of the mind's way of seeing and ordering experience. Nevertheless, throughout the book, Melville is constantly making shift
to allow for man's physical and sensuous nature. The mental character of the book is offset by a lavish sensuousness of decor un-
paralleled in Melville's writings. Then, too, the endless speculation
on the soul is accompanied by almost endless feasting. To counter-
balance the soul's sad importunities, there is a continual crying up

of the joys of the belly, of deep belly laughter and the sensuous indolence of smoking. *Mardi* presents an image in the individual's consciousness of the millenium, of which there is a fleeting vision in the opening pages, in which human opposites will harmonize and Dante, for example, will "shake sides with fat Rabelais."

All this gives weight to the contention that *Mardi* is a heroic undertaking, in which Melville takes on the full weight of what it is to be a man and struggles to embrace in a noble synthesis all the mixed elements in man's nature. The form proposed for this synthesis is the pursuit of truth. *Mardi's* tragedy, or Melville's tragic experience in *Mardi*, is to discover that the exertion to action in this synthesis produces the opposite of the end in view.

Mardi has force, yet it fails of the force which we are entitled to expect of tragedy, of whatever kind, and the reason for this failure is not far to seek. To say that the weakness lies in the unreality of Yillah or any of the characters only touches the surface of what is wanting. It presents an image of harmonious being. Yet the image is partial. More important, it is incomplete as an exertion of being or consciousness. There is what strikes one as muscular action to the book; yet, on the whole, it has no sensational body. I would say of *Mardi* exactly what Melville once said of Hawthorne's *Twice Told Tales*, "Their deeper meanings are worthy of a Brahmin," yet "there is something lacking—a good deal lacking to the plump sphericity of the man." In spite of Melville's insistence on man's sensuous nature, that nature is not integral in the book, but counts as decor only. Something else still, and something more important, is lacking in *Mardi*. It has all the lopsidedness of precocity. It has brilliance without warmth. It is emotionally immature. Underneath the intellectual juggling, there are the tensions of profoundly serious intellectual aspirations, and we feel the reality of the mind in the throes of its noble importunity after the truth, but the realities of life and being which Melville identified with the heart—these are not there. "I am certain of nothing but of the holyness of the Heart's affections, and the truth of Imagination," wrote John Keats.

In *Mardi* the truth of imagination is partial because the heart's affections have not been counted in. The realities of the heart's affections, which are sacrificed by the mind to its infinite aspirations, are not felt. Or if felt—if, in other words, there is a victim, as tragedy requires that there should be—then the victim in *Mardi* is felt as such a one as Fayaway in *Typee* at the very most. But tragedy requires more heft than our sympathies for such a one can give. Tragedy requires a more poignant, a more human victim. In *Mardi* it is as in the story of Abraham when commanded to sacrifice Isaac; there was no tragedy because a sheep was substituted as the victim of the "exacting behest."

The tragic necessity that the mind is under to reach for the infinite is present in *Mardi.* But the tragedy of mind involves another victim of the mind's aspirations than the mind itself. Without this victim the tragic force is less than it should be by more than a half. Before Melville could imbue tragedy with the force which tragedy requires, he would have to command pity. He would have to realize the realities of the heart's attachments, or, in Keats's phrase, "the holyness of the Heart's affections."

CHAPTER FOUR

Redburn – White Jacket

IN 1849 Melville was writing at top speed. In April he published *Mardi*, in November, *Redburn*. By the time *Redburn* made its appearance, Melville was in London, arranging for the publication of *White Jacket*, published there in January and in New York in March, 1850. By the end of 1850 Melville was well along with *Moby Dick*. The unfolding within himself, of which Melville had written to Hawthorne, was rapidly taking place. "But I feel," he wrote, "that I am now come to the inmost leaf of the bulb, and that shortly the flower must fall to the mould."

Among Melville's books of this period *Redburn* makes a dingy, poor-relation's appearance. It alone in the company does not reflect in any way the glamor of the South Seas or the almost final waters of the Pacific. The story of a voyage, like *Typee*—"His First Voyage" is its subtitle—Melville's destination was not the Marquesas nor Tahiti where "Eden, isled, empurpled glows." The voyage was no less prosaic than aboard a merchantman bound from New York to Liverpool and back. To Melville, who had bled *Mardi*, *Redburn* was only a pot-boiler which he wrote to provide himself with tobacco. What can a poor man do, he asked, "with duns all around him . . . like the devils about St. Anthony—what can you expect of that poor devil?—What but a beggarly *Redburn*?" Nevertheless, *Redburn* possesses great significance in Melville's unfolding development. What is more, *Redburn* is charming. I am not sure that it is not the most charming of all his books. In any case, its charm is peculiar, a combination of liveliness and wistfulness.

Melville, now close to thirty, looks back upon his younger self, aged eighteen, fatherless, his family left in a penurious gentility, undergoing his first experience of the world, in a mood in which melancholy and self-pity are mixed with irony. "I had learned to think much and bitterly before my time," he wrote. As his name would indicate, Wellingborough Redburn, as Melville calls his younger self, makes an incongruous figure in the forecastle of a merchantman. He is very conscious of being a gentleman's son and of what is due to him on this account. He has also been taught in the Presbyterian Sunday school at home exactly what is right and wrong to do. He belonged to the Juvenile Total Abstinence Society in his village. Young Wellingborough is bound to have some shocking revelations. When he comes aboard ship he asks for a light, so that he may find his way to his quarters, and has for answer, "Strike your eyes together and make one . . . we don't have any lights here." After several hours out, some of the sailors are still sleeping off their liquor. One sailor among these is seized with delirium tremens and rushes shrieking to the deck and plunges overboard. Wellingborough is horrified by this, and horrified again when he finds he is assigned to the suicide's bunk. The sailors are delighted to see the boy frightened and take the opportunity to tell him "what a hard and wicked life [he] had entered upon, and how that such things happened frequently at sea, and that they were used to it."

Not once all the way across does Redburn meet with any kindness. The captain of whom he hoped so much is the worst bully of them all and cheats him of his wages. The worst thing about the sailors lies in that they are all dominated by the most vicious man among them, a man who instinctively hates Wellingborough and sets the rest of the crew against him. This is the sailor Jackson. "In fact he was a great bully . . . [his eye] was a horrible thing; and I would give much to forget that I have ever seen it."

In his wretchedness on the ship, Wellingborough Redburn looks forward all the more breathlessly to Europe and to setting foot on English soil. His father, in his affluence, had travelled much abroad and had told his son about Liverpool and Havre and St. Paul's in London. Wellingborough thinks of Europe and of fine old lands and mossy ruins and noble cathedrals rising above crooked streets. What should he, brought up as he had been, expect to find in England but old minsters and Lord Mayor's dinners and coronations, May-poles, jolly fox-hunting squires and Derby races? His first sight of Liverpool gave his expectations the lie. "Looking shoreward, I beheld ranges of dingy warehouses, which seemed very deficient in the elements of the marvellous; and bore a most unexpected resemblance to the warehouses along South Street in New York." After days spent walking about the city, his first impression had broadened and grown blacker. "Poverty, poverty, poverty, in almost endless vistas: and want and woe staggered arm in arm along these miserable streets."

Beside the character of Jackson, another impression that revealed itself in Redburn's mind and remained at the back of his speculations for years to come was of a woman and her three small children starving in a warehouse cellar. At the sight of them he hurried after bread and water and descended with it to where they were. Then "I crawled up. . . . For I well knew that the law, which would let them perish of themselves without giving them one cup of water, would spend a thousand pounds, if necessary, in convicting him who should so much as offer to relieve them from their miserable existence." The next day and the next he passed by and dropped more bread down to them. The third day the cellar was empty. In place of the woman and her children "a heap of quick lime was glistening."

The crucial episode in *Redburn* is connected with an old guidebook which had belonged to Wellingborough's father, and which he had taken lovingly along with him, so that he might see the fine sights which his father used to talk about. With this guide-book to direct him, he set off one morning to find the very hotel where his father "slept and dined, smoked his cigar, and read the papers." Since he was too poor and shabby to expect to be admitted himself into the hotel, this was a purely spiritual and sentimental pilgrim-age. Following his guide-book, he arrived where the hotel should have stood. There was nothing there that even resembled a hotel. A passerby whom he dared question answered that he thought he had heard the name of the hotel—yes, and if he was not mistaken, his own father had been one of the workmen engaged to tear it down. "Then, indeed, a new light broke in upon me concerning my guide-book, and all my previous dim suspicions were almost con-firmed. It was nearly half a century behind the age! and no more fit to guide me about the town than the map of Pompeii."

This crucial episode is carefully placed just halfway through the book. Whether the literal truth or not, it served to focus the sig-nificance of his first voyage, as it emerged for Melville from his re-capitulation of it. According to the story, immediately upon this revelation Wellingborough took counsel with himself. "Here, now, oh Wellingborough . . . learn a lesson and never forget it. This world, my boy, is a moving world; its Riddough's Hotels are for-ever being pulled down; it never stands still; and its sands are for-ever shifting. . . . And, Wellingborough, as your father's guide-book is no guide for you, neither would yours (could you afford to buy a modern one today) be a true guide to those who come after you. Guide-books, Wellingborough, are the least reliable books in all literature; and nearly all literature, in one sense, is made up of guide-books. . . . Every age makes its own guide-books, and the old ones are used for wastepaper."

Here, out of the mouth of young Redburn, is a generalization such as *Mardi*, out of the mouth of Babbalanja, abounds in. Also, like many of Babbalanja's, this of Redburn resembles one of the generalizations to which Emerson had given currency in the 1840's. The books of the past cannot serve the present, Emerson had writ-ten; each generation must write its own books. The point of dif-ference in the resemblance here between *Mardi* and *Redburn* is that in *Redburn* the generalization is embodied in terms of the hero's personal experience; it is compelled out of the tension of that experience. Therefore, it is organically related to fact. Whether the episode is fiction or not, the discovery that this book on which he had relied so much, "the book full of fine old family associations . . . was next to useless," shows that Melville had glimpsed, in his initial experience of the world, that his father's world of social privilege and economic security, of right and wrong firmly established by the sanctions and prescriptions of Presbyterian orthodoxy (or, as it had become, Presbyterian respectability), did not rest on immutable foundations. It is in the nature of things that the landmarks and signposts which men set up for their comfort and salvation have a temporary value at best. The world he had to face was not his father's. It was a wider and vaguer, a more indefinite and dangerous world than his father's. This "was a sad, a solemn, and a most melancholy thought."

Like *Typee, Redburn* is a story of discovery, or what, in this case, is another aspect of the same thing—it is a story of disillusionment. The young hero comes quickly to understand that the world of his childhood is a painted fiction, that sailors and seafaring are not what his fancy pictured them, and that reality everywhere is harsh and cruel, in Europe as in America. Truth, however, has its way of giving a hand to him who can face it. Young Redburn, suddenly stripped bare of all illusions, does not face the truth about the world without putting on stature. On the voyage home he is on his own feet and shifts for himself. At the same time his sympathies are no longer adolescently self-centred. He sympathizes with, and manfully befriends young Harry Bolton, another gentleman's son, who is, on the way back, in just the same pitiful plight that Redburn has been in on the way over. (The sailors instinctively disliked Harry, too.) His sympathies reach further than this. He has shaken off "those local and social prejudices, that are the marring of most men, and from which, for the mass, there seems no possible escape," and to which, it would seem, Americans are peculiarly subject, so that we "leave to other countries the carrying out of the principle that stands at the head of our Declaration of Independence." Now young Wellingborough sees that even the nigger ship's cook "has his claims to humanity and normal equality." He sympathizes with the poor immigrants cut off in the steerage "from the most indispensable conveniences" and facing the terrors of an unknown world. And finally Redburn comes to know "the natural antipathy with which almost all seamen and steerage passengers regard the inmates of the cabin [cabin passengers] . . ." He himself did not feel charitably disposed to these gentry, "not because they happened to be cabin passengers: not at all: but only because they seemed the most finical, miserly, mean men and women that ever stepped over the Atlantic." Not once does Melville relax his realistic view of the sailors to paint them in more engaging and romantic colors. He shows them to be both weak and brutal. Nevertheless, his mature sympathies are with the sailors, or, what is the same thing, his mature indignation is not directed at the sailors at whose hands he suffered, but at the genteel well-to-do of the world, who deny their common humanity by withholding this humanity even in the act of dispensing charity to sailors. "Will you throw open your parlors to him; invite him to dinner? or give him a season ticket to your pew in church?—No, You will do no such thing; but at a distance you will perhaps subscribe a dollar or two for the building of a hospital to accommodate sailors already broken down; or for the distribution of excellent books among tars who cannot read." Presently, setting forth the perception which released his sympathy, Melville wrote (he was maintaining the fact that Byron's small hands betokened his noble birth): "And so it did: for Lord Byron was as all the rest of us—the son of a *man*. And so are the dainty-handed, and wee-footed half-caste paupers in Lima; who, if their hands and feet are entitled to consideration, would constitute the oligarchy of all Peru. . . .

"Dandies! amputate yourselves, if you will; but know, and be assured, oh democrats, that, like a pyramid, a great man stands on a broad base."

Between *Redburn* and *Typee* there is a similarity the more striking because it is checked and crossed by dissimilarities. What would seem to be the same waywardness is in both. In the one he found natural goodness in a tribe of cannibals. More normally, one would say of the other, he found natural depravity in the forecastle of merchantmen. But in this same forecastle, as he came to understand when he wrote *Redburn*, he found the natural dignity of humanity—the common, suffering, tragic dignity of man.

2

"Yet so untouchable is true dignity," he wrote in *White Jacket*, "that there are cases wherein to be flogged at the gangway is no dishonor; though, to abase and hurl down the last pride of some sailor who has piqued him, be sometimes the secret motive, with some malicious officer, in procuring him to be condemned to the lash. But this feeling of the innate dignity remaining untouched, though outwardly the body be scarred for the whole term of the natural life, is one of the hushed things, buried among the holiest privacies of the soul." In *White Jacket*, Melville's book about his life on board a United States man-of-war, which followed on *Redburn*'s heels, Melville was groping to the sensational realities back of his remark in the earlier book, that it is the noble lineage of us all that we are each of us "the son of a *man*."

I spoke in the last chapter of Melville's use of the antithesis of heart and mind. In terms of this antithesis, whereas *Mardi* was a book of the mind, *White Jacket*, like *Redburn* just before it, follows the heart. An antiphonal movement, begun in muted and tentative manner in *Redburn*, has gathered in force and volume, and, in consequence, *White Jacket* is the ruddiest of Melville's books; it possesses the heartiest humanity. I do not wish to imply that Melville's realism in *White Jacket* debilitates itself by blinking the ugly realities which fall within its view. Nor do I mean that Melville's humanity in *White Jacket* is like Walt Whitman's: Melville does not bolt down his fellow beings, good, bad and indifferent, all with the same relish. In *White Jacket* Melville sticks to what he had declared in *Typee*, that the "pent up wickedness of five hundred men" on a man-of-war nearly overturned all his previous belief in men's goodness. In *White Jacket*, although his soul shuddered at his revelations, he set before himself, for us to see, all of what he called "the knotted, trebly intertwisted villainy, accumulating at a sort of compound interest in a man-of-war."

Nevertheless, the whole force and direction of the book is prompted by the human heart's democracy. Here is an act of recognition, in which to see is to feel. The recognition that all men are one preserves itself and grows stronger in the teeth of all that attests the imbecility and depravity of men. And here it is further seen that only in this recognition and acceptance can the individual fulfill his humanity. That is, the man who keeps his feet out of the mud of common humanity, who does not plant them firmly on the common ground, cannot be a great man, standing like a pyramid "on a broad base"; he "is only the brittle porcelain pagoda that tottles on a toe."

It is a superficial criticism of *White Jacket* that dismisses everything Melville says about Christianity and democracy as palatable platitudes intended to secure popularity. To the Articles of War he opposes the Sermon on the Mount and the Declaration of Independence. The Articles of War, cataloguing the crimes for which the offenders shall suffer death or ignominy, is the instrument of disunion, arbitrarily setting up some men to judge others and, in the spirit of war itself, setting men against themselves. On the other hand, the Sermon on the Mount and the Declaration of Independence are great affirmations of the unity and the brotherhood of man. From the heartless beneficence which he condemned in *Redburn* he distinguishes true virtue. In *White Jacket* he writes, "When Virtue sits high aloft on a frigate's poop, when Virtue is crowned in the cabin a commodore, when Virtue rules by compulsion, and domineers over Vice as a slave, then Virtue, though her mandates be outwardly observed, bears little interior sway. To be efficacious,

Virtue must come down from aloft, even as our blessed Redeemer came down to redeem our whole man-of-war world; to that end, mixing with its sailors and sinners as equals."

Far from being extraneous, or put in only to win popularity, Melville's devotion to Christianity and democracy in *White Jacket* proceeds from what lies deeper than Melville's conviction in the book; it proceeds from his deepest sensibility. If there is any doubt of this, it is only necessary to look at a critical essay of Melville's written in the following summer, in every word of which he was profoundly serious. There he lays it down that what distinguishes the new and the best literature of his time and land is that "which now takes the practical lead in this world," namely, "the unshackled, democratic spirit of Christianity in all things." In other words, the best literature of his day, and that most deserving reception, has and will have the force of universal sympathy, of which Christianity and democracy are the great affirmations and vehicles. It has, and will have, precisely the force of the heart which Melville was expressing in *White Jacket*.

White Jacket follows *Redburn* and has the same sombre realism, but the maturity which was only anticipated in *Redburn* is a fact in *White Jacket*. On the dark ground of reality Melville's sympathies have taken life and a reality of their own. All that is affirmative and radical and warm-blooded about *White Jacket* centers upon the hero of the book, Jack Chase, an actual seaman whom Melville had known aboard the *United States*. Melville's friendship for him, recovered, re-lived and idealized, is crucial in *White Jacket*. In contrast with Captain Claret, who commands the frigate, Jack Chase has an essential superiority as compared with the factitious superiority of the captain. Jack was "better than a hundred common mortals." He was "an entire army; Jack was a thousand-strong." He was "tall and well-knit, with a clear, open eye, a fine broad brow, and an abounding nut-brown beard. No man ever had a better heart or a bolder. He was loved as a seaman, and admired by the officers; and even when the captain spoke to him, it was with a

slight air of respect. . . . There was such an abounding air of
good sense and good feeling about the man that he who could not
love him would thereby pronounce himself a knave. I thanked my
sweet stars that kind fortune had placed me near him, though under
him, in the frigate; and from the outset Jack and I were fast
friends . . . we maintop men were brothers, one and all; and we
loaned ourselves to each other with all the freedom in the world."
Jack was a "stickler for the Rights of Man and the liberties of the
world." He had taken part in a civil war in South America, be-
friending "heart and soul what he deemed the cause of the Right."
On one occasion when the crew was mustered for the flogging of
an old seaman, Jack was held back by force from striking the captain. "By God, I can't stand it," he cried. Jack had the air and
easy good manners of the true gentleman. He must, says Melville,
"have been a by-blow of some British Admiral of the Blue."

Yet he was the people's man. His friend, a fore-top-man who
writes poetry which finds no readers, calls the public a monster with
the head of a jackass. Jack demurs; he does not like that. He himself, when on shore, is "part of the public." No, says the poet,
"You are then a part of the people." Right, says Jack, "right as this
leg . . . the public and the people! Ay, ay, my lads, let us hate the
one and cleave to the other." When the ship has been for some
time in the harbor of Rio and liberty to go ashore has not been
granted, it is Jack who puts himself at the head of the crew—"I'm
your tribune, boys; I'm your Rienzi." And it is Jack whose polite
audacity wrests from the captain the "liberty" they demand. It is
of his generous abundant nature that he loves poetry and shouts
Byron's verses in the rigging. He has that in him, he tells White
Jacket, "which under happier skies . . . might have made a Homer
of me." Nothing subdues his exuberance or dims his radiance. He
has "a heart in him like a mastodon." Within his capacious heart
there blazes a veritable bonfire of good feeling and fellowship. In
the warmth that he irradiates, the members of the crew melt down
into unity and unison. The "martial formalities" of life in a man-

of-war lose something of their force of barbed-wire entanglements. Under his influence the officers show human countenances. They *"shipped their quarterdeck faces."* The unwonted spectacle was presented "of gun-room officers mingling with *the people* in applauding a mere seaman like Jack Chase. . . ."

Besides Jack Chase, there is another Jack, Mad Jack, a lieutenant, who is also on board. "Mad Jack is in his saddle on the sea. *That* is his home; he would not care much, if another flood came and overflowed the dry land. . . . Mad Jack was expressly created and labelled for a tar." He is all compact of muscle and physical courage; for the rest, he is hard common sense. His true ability compares with the captain's in a sudden, furious gale "one terrific night," when the ship is rounding Cape Horn and all seems on the point of being lost. Mad Jack assumes authority: "'Hard *up* the helm!' shouted Captain Claret. 'Damn you,' raged Mad Jack, 'Hard down,— hard down I say, and be damned to you!' Contrary orders! but Mad Jack's were obeyed." Because of his command, the opposite of the captain's, Mad Jack is the saving genius of the ship.

White Jacket is a book of the heart in Melville's sense of the word; the heart as opposed to the head. As such, it is concentrated on Jack Chase. We are to notice, further, that the world of *White Jacket*, unlike that of *Mardi's* world of mind, is the world of facts and actualities, the world of sensuous impressions, human affections and common sense. Mad Jack, the exponent of common sense, belongs, as we see him, side by side with Jack Chase. This external view of the book only reflects the interior view. In no other of his books is there such a cordial glow of fellow feeling, and such a ripe humanity. What is more, this humanity, this love of kind, is directed to a practical purpose.

White Jacket was written with a practical intention. It was written to reveal the abuses of authority in the American Navy and to plead for the reform of these abuses. A book of the heart, it is also a book of reform, or of common sense, since it pleads for reform within the sphere of the actual. It is very possible that *White*

Jacket prompted action to ameliorate conditions and practices in our navy. A book of the heart, it accepts the actual and the possible, the two opposite sides of this acceptance being common sense, or prudence, and faith. "Fate is Fate," confides Jack Chase to White Jacket; and "Don't deny the blessed Bible now! don't do it." So Melville concludes *White Jacket* with these words, in which a realistic view of the world does not shake his faith: "Oh, shipmates . . . Life is a voyage that's homeward bound!"

3

We see only a part of the truth about *Redburn* and *White Jacket* if we see them in relation to *Mardi*. We get a fuller view of them if we look at them retrospectively, that is, from the point of view of all Melville wrote after them. Of course, we shall only be able to command this point of view when we shall have connected *Moby Dick* to everything else that Melville wrote after *White Jacket* to the last year of his life. Yet, to get some benefit from this point of view, we need not go even so far ahead as *Moby Dick*. In the summer of 1850—that is, in the interim between *White Jacket* and *Moby Dick*—Melville wrote a critical essay called "Hawthorne and His Mosses," which is as self-revealing as any short piece he ever wrote.

In this essay Melville speaks beautifully of the "wild moonlight of contemplative humor that bathes" Hawthorne's "Mosses." He speaks of "the enchanting landscape in the soul of this Hawthorne, this most excellent man of Mosses." He does reverence (but with no trace of obsequiousness to the older author) to the charm that the public had come to recognize in Hawthorne. But Melville does not stop where the popular approval of Hawthorne stopped. "It is," he writes, "the least part of genius that attracts admiration. Where Hawthorne is known, he seems to be deemed a pleasant writer, with a pleasant style,—a sequestered, harmless man." Then, speaking for himself and shouting himself to be one who had drastically parted from the average reader, even the average reader of Hawthorne, Melville goes on to say: "But there is no man in whom humor and love, like mountain peaks, soar to such a rapt height as to receive the irradiations of the upper skies;—there is no man in whom humor and love are developed in that high form called genius; no such man can exist without also possessing, as the indispensable complement of these, a great, deep intellect, which drops down into the universe like a plummet. Or, love and humor are only the eyes through which such an intellect views this world. The great beauty in such a mind is but the product of its strength."

Melville's meaning when he speaks of "a great, deep intellect, which drops down into the universe like a plummet" is explained in the next page. Referring to Hawthorne again, he writes, "For spite of all the Indian summer sunlight on the hither side of Hawthorne's soul, the other side—like the dark half of the physical sphere—is shrouded in a blackness, ten times black. . . . You may be witched by his sunlight . . . but there is the blackness of darkness beyond. . . . Now, it is that blackness in Hawthorne, of which I have spoken, that so fixes and fascinates me."

Whatever their truth with respect to Hawthorne, Melville's words throw an illuminating light on the whole course of his own development as it lay behind him at the time and, also, as it led almost directly to his wonderful maturity. *Typee* had been a poem in praise of the sensuous, sunny side of life. To be sure, it contains overtures and even vistas which betray the knowledge of "the other side—like the dark half of the physical sphere," but this side is not explored; it is not strictly pondered. To overlook *Mardi* for the moment, in *Redburn* and *White Jacket* Melville begins to explore the dark side of things. But this exploration of the dark, as opposed to the sunny, sensuous, side of life, must be understood, as Melville recognized it in the mirror which all unconsciously he held up to himself, namely, as an integral part of his growth from *Typee* on. It is a manifestation of that strength of which love is the eyes. The strong mature heart, Melville would say, takes on its own self-knowledge. It takes up its burden of love and, simultaneously, its burden of pain and mystery. The heart, "the all engendering heart of man," reveals the mystery of life. Man's darkness "is immeasurably deeper than the plummet of the mere critic. For it is not the brain that can test such a man; it is only the heart." The heart, I repeat, reveals the mystery; the stronger the heart, the more it reveals. The mind, however—being, in Melville's words "the indispensable complement"—sharing this same strength, faces this mystery. Faces? Rather, fathoms into it like a plummet and in innumerable forms bodies it forth.

At one point in this essay Melville speculates as to whether Hawthorne's darkness is simply a paint to dip his brush in so that he can get certain chiaroscuro effects, or "whether there really lurks in him, perhaps unknown to himself, a touch of Puritanic gloom." Then Melville adds what is perhaps the most striking statement in the whole striking essay: "Certain it is," he writes, "that this great power of blackness in him derives its force from its appeals to the Calvinistic sense of Innate Depravity and Original Sin, from whose visitations, in some shape or other no deeply thinking mind is always and wholly free. For, in certain moods, no man can weigh this world without throwing in something, somehow like Original Sin, to strike the uneven balance."

Certain it is that, as the child of orthodox Presbyterian parents, Melville was early acquainted with some notion of original sin. Certain it is, moreover, that while still in his formative years, his notion of original sin was horribly realized for him in the impressions which he drew from his characterization of the sailor Jackson. Jackson's nature was depraved. In him there was nothing left but "the foul lees and dregs of a man." An object of terror and loathing, as Melville drew him, Jackson is also—a point not to be missed—something of an object of pity. What Melville barely hints in this respect about Jackson he says explicitly about another example of depravity, Bland, the master-at-arms in *White Jacket*. Like Jackson, Bland has a snaky eye. "I could not," writes Melville, "I could not but abominate him when I thought of his conduct; but I pitied the continual gnawing which, under all his deftly donned disguises, I saw lying at the bottom of his soul. . . . Besides, a studied observation of Bland convinced me that he was an organic and irreclaimable scoundrel, who did wicked deeds as the cattle browse the herbage, because wicked deeds seemed the legitimate operation of his whole infernal organisation. Phrenologically, he was without a soul. Is it to be wondered at, that the devils are irreligious? What, then, thought I, who is to blame in this matter?"

Who is to blame in the matter, Melville asks in *White Jacket*, since the individuals in question do not will their wickedness. "For one, I will not take the Day of Judgment upon me by authoritatively pronouncing upon the essential criminality of any man-of-war's man; and Christianity has taught me that, at the Last Day, man-of-war's men will not be judged by the Articles of War nor by the *United States Statutes at Large*, but by immutable laws, ineffably beyond the comprehension of the Honorable Board of Commodores and Navy Commissioners."

And yet he does not leave the matter here. Once more in *White Jacket*, and in a curious context, he casts his eyes into the infinite obscure which shrouds the origin of evil. It happens that the ship's surgeon, one Cadawallader Cuticle, M.D., has a collection of Parisian casts in his stateroom, "representing all imaginable malformations of the human members, both organic and induced by disease." Chief among them is the head of an elderly woman, "with an aspect singularly gentle and meek, but at the same time wonderfully expressive of a gnawing sorrow, never to be relieved." A face, one would say, to arouse all a man's compassion, "but when you first beheld it, no such emotions ever crossed your mind. All your eyes and all your horrified soul were fast fascinated and frozen by the sight of a hideous, crumpled horn, like that of a ram, downward growing out from the forehead, and partly shadowing the face. . . . The horn seemed the mark of a curse for some mysterious sin, conceived and committed before the spirit had entered the flesh. Yet that sin seemed something imposed and not voluntarily sought: some sin growing out of the heartless necessities of the predestination of things; some sin under which the sinner sank in sinless woe."

It would be unreasonable to expect consistency of Melville in his treatment of evil. The fact that evil is, this was all-important to him. It was this recognition that largely determined his intellectual affinities. Soon after the publication of *Mardi*, Melville wrote to Evert Duyckinck: "Nay, I do not oscillate in Emerson's rainbow, but prefer rather to hang myself in mine own halter than swing in any other man's swing. Yet I think Emerson is more than a brilliant fellow." In *Mardi*, really in the course of writing *Mardi*, he had broken from all premises on which an extensive sympathy between himself and Emerson could be based. "Our young people," Emerson had written, "are diseased with the theological problems of original sin, origin of evil, predestination and the like. These never presented a practical difficulty to any man,—never darkened across any man's road who did not go out of his way to seek them. These are the soul's mumps and measles. . . ."

In *Mardi* Melville wrote, "For evil is the chronic malady of the universe; and checked in one place, breaks forth in another." He had started out on the Emersonian assumptions that the soul can be a harmonious entity and that between a man's soul and the universe there can exist a perfect harmony. "The waving of the boughs in the storm is new to me and old. It takes me by surprise, and yet it is not unknown . . . yet it is certain that the power to produce the delight does not result in nature but in man, or in a harmony of both." So Emerson wrote in his first book *Nature*, and, much later, "I believe . . . in the moral design of the universe, it exists hospitably for the weal of souls." Melville started off in *Mardi* from just such assumptions as these and came, as we know, to conclusions the opposite of those to which one would expect them to lead. That Emerson could affirm a radiant and harmonious universe argued for Melville that something was missing in his human make-up: "His belly is in his chest and his brains descend down into his neck," he wrote to Duyckinck in the letter which I quoted above, adding, "I could readily see in Emerson, notwithstanding his merit, a gaping flaw. It was, the insinuation, that had he lived in those days when the world was made, he might have offered some valuable suggestions."

Because Emerson ignored the reality of evil, his views in all directions were vitiated. His light could not illumine, much less give any warmth. On the other hand, Melville was drawn to Calvinism because it recognized the cardinal fact of evil. He did not subscribe to the dogma which Calvinism fastened to the fact, but inasmuch as it recognized the fact it was truthful and commanded Melville's respect as Emerson did not. For the same reason, fundamentally, he was drawn to Hawthorne. But there were other than intellectual considerations for Hawthorne's magnetic influence upon him. An artist cannot face a void. In *Mardi,* where he had turned from the Emersonian universe, he had ended up in a void. In Hawthorne, he found in the place of that void a tingling and universal presentiment of evil. He found in recognizable form the truth of darkness which, as he already knew, cannot be ignored but at the price of light. He found darkness palpable; in Hawthorne it was part of the life-blood of poetry and tragedy.

For Melville the dark side of life included the mysterious necessity for sin and suffering. Whatever the explanation for the necessity, the fact of sin presents one definite aspect. It involves separation from one's kind, separation it may be, by "fate and ban." Captain Claret in *White Jacket* is a dull and brutal man, still "of whatever acts Captain Claret might have been guilty . . . perhaps none of them proceeded from any personal, organic hard-heartedness." Captain Claret, then, was not banned of inscrutable laws but of man-made laws. His position of authority had shut him out from common sympathies. Mr. Cuticle is shut off from his fellow men in another way. He is "the meagre death's head of a [man]." About to operate on a young sailor, he removes first his wig, then his false teeth and then his glass eye. They are all outward tokens of Dr. Cuticle's character. For he is spiritually dead. It is of no human concern to him when he is told soon after the operation that the young sailor has died. If he feels it at all, he feels it as a blow to his professional prestige, for, as he confesses, he would rather cut off a man's arm than dismember the wing of the most delicate pheasant. From vulgar vanity and from professional pride, he too has cut himself off from the common heart of man. We should remember Hautia in *Mardi*, a symbol of evil and spiritual death in whom pride and sensual lust had excluded the affections that bind men and women together in an organic whole. Hautia looks forward to Mrs. Glendinning in *Pierre*, another symbol of evil. She is proud, with the pride of wealth, of beauty, of station, and of superior intellect and will. Yea, "the Infinite Haughtiness had first fashioned her; and the haughty world had further moulded her." She moved to the outward eye in "the gilded prosperities of life," and to the inward eye of truth, "in the dreary heart vacancies of the conventional life."

4

A sense of evil is not simply the knowledge that evil is in the universe. It is the stuff of consciousness. A man who has no sense of evil is spiritually dead; his emotional experience as a whole is torpid, like a body which has a deficient nervous system. For the imaginative writer it is the most effective principle of control. It puts him in a strong, primitive relation to his fellow men.

A sense of evil is a dimension of consciousness like depth added to height and breadth, in which all objects as items of consciousness can share. It is the possibility of complete plasticity, being a shaping vision that gives the greatest human significance to its materials, at the same time rendering these materials wholly tractable to its vision. For it implies an equilibrium in the consciousness which can resolve the stiffest opposites in terms of sensation. Fundamentally, a sense of evil implies a sense of otherness, a sense of the non-human, the utterly alien and, at once with this, the recognition of terrifying intimacy. And from this source follows the reconciliation of the far and the near, the abstract and the concrete, the within and the without, horror and tenderness, pity and fear.

Melville's sense of evil was of his maturity just as a greater capacity to love and pity was of his maturity. Evil, he came to understand, was of the same reality as love, and in the man who ignores evil love is less real by half. The love of such a man is sub-human and nothing poignant. If the whole truth was embodied or exemplified in any man, that man was Shakespeare. Shakespeare, Melville wrote, was to be adored for "those occasional flashings forth of the intuitive Truth in him" out of "the infinite obscure of his background." Shakespeare's "darkness" was of his truth—of his reality. So, too, was his compassion; "Ah, he's full of sermons-on-the-mount, and gentle, aye, almost as Jesus." Melville could respond the more wholeheartedly to Shakespeare now that he, too, had come to realize the human reality—the human predicament. He had come to realize the substance of tragedy, without which the formulas for tragedy are of no force. In *Mardi* he had projected as a form the tragedy of mind. Now he commanded the substance to add to the form. Now he knew all that was at stake in the tragedy of mind.

Man's life is enacted against a mysterious, inscrutable backdrop. He makes his foreground world of human values. From innocence and joy of sensuous life he grows up to love and to the deeper ties of his emotional nature. He makes a little world of love grounded in the organic unity of man, that brotherhood of man which bespeaks the fatherhood of God. This little world of color and human warmth hangs perilously among "the heartless necessities of the predestination of things," or what he called in *Moby Dick* "the heartless voids and immensities of the universe." But, alas, the perils of the unknown life are not all outside. Evil is the chronic malady of the world. Evil, as Melville had come to see, is a league of destruction, either fated or artfully entered into as a dark partnership, between men and the heartless voids and immensities of the universe.

CHAPTER FIVE

Moby Dick

ABOUT HALF WAY through *Moby Dick* there is a passage of description and commentary which must stand at the head of this chapter. In "The Funeral" Melville speaks of the enormous carcass of a whale, stripped of its blubber and finally cut loose from the whaler which has despoiled it:

"For hours and hours from the almost stationary ship that hideous sight is seen. Beneath the unclouded and mild azure sky, upon the fair face of the pleasant sea, wafted by the joyous breezes, that great mass of death floats on and on, till lost in infinite perspectives. There's a most doleful and most mocking funeral! The sea-vultures all in pious mourning, the air-sharks all punctiliously in black or speckled. . . . Oh, horrible vulturism of earth! from which not the mightiest whale is free."

This is not the end, however. "Desecrated as the body is, a vengeful ghost survives and hovers over it to scare." Espied in the distance by some passing vessel, with the white spray heaving high against it, straightway the harmless corpse is set down in the log, "*shoals, rocks and breakers hereabouts: beware!*" For years afterwards ships shun the place, "leaping over it as silly sheep leap over a vacuum, because their leader originally leaped there when a stick was held out. There's your law of precedents; there's your utility of traditions; there's the story of your obstinate survival of old beliefs never bottomed on the earth, and now not even hovering in the air! There's orthodoxy!"

Passing from solid matter of fact to poetry of a beauty and irony in various shades and degrees, betraying in every particular a profound awareness of life as a whole, the passage contains the spectrum of the book, of which it is so small a particle. It also may stand as a warning which no critic of *Moby Dick* can afford to disregard. For there are no established definitions to apply to *Moby Dick.* Where one critic has held out his critical yard-stick, just there a succeeding critic should be most on his guard and not follow blindly. Is *Moby Dick* a novel? It is no more a novel than it is an epic and no more an epic than a tragedy—in the sense that Shakespeare, for instance, conceived tragedy. *Moby Dick* is not to be comprehended unless, like the dead whale in the distance, it is seen in infinite perspectives.

Moby Dick bears a family resemblance to all its predecessors among Melville's books. It has the narrative strength of limb and brilliance of *Typee, Omoo,* and the first part of *Mardi.* It has the poignant, penetrating spirituality of *Redburn.* It has the compact physical organization of *White Jacket.* In this limited perspective, the readiest way of describing it is to say that it joins the corporeal weight of *White Jacket,* including what is of the "heart" in *Redburn,* with the momentum and the intellectual reaches of *Mardi.*

"What things real are there, but imponderable thoughts?" asks Ahab, the hero. The crew of the *Pequod* is "an Anacharsis Clootz deputation" accompanying Old Ahab "to lay the world's grievances before that bar from which not very many of them ever come back." The *Pequod* sails out of Nantucket with these ultimate, these infinite and impossible ends in view. Nevertheless, the *Pequod,* we are told—and we come to know all the details of this truth—"is ballasted with utilities." So *Moby Dick,* the book, like *Mardi,* is an assault upon the ultimate truth of creation, yet, like the *Pequod,* it is ballasted with utilities. Its manifold character is such that along with so many other things it is both an encyclopaedia of whaling and a practical manual for whalemen.

Melville has just got his story under way when he introduces a chapter, entitled "The Advocate," in which he avows the honor and glory of whaling: "And, as for me," he says, "if, by any possibility, there be any as yet undiscovered prime thing in me; if I shall ever deserve any real repute in that small but high hushed world which I might not be unreasonably ambitious of; if hereafter I shall do anything that, upon the whole, a man might rather have done than to have left undone; if, at my death, my executors, or more properly my creditors, find any precious MSS. in my desk, then here I prospectively ascribe all the honor and the glory to whaling; for a whale-ship was my Yale College and my Harvard."

There is a profound sincerity in these words; and they are truthful both as statement of fact and as supposition. *Moby Dick* is founded on the realities of whaling. But these realities have become an internal structure, as of bones, joints and muscles, to articulate the whole vast and varied body of reality that Melville, out of his experience, out of his reading and out of the five books which lay behind him, had come slowly to encompass. Could any education, then, serve a man in better stead? Organically related to them in the process of Melville's growth, *Moby Dick* was bound to bear a deep-seated likeness to all his previous books. But it is a consummation of so much more than all of them put together that hardly is its impact felt than it removes itself from the family circle to take a place in that "small but high hushed world" which a man might not be unreasonably ambitious of entering. In the world of books *Moby Dick* takes its place in the most august, the most exclusive and the most cosmopolitan society.

I do not care to insist further on this claim, and it is for other reasons that I shall now enter *Moby Dick* in a comparison involving two of the greatest names in all literature. My purpose here is practical. I want to show to what lengths *Moby Dick* escapes all classification, and at the same time to explore a little into its labyrinthine interior. A cosmopolite, it is not to be pinned down by easy definitions. On the other hand, just because it is so thorough a cosmopolite, it lends itself on all sides to illuminating comparisons.

By December, 1850, Melville was well along with *Moby Dick*

When in the summer of this year he wrote his essay on Hawthorne's *Mosses*, he was composing himself for the great task which lay ahead of him. In what he wrote in this essay about Hawthorne and Shakespeare he was, at bottom, envisaging his own development. He was feeling out his own equilibrium in virtue of which all his experience and all the aspects of his consciousness were available to him; to serve, respectively, as his materials and as so many different look-outs over his materials. The essay also shows that of all the forces outside himself which helped him to a full awareness of his own resources, the greatest by far was Shakespeare. What the essay shows in this respect is borne out in abounding measure in *Moby Dick*.

The influence of Shakespeare on Melville was fundamentally a profound and pervasive act of fertilization. There are many indications of this that one can point to, some of them important and others superficial. That is, there are numerous and diverse parallels in language, in emotional effect, in situation and tragic action between *Moby Dick* on the one hand, and, on the other, *King Lear, Hamlet, Macbeth, Othello* and *Timon*. I must repeat what I quoted in the last chapter from Melville's remarks on Shakespeare: "those deep faraway things in him; those occasional flashings-forth of the intuitive Truth in him; those short, quick probings at the very axis of reality;—these are the things that make Shakespeare, Shakespeare." Now look at *Moby Dick*. "Oh God!" cries Ahab, "Oh God! that man should be a thing for immortal souls to sieve through!" There is Ahab's angry retort to the ship's carpenter, "Thou art as unprincipled as the gods, and as much of a jack-of-all-trades." And I might add any number of other instances where Melville, following Shakespeare, put in the mouths of his own "dark" characters words which probe jaggedly at the very axis of reality.

A point of difference must come up first which is high-lighted by the many similarities between them. This difference might have been expected from the peculiarity of Melville's response to Shakespeare, his response to him primarily as a seer or truthteller. This was Melville's first criterion in estimating a poet's worth. How independent and rigorous he was in applying this criterion of truthfulness can be seen in his letter to Evert Duyckinck of March, 1849, in which he wrote, "Now I hold it a verity, that even Shakespeare, was not a frank man to the uttermost." Shakespeare, he granted, was handicapped by the prejudices of his time when all men were forced to wear a muzzle on their souls. Thereupon Melville added, with an optimism which his own experience was to belie, "but the Declaration of Independence makes a difference."

In *Moby Dick,* as in Shakespeare's tragedies, there is a solid, crowded foreground of material things and of human characters and actions. Yet this solid ground will suddenly seem to give under our feet, so that we feel ourselves hung momentarily over the abyss. We owe this sensation to the fact that solidity has been sacrificed to transparency for the sake of a more immediate view into the ultimate. Shakespeare was satisfied to leave the mysterious background of life to random probings or to inference. Melville could not. He was bound by many diverse considerations—by his inherited and his temperamental Calvinism, by the American pioneer in him as well as the Puritan—to confront the truth as directly and comprehensively as possible. In *Moby Dick* the mysterious background truth looms in the foreground of palpable facts. It articulates itself in those facts and by so doing it confers upon them something of an apocalyptic scale and intensity foreign to Shakespeare's prevailing naturalism.

Melville's headstrong preoccupation with the truth was served by the form he chose for *Moby Dick,* the narrative instead of the dramatic, and by the intervention of Ishmael, the ubiquitous "I" who tells the story. But such shifts are not sufficient. This preoccupation diffuses a settled character throughout *Moby Dick* which, while removing it from Shakespeare's tragedies, relates it to the "visions" of mediaeval literature of which Dante's *Divine Comedy* is the commanding masterpiece.

The comparison of *Moby Dick* with the *Divine Comedy* should not come as a surprise. In *Mardi,* as we know, the harmony of consciousness which Melville aspired to was imaged by "grim Dante" shaking sides with fat Rabelais. In *Mardi,* too, Babbalanja discourses at length on the great poet Lombardo, and his words show that Melville felt a kinship with Dante, if not in the substance, at any rate in the process of his unfolding vision. ("And ere Necessity plunged spur and rowel into him," Babbalanja says of Lombardo, "he knew not his own paces. *That* churned him into consciousness; and brought ambition, ere then dormant, seething to the top, till he trembled at himself.") Moreover, the comparison between *Moby Dick* and the *Divine Comedy* does not rest on the bare fact that both are cosmic visions. There are some further details which add not a little to the light this comparison can shed.

In the *Divine Comedy* the vision focusses ultimately on the will of God in his creation. In *Moby Dick* the vision focusses on the mystery of creation, the chief emblem of which is the terrible White Whale. However, just as in Dante's poem all men are classified as they stand in relation to the will of God, so in *Moby Dick* the characters are classified in relation to the Whale—according to whether they fear him, worship him, or ignore him.

From this view of *Moby Dick,* it would appear that Melville aimed to strike a balance between Dante and Shakespeare. Certainly, there are two actions in the book which although they mesh are distinct from one another, one of which is Shakespearean, the other Dantesque. The Shakespearean or outward tragic action includes Ahab's conflict with forces outside himself and, also, the bitter, agonizing self-conflict which follows on its heels. All the other characters are caught up in this action, but it centers in Ahab. The other action, the Dantesque, lies entirely with Ishmael, who, let me say for the moment, stands to Ahab as the shadow to the object which casts it. Pushing a paradox, I shall call this action passive as well as inward—inward, that is, with respect to the book as a whole. Like the action that extends from first to last in the *Divine Comedy,* it is the action of man's comprehension slowly completing itself. In Dante each incident, each observation that adds to his comprehension gains from the next; each shares in the accruing interest of his unfolding vision, and each participates by undergoing a transfiguration in the completion of the whole. It is much the same in point of action with Ishmael. His every realization gains from the next and each is the more realized by the completion of his comprehension of things. But how appallingly different is the substance of his vision! Dante came at last to the beatific vision and beheld the divine love enfolding the orders of creation as a lordly rose enfolds its own petals. The long accumulation of Ishmael's comprehension of things rolls back along the dark interior windings of *Moby Dick*. From his last word of all Ishmael has seen into a sundered or cloven universe and he ends by calling himself "another orphan." His vision takes a direction opposite to Dante's; it shows him at the core of creation, not love but destruction. His vision has bereft him of all sense of kinship either below, among bodies terrestrial, or on high, among the celestial orders.

2

"Believe me, my friends," wrote Melville in his essay on Hawthorne, "that men not very much inferior to Shakespeare are this day being born on the banks of the Ohio. And the day will come when you shall say, Who reads a book by an Englishman that is a modern? The great mistake seems to be, that even with those Americans who look forward to the coming of a great literary genius among us, they somehow fancy he will come in the costume of Queen Elizabeth's day: be a writer of dramas founded upon old English history or the tales of Boccaccio. Whereas, great geniuses are parts of the times . . . and possess a corresponding coloring."

No book of its age, not *Leaves of Grass*, is more thoroughly American than *Moby Dick*, and no book of any age is more greatly American. Melville dispensed with all the fancy dress and masquerade that Whitman called the "feudalism" of poetry as drastically as Whitman did himself. "I must not conceal," wrote Melville of his hero, "that I have only to do with a poor old whale hunter . . . and, therefore, all outward majestical trappings and housings are denied me." Ahab stands before us with nothing to adorn "his Nantucket grimness and shagginess."

Body and soul, *Moby Dick* comes out of the non-feudal American past. There is behind it the determination of generations of Puritans to confront the ultimate without benefit of mediator or intercessor. There is the experience of generations of pioneers bred to set aside all traditional securities and landmarks, and to the Puritan's pursuit of truth has been added a body of physical action. *Moby Dick* is pervaded with a sense of American place. When Melville refers to an eagle in a simile for spiritual daring, it is a Catskill eagle. When he wants an image for Ahab's shagginess, he writes, "He lived in the world, as the last of the grizzly bears lived in settled Missouri." His sense of the sweep and variety of American geography was equal to Whitman's. He wove into the fabric of his materials whatever offered of American reference and allusion.

I made a point, in the last chapter, of Melville's heartiness. One form which this heartiness took was an exuberant patriotism. The future lay with America; "to her was given an express dispensation; to her were given new things under the sun. And we Americans are the peculiar, chosen people—the Israel of our time; we bear the ark of the liberties of the world." Not for ourselves only were these liberties entrusted to us, but to be dispensed among all mankind; "let us always remember that with ourselves, almost for the first time in the history of earth, national selfishness is unbounded philanthropy; for we cannot do a good to America, but we give alms to the world." The same patriotism reappears in *Moby Dick*, the happier because it is identified not with a warlike navy but the great American whale fishery, which exemplified American daring and democratic independence and, also, a peaceful, enlightened bearing toward other nations. It was the whale fishery which rounded Cape Horn and brought the Pacific coast into liberalizing intercourse with the rest of the world. It was the whalemen who first circumvented the jealous policy of the Spanish crown "and, if space permitted, it might be distinctly shown how from those whalemen at last eventuated the liberation of Peru, Chili, and Bolivia . . . and the establishment of the eternal democracy in those parts."

When Melville wrote *Moby Dick*, whaling was an American tradition still serving the country, and, touching the country's vital needs, it occupied a more central position than the American navy. The American whale fishery expressed the best in the American character. It also exemplified the peculiarities of our national life. Like the country itself it drew from all corners of the earth for its man power, so that New Bedford, the capital city of the fishery, showed a greater motley of nationalities than New York. The *Pequod*'s crew of red, white, yellow, black and dusky men emphasized the fact "that at the present day not one in two of the many thousand men before the mast employed in the American whale fishery are Americans born, though pretty nearly all the officers are. Herein it is the same with the American whale fishery as with the American army and military and merchant navies, and the engineering forces employed in the construction of the American canals and railroads. The same, I say, because in all these cases the native American liberally provides the brains, the rest of the world as generally supplying the muscles."

Whaling could boast of an ancient and world-wide history. "Who wrote the first account of our leviathan? Who but mighty Job! And who composed the first narrative of a whaling voyage? Who, but no less a prince than Alfred the Great . . . !" By the mid-nineteenth century it had arrived at its period of greatest vigor. By this time the whalemen of America outnumbered "all the rest of the banded whalemen of the world." Whaling had become a fit emblem or symbol of American enterprise. For two hundred years the Nantucketers had shown more and more daring in the chase of the whale. It had remained for them to seek him out in all the watery wastes and corners of the world and "put an incessant belt of circumnavigations round it." They first "peeped in at Behring Straits; and in all seasons and all oceans declared everlasting war with the mightiest animated mass that has survived the Flood; most monstrous and most mountainous!"

American daring and perseverance, the same that Americans honored in their first pioneers and explorers, in Washington's army at Valley Forge, and Andrew Jackson's at New Orleans, had, in the nineteenth century, before the Civil War, a fitting symbol and vehicle in the American whale fishery. Still there was something else to American enterprise than daring and perseverance. It had another trait, just as old and as generally recognized. This trait, too, could be identified in whaling. Not for nothing does Melville claim kinship in behalf of a long line of harpooners with Benjamin Franklin. The inventive genius and practical sagacity of the American character, of which Franklin had been, from the birth of the nation, and still remains the most universal symbol, had gone step by step with daring and perseverance to bring the American whale fishery to its position of world preëminence. I have called *Moby Dick* a practical manual for whalemen. There is hardly a detail of a whaleship's gear and tackle and hardly a point of usage among whalers which Melville does not describe from the practical point of view, at the same time giving a tremendous sense of the resourceful and inventive use of experience to a given end. Combining this practical sagacity with courage and perseverance, Melville could present the whale fishery of America as a symbol of American enterprise. It symbolized that enterprise which so far had bowed to no earthly obstacle and on the strength of which America as a nation affirmed her belief in progress and laid claim to the future as her own Promised Land.

It is not possible at any time to distinguish any one chord from all the others in *Moby Dick*. But certainly the patriotic chord makes itself heard along with others when Ahab, in his representative capacity as the greatest whaling captain who ever sailed out of Nantucket, soliloquizes:

"Swerve me? . . . The path to my fixed purpose is laid with iron rails, whereon my soul is grooved to run. Over unsounded gorges, through the rifled hearts of mountains, under torrents' beds, un-erringly I rush! Naught's an obstacle, naught's an angle to the iron way!"

3

The future is an open window to let in light and air and as necessary to man's consciousness as oxygen. In terms of life it is not so much a view of its own as it is the fine edge to a man's aware-ness of the present. But then, it is as difficult to draw the line be-tween his awareness of the present and his sense of the past. We feel that there exists between the two the interdependence of form and substance. But which is form and which substance? In *Moby Dick* the future complements the present view of things which in turn complements Melville's sense of the past. This statement is true although it misses the *force* of the truth. The more Melville thrusts his vision forward into the future; so much the more, and in consequence of the same exertion, the past opens backward in his view. It might do to speak of this twofold action as action and reaction—but with this addition, that in violation of the law of physics the reaction exceeds the action which produced it. Dura-tion, Melville had written in *Mardi*, "is not of the future, but of the past; and eternity is eternal, because it has been. . . . Thus deeper and deeper into Time's endless tunnel, does the winged soul, like a night-hawk, wend her wild way; and finds eternities before and behind; and her last limit is her everlasting beginning." What was barely surmise in *Mardi* has become the organic law of *Moby Dick* as an exertion of Melville's imagination and consciousness.

An admiring critic has written that *Moby Dick* "is one of the first great mythologies to be created in the modern world, created, that is, out of the stuff of that world, its science, its exploration, its ter-restrial daring, its concentration upon power and dominion over na-ture, and not out of ancient symbols, Prometheus, Endymion, Orestes,

or mediaeval folk-legends, like Dr. Faustus." * Unfortunately
the truth in these words is more than matched by the truth which
they miss. For they do not take into account that the backward pull
in *Moby Dick* is greater than the forward thrust—that not the
foreground truth about men in the nineteenth century but the
eternal background truth of man was Melville's chief preoccupation. *Moby Dick* is, if one wishes, a mythology. It dispenses with
the whole outworn miscellany of poetic archaisms. It is nineteenth
century in costume. It uses nineteenth-century means and references.
It is no exaggeration to say that when Melville wrote *Moby Dick,*
whaling was a triumph of human ingenuity or science quite as
much as the armament of a dreadnaught and the mechanics of a
bomber are today. Nevertheless, superficial coloring aside, the
mythology of *Moby Dick* was born of the age-old presentiments of
the human consciousness, out of which Shakespeare wrought his
contrasts and chiaroscuro of light and dark, which Dante erected
into the most imposing façade in all literature and which gave birth
to the oldest mythologies of the race.

"The classification of the constituents of a chaos," Melville wrote
in *Moby Dick,* "nothing less is here essayed." "To grope down into
the bottom of the sea . . . to have one's hands among the unspeakable foundations, ribs, and very pelvis of the world; this is a fearful thing." It is legitimate to take these words from their context
and apply them to *Moby Dick,* the total effort. Melville's symbols
are new in a sense, but what they symbolize is as old as man. Therefore, in another sense they are not new. And though there is no
resemblance worth remarking between Ahab and Endymion, each
of the other "ancient symbols" named above bears comparison with
Ahab and conveys something of his significance.

He is a shaggy, a battered and misanthropic Prometheus out of
Nantucket. He is like Faustus, whose soul rebelled at the bondage of
its own self-commitment to the denying spirit of Mephistopheles.
He is like Orestes, caught in the conflict between the dark vindictive

* Lewis Mumford, *Herman Melville,* Harcourt, Brace and Co., 1929, p. 193.

Eumenides of an older creation and the bright Olympian deities, Athena and Apollo. A cosmic vision, *Moby Dick* has affinities with the *Divine Comedy*. The substance of its vision, however, is much closer to Aeschylus than Dante. Ahab is caught up in the same terrible web of aboriginal conflict which, according to Aeschylus, caught Agamemnon and Clytemnestra and then Orestes.

There are, of course, plenty of Biblical parallels. Ahab is like Moses trying to mediate between an exacting Jehovah and the recusant Israelites. He is like Job, whose soul hung suspended between God and Satan. In the furthest view we have of Ahab he is enmeshed in a conflict as old as the second act of creation. "And God said, Let there be light: and there was light. And God saw the light, that it was good: And God divided the light from the darkness." That is how it was according to Genesis. But according to "the uncanonical Rabbins," of whom Ishmael had knowledge, whose truth was borne out in the ultimate meaning of the "whiteness" of the White Whale, the light parted the body of primordial darkness, implanting the seed of death, division and eternal enmity throughout creation. Here, according to the revelation of *Moby Dick,* is the origin of the eternal feud between the white and the dark races, and the origin of the feud between a man's intellectual and spiritual and his instinctive, sensuous consciousness. No consciousness can escape it. No consciousness or soul is so light but that its light has its own dark antagonist. No consciousness is so dark but that it encompasses the light which would destroy its dark. Fedallah, the Parsee harpooner, is Ahab's evil spirit. Ahab has smuggled him on board and kept him hidden in the *Pequod*'s hold until halfway through the voyage. At the first command to lower for a whale Fedallah appears on deck with four other mysterious strangers. The crew is astounded by the apparition. "With a start all glared at dark Ahab, who was surrounded by five dusky phantoms that seemed fresh formed out of air." Fedallah was "tall and swart, with one white tooth evilly protruding from its steel-like lips. A rumpled Chinese jacket of black cotton funereally invested him . . . But strangely crowning this ebonness was a glistening white plaited turban, the living hair braided and coiled round and round upon his head." "He was such a creature as civilized, domestic people in the temperate zone only see in their dreams, and that but dimly; but the like of whom now and then glide among the unchanging, Asiatic communities . . . those insulated, immemorial, unalterable countries, which even in these modern days still preserve much of the ghostly aboriginalness of earth's primal generations, when the memory of the first man was a distinct recollection, and all men his descendants, unknowing whence he came, eyed each other as real phantoms, and asked of the sun and the moon why they were created and to what end; when though, according to Genesis, the angels indeed consorted with the daughters of men, the devils also, add the uncanonical Rabbins, indulged in mundane amours."

The richness of *Moby Dick* consists in its combination of this deep insight with a young athletic and sensuous spirituality that manifests itself constantly in the fullness of its vision of things. American writers—as if the air of a new continent had cut their sight sharp and clear—have shown a peculiar gift for seeing things out-of-doors immediately and concretely, even to the point of feeling the pungency of them, and the damp or the dry warmth of the sun upon them. Thoreau, Whitman, Emily Dickinson are examples among writers of the last century. And Melville was with the best of them for his vivid visualizations. To this freshness he adds a wholeness of vision which is not found elsewhere in American literature, and which might be summed up roughly by adding Hawthorne's human interiors to Thoreau's nature. The best American trait in *Moby Dick* finally distinguishes it from all other American books. It is this: with the same absence of bookishness that we recognize in Thoreau's description of the Maine woods, Melville saw anew and represented in *Moby Dick* the matter of the world's oldest books. With the same penetrating freshness with which Thoreau looked about him on Mount Katahdin, Melville looked into the oldest and darkest recesses in the human soul, which open backward beyond our individualities, beyond the different generations into the dim beginnings of the race.

4

Captain Ahab, the hero of *Moby Dick,* is the best whaling captain out of Nantucket. "Ahab's above the common," says Captain Peleg, another veteran of the fishery and now part owner of the *Pequod,* which Ahab commands; "His lance! ay, the keenest and the surest that out of all our isle . . ." Opposite, concealed somewhere in the ocean, is Moby Dick, the great White Whale. Any sperm whale was a mighty antagonist to men who chased him in small boats that bobbed, like chamois leaping, from wave to wave. Still, about certain whales "from the fatal experiences of the fishery there hung a terrible prestige of perilousness." Such was Timor Tom, New Zealand Jack, Don Miguel, the Chilean Whale, the Morquan. Most fearful of all, because of his huge strength and ferocity, and his reputed "intelligent malignity," and his way of turning up at widely separated points on the watery globe, was Moby Dick, to those other whales like Charlemagne among his peers. The two adversaries, Ahab and Moby Dick, come face to face at last in the midmost Pacific, those "almost final waters."

Ahab will sail like any other captain, with a commission to cruise in the usual whaling waters and will be expected home in the usual time of about three years, the hold of the *Pequod* loaded with valuable sperm oil. The usual preparations for such a voyage have been completed, when on a short, cold winter day, says Ishmael, "we gave three heavy-hearted cheers, and blindly plunged like fate into the lone Atlantic." The words have a ring like Francesco's at the beginning of *Hamlet:* " 'Tis bitter cold, and I am sick at heart."

The *Pequod* has been out many days and has entered southerly waters before moody Ahab makes his appearance on deck. Then he announces that regardless of his commission, he has undertaken the voyage with a secret purpose at heart. On his last voyage, when sailing homeward, he ordered the boats lowered for a whale and he himself, contrary to the custom of captains, led the chase. Suddenly the whale turned on his assailants, spilling them into the ocean and making chips of the boats. The whale was Moby Dick; "And then it was, that suddenly sweeping his sickle-shaped jaw beneath him, Moby Dick had reaped away Ahab's leg, as a mower a blade of grass in the field." Ahab's secret purpose is to have his revenge for that mutilation. Standing before the crew, he holds up a great gold coin and promises it to the man who raises him the "white-headed whale with a wrinkled brow and a crooked jaw." "And this is what ye have shipped for, men! to chase that white whale on both sides of land, and over all sides of earth, till he spouts black blood and rolls fin out." He has the gold coin nailed to the main-mast in order to hold his men to his purpose. It was on Christmas of all days when the *Pequod* plunged into the lone Atlantic. In line with the same perversity, Ahab now sails the *Pequod* on the opposite course to the common one of whalers. Instead of continuing southward and rounding Cape Horn, he sails easterly, across the Atlantic and Indian Oceans, thence, through the Straits of Sunda, into the Pacific.

Ahab, the White Whale, the sea—these are Melville's greatest creations in *Moby Dick*. Ahab is the hero, but the White Whale is the central character. The sea embraces them both and brings them face to face with one another. Here is a trinity, a three in one. , Ahab is more than a whaling captain; he is man. He is man sentient, speculative, purposive, religious, standing his full human stature against the immense mystery of creation. His antagonist, Moby Dick, is that immense mystery. He is not the author of it but he is identical with that galling impartiality and indifference in the laws or lawlessness of the universe which Isaiah devoutly fathered on the Creator: "I form the light, and create darkness: I make peace and create evil: I the Lord do all these things." From time out of mind the White Whale has descended in non-canonical generations. His form will be found imbedded or repeated in every prospect of antiquity and magnitude: "Then, again, in mountainous countries . . . you will catch passing glimpses of the profiles of whales defined along the undulating ridges . . . Nor when expandingly lifted by your subject, can you fail to trace out great whales in the starry heavens, and boats in pursuit of them; as when long filled with thoughts of war the Eastern nations saw armies locked in battle among the clouds."

Moby Dick stands for the mystery of creation which confronts and challenges the mind of man at the same time that it lies ambushed in the process of his own consciousness. He is significant of the massive inertia in things, and of the blind beauty and violence of nature—all that ignores or twists or betrays or otherwise does outrage to man's purposes.

In the third place there is the sea, perhaps the most wonderful of Melville's symbols. The sea is the element of truth as also of man's greatness and infinite aspirations. It is the ubiquitous hide-out of Moby Dick. It leads away from all definitions, all traditional sanctities, all securities.

Ishmael will help us here. His·decision to go to sea leads to his partnership with Ahab. On his way to the ship he receives certain pointed impressions. In New Bedford he puts up at the Spouter Inn and while he waits for his supper, he is struck by the appearance of a sailor, one in a group just off a whaler who burst in and gather at the bar. The man is Bulkington. He is nobly built, his face deeply tanned, "while in the deep shadows of his eyes floated some reminiscences that did not seem to give him much joy." He turns up only a few days later in the crew of the *Pequod*, bound on another long voyage. "The land seemed scorching to his feet." I have already quoted the apostrophe to Bulkington, type of the sea man, with the pronouncement "that all deep, earnest thinking is but the intrepid effort of the soul to keep the open independence of her sea." "Terrors of the terrible! is all this agony in vain? Take heart, take heart, O Bulkington! Bear thee grimly, demi god! Up from the spray of thy ocean-perishing—straight up, leaps thy apotheosis!"

The sea, the element of truth, is the dangerous element. It is very close to death, which is "only a launching into the region of the strange Untried; . . . the immense Remote, the Wild, the Watery, the Unshored." Suggestions and images of death cluster in Ishmael's mind as the time draws near for him to sail to sea. His landlord in New Bedford is one Peter Coffin. The sign of his inn, the Try Pots, in Nantucket, is so rigged up that it looks like a gallows. Dropping into the whalemen's chapel in New Bedford, Ishmael considers the white memorial tablets to the lost at sea: "What deadly voids and unbidden infidelities in the lines that seem to gnaw upon all Faith, and refuse resurrections to the beings who have placelessly perished without a grave . . . Yes, there is a death in this business of whaling—a speechlessly quick chaotic bundling of a man into Eternity."

There is death and nameless perishing in this sea calling—death of a man's body, death, it may be, of his faith. There is also glory to it. Bulkington is promised an apotheosis. In the chapter which follows immediately Melville affirms the honor and glory of whaling. "But though the world scouts at us whale-hunters, yet does it unwittingly pay us the profoundest homage; yea, an all-abounding adoration! for almost all the tapers, lamps, and candles that burn round the globe, burn, as before so many shrines, to our glory!" Whaling gives light to the world. Sperm oil is the "coronation stuff" for kings.

The land has its perils too. As Ahab says after his thoughts have turned landward for a moment, "Sleep? Ay, and rust amid greenness." On land is "safety, comfort, hearthstone, supper, warm blankets, friends, all that's kind to our mortalities." And there is mortal danger from apathy, dry rot, decay. On land men drink and drug themselves to spiritual death. Yet the land is life-giving and life-nourishing, and throughout *Moby Dick* the salt-bleached sea imagery of death is crossed with a land imagery of life—meadows and "glades eternally vernal," April butter, cherries.

The land stands for the Typee side of life. It also stands for this side grown up and includes the deepest human affections. It is the proper sphere for that soundness of heart which Melville dramatized in *Mardi* and weighed . in *White Jacket* against the demands of man's infinite nature. The landsman puts aside the indefinite heights of human nature (and the depths likewise as it will appear) for soundness at the core of his being and "red-ripe of the heart." He accepts the limitations which have been ordained for men, his acceptation taking the twin forms of pity and common sense. We must not allow ourselves to be put off by any unpleasant associations of our own and underestimate these two virtues. In *Moby Dick* they are represented as vital safeguards of the deepest and tenderest ties of man's nature, including what is the fine flowering of all of them—his faith.

Starbuck, the first mate on the *Pequod,* is a good landsman. A brave man, his courage "was not a sentiment; but a thing simply useful to him, and always at hand upon all mortally practical occasions." He thinks lovingly of his wife and little boy back home in Nantucket. Without heroism, he is virtuous and right-minded. To him Ahab's infuriated will is "heaven-insulting." He implores Ahab, "in Jesus' name, no more of this, that's worse than devil's madness." He prays, "O life! 'tis now that I do feel the latent horror in thee! but 'tis not in me! that horror's out of me! and with the soft feelings of the human in me, yet will I try to fight ye, ye grim, phantom futures! Stand by me, hold me, bind me, O ye blessed influences!"

In the language of Melville's symbolism man is an amphibious creature. "Why," he asks, "is almost every robust healthy boy with a robust healthy soul in him, at some time or other crazy to go to sea?" At some time or other in everyone who comes to manhood the sea instinct plays a vital part. But his sea instinct must be checked and countered by his land sense if he is not to expose himself to horrible dangers. Human greatness carries heavy penalties, and not every "ocean-perishing" has its straight up apotheosis. "Consider," writes Melville, "the subtleness of the sea; how its most dreaded creatures glide under water, unapparent for the most part, and treacherously hidden beneath the loveliest tints of azure . . . Consider, once more, the universal cannibalism of the sea . . . Consider all this; and then turn to the green, gentle, and most docile earth; consider them both, the sea and the land; and do you not find a strange analogy to something in yourself?"

I said that Ahab stands for man. At closer view we become aware of certain more individualizing traits. Like Bulkington he is a sea man. But there is an important difference between them. To understand the difference we must retrace Ishmael's impressions. In search of cheap lodgings in New Bedford, he walks accidentally into a negro church. The preacher is in his pulpit. Ishmael withdraws hastily and a few minutes later he is in the low, straggling entry of the Spouter-Inn, looking at the curious trophies hung on the walls. On one was a "heathenish array of monstrous clubs and spears." That night he shares a bed with a cannibal harpooner, Queequeg, whose fast friend he becomes. Next morning, having time on his hands, he attends divine service in the whalemen's chapel. He and Queequeg go on to Nantucket together and put up at the Try Pots. They have promised to share their luck and will sign on the same ship. The day after their arrival in Nantucket happens to be a day of fasting, humiliation and prayer in the calendar of Queequeg's religion. He must keep his room while Ishmael goes to pick out a ship. Ishmael chooses the *Pequod*. "Her ancient decks were worn and wrinkled, like the pilgrim-worshipped flag-stone in Canterbury Cathedral . . . She was apparelled like any barbaric Ethiopian emperor, his neck heavy with pendants of polished ivory. She was a thing of trophies. A cannibal of a craft, tricking herself forth in the chased bones of her enemies."

Weaving through Ishmael's initial impressions we can see a contrast which relates to the apparently opposite ideas of worship and antagonism. Worship and antagonism, however, are intimately identified with each other in the soul: they are its oldest postures in front of the unknown. The mass of men conspire to ignore or gloss over the intimate link between them. Indeed, worship is usually disguised enmity. But the great man faces the truth and dares to choose between worship, the way of faith in the face of the unknown, and undisguised antagonism. Faith is of the heart. "Take heart, take heart, O Bulkington!" Bulkington was Ishmael's ship-mate, "though but a sleeping-partner one," Ishmael adds, "so far as this narrative is concerned." As to Ahab, the hero of the narrative, we must bear his friend Peleg's words in mind, "He's a queer man . . . He's a grand ungodly, god-like man . . . Ahab's been in colleges, as well as 'mong the cannibals; been used to deeper wonders than the waves; fixed his fiery lance in mightier, stranger foes than whales." And Melville added presently, while explaining that whalemen are called upon to show the utmost courage, "For what are the comprehensible terrors of man compared with the interlinked terrors and wonders of God?"

Ahab is not one to make Babbalanja's renunciation of all "arrogance of knowing," and acknowledge that "some things there are we must not think of. Beyond one obvious mark all human law is vain." For forty years he has followed the sea and still he cannot tame the sea instinct in him. What is it, he asks, "what is it . . . commands me; . . . recklessly making me ready to do what in my own proper, natural heart, I durst not so much as dare?" "His whole high, broad form seemed made of solid bronze, and shaped in an unalterable mould." He wears a scar, "a slender, rod-like mark, lividly whitish, that runs from among his white hairs down his "tawny, scorched face and neck, till it disappeared in his clothing." How and when he got this scar no one knows, but according to an old Gay-Head Indian in the crew, not until he was forty was Ahab that way branded, and then it came upon him, "not in the fury of any mortal fray, but in an elemental strife at sea." Beside this, he has lost one leg and uses an ivory one in its place. This mutilation, as we know, dates from his previous voyage and was inflicted in his first body-to-body encounter with the White Whale.

His "compacted aged robustness" shows him to be a man of indomitable will and strength of mind. But we shall miss the point of his tragedy if we forget that Ahab combined "a ponderous heart" with "a globular brain." There lies his anguish. "This lovely light, it lights not me; all loveliness is anguish to me, since I can ne'er enjoy. Gifted with the high perception, I lack the low, enjoying power; damned, most subtly and most malignantly!" Near the end of the book, in the chapter called "The Symphony," Ahab opens his heart to Starbuck, the first and last time, "When I think of this life I have led; the desolation of solitude it has been; the masoned, walled-town of a captain's exclusiveness, which admits but small entrance to any sympathy from the green country without—oh, weariness! heaviness!"

Ahab is blasphemous and he is called atheistical. He appears atheistical to such a man as Starbuck. Nevertheless, we shall go all wrong if we take Starbuck's opinion here. Captain Peleg knew better, "stricken, blasted, if he be, Ahab has his humanities!" "Ungodly," Peleg calls him, but also "godlike." Ahab has a great soul. Although maimed and wrenched, its strength remains unimpaired. He has his moment of skepticism. "Sometimes I think there's naught beyond," he says to Starbuck. Yet skepticism goes against the grain of his being. His religious sense is as strenuous and importunate as that of the first generation of Puritans and, like them, it is almost impossible for him not to see all things as the manifestation of a divine will at work in creation. Still the main point about Ahab's soul and his religious sense refers us back to the main view that Melville takes of his hero, the view on which his tragedy hinges. That is, Ahab is the grand human thing itself. He will not abate one inch of his whole high broad human form. He will not renounce his speculative intellect. Neither, on the other hand, will he abase himself by denying his spiritual nature. His soul is part of his royal crown of a man. Is it, he asks, too heavy? "this Iron Crown of Lombardy. Yet is it bright with many a gem; I, the wearer, see not its far flashings; but darkly feel that I wear that, that dazzlingly confounds."

We cannot get Ahab's force and stature, his human weight, unless we take him in the sense in which he is presented, with its carefully contrived juxtapositions. Starbuck stands nearest to him in a way. Only Starbuck thinks of opposing him. "Vengeance on a dumb brute!" cried Starbuck, "that simply smote thee from blindest instinct! Madness! To be enraged with a dumb thing, Captain Ahab, seems blasphemous." Starbuck has soul enough to catch sight of Ahab's purport. He is horrified. Yet though he would, he cannot oppose him. His courage was of that sort, "which, while generally abiding firm in the conflict with seas, or winds, or whales, or any of the ordinary irrational horrors of the world, yet cannot withstand those more terrific, because more spiritual terrors, which sometimes menace you from the concentrating brow of an enraged and mighty man."

The other two mates of the *Pequod* are Stubb and Flask. They fall far short of Starbuck's humanity and are blind to Ahab's incentives. "Long usage had, for this Stubb, converted the jaws of death into an easy chair. What he thought of death itself, there is no telling." To him Ahab is "a hot old man! I guess he's got what some folks ashore call a conscience; it's a kind of Tic-Dolly-row they say—worse nor a toothache." As for Flask, "So utterly lost was he to all sense of reverence for the many marvels of their majestic bulk and mystic ways . . . that in his poor opinion, the wondrous whale was but a species of magnified mouse, or at least water-rat, requiring only a little circumvention and some small application of time and trouble in order to kill and boil."

Another variety of mankind aboard the *Pequod* is the ship's carpenter. We know little about him until more than three-fourths of the way through the book, when he is called upon to fashion a new ivory leg for Ahab. This carpenter "was prepared at all points, and alike indifferent and without respect in all. Teeth he accounted bits of ivory; heads he deemed but top-blocks; men themselves he lightly held for capstans. . . . Yet was this half-horrible stolidity in him, involving, too, as it appeared, an all-ramifying heartlessness . . . not unstreaked now and then with a grizzled wittiness. . . . He was a stript abstract; an unfractioned integral; uncompromised as a newborn babe; living without premeditated reference to this world or the next. You might almost say, that this strange uncompromisedness in him involved a sort of unintelligence; for in his numerous trades, he did not seem to work so much by reason or by instinct . . . but merely by a deaf and dumb, spontaneous literal process. . . . If he did not have a common soul in him, he had a subtle something that somehow anomalously did its duty."

This description performs a complex duty. By contrast it throws light on Ahab's humanity, to whom nothing matters which is not infused with the warm stuff of human consciousness. Not long after the introduction of the carpenter, Ahab is angered by his quadrant, "Thou canst not tell where one drop of water or one grain of sand will be tomorrow noon; and yet with thy impotence thou insultest the sun! Science! Curse thee, thou vain toy." He rebukes Stubb for his "mechanical" courage. "What soulless thing is this that laughs before a wreck?" Not to have a sense of danger, as not to have a sense of evil, is to be less than human and to act like an automaton. Yet antipathetical to Ahab as the carpenter is, he is not altogether so. He approximates him as a parody approximates the poem which is its butt. In so doing he is like a light held on the inside of Ahab's tragedy, at the same time that he spotlights him from the outside as a tragic human figure. And this carpenter, while he bears a backstairs resemblance to Ahab, is also an image that lends itself to those vague and vast forces of creation against whose hateful inhumanity Ahab pits his throbbing humanity. He is, in Ahab's words (not about him, however), "the personified impersonal." The same trait behind the carpenter's indifference and impartiality, his "impersonal stolidity as it were," is reflected in Moby Dick's ubiquity and that something else about him that infuriated Ahab. "That inscrutable thing is chiefly what I hate." The same trait was reflected in the common sunlight the day Moby Dick turned on his assailants, Captain Ahab at their head, with such "aforethought of ferocity" as a man could hardly impute to "an unintelligent agent." "Judge, then, to what pitches of inflamed, distracted fury the minds of his more desperate hunters were impelled, when amid the chips of chewed boats, and the sinking limbs of torn comrades, they swam out of . . . the whale's direful wrath into the serene, exasperating sunlight, that smiled on, as if at a birth or a bridal."

On another occasion the carpenter displays his impartial and impersonal stolidity. He undertakes to convert a coffin which he had built and which it turned out was not needed into a life preserver. Finding him at this task, Ahab calls him an "all-grasping, intermeddling, monopolising heathenish old scamp, to be one day making legs, and the next day coffins to clap them in, and yet again lifebuoys out of those same coffins. Thou art as unprincipled as the gods," says Ahab, "and as much of a jack-of-all-trades." Here Melville begins to glimpse the irresponsibility of God. As Emily Dickinson was to say:—

> It's easy to invent a life,
> God does it every day—
> Creation but a gambol
> Of His authority . . .
> The Perished Patterns murmur,
> But His perturbless plan
> Proceed—inserting here a Sun—
> There—leaving out a Man.

The crew of the *Pequod* is "chiefly made up of mongrel renegades, and castaways and cannibals." It is about evenly divided between the white and dark races. The three harpooners are of the dark; Ahab calls them his "three pagan kinsmen" and "my sweet cardinals." Queequeg is a cannibal from the South Seas. Daggoo is "a gigantic, coal-black negro-savage." Tashtego is an unmixed

Indian from Gay Head on Martha's Vineyard. The fourth harpooner, a Parsee, called Fedallah, has been already mentioned. There is the cabin boy. Ordered to take a place in one of the boats, in the commotion of the chase, he gets thrown out and goes mad from terror. Then always there is Ishmael.

Ahab towers above his crew. "The pagan leopards," he calls them, "the unrecking and unworshipping things, that live; and seek, and give no reasons for the torrid life they feel." He is speaking to Starbuck who, as I said, stands nearest to Ahab in some respects. Nevertheless, the crew has a compact animal or instinctive integrity which gives them a strength that Starbuck lacks, and which sets them off from the slack vulgarity of Stubb and Flask. Ahab's dramatic announcement of his purpose on the voyage is taken by these two with hardly so much as a shrug of the shoulders. The crew respond differently. "How it was that they so aboundingly responded to the old man's ire—by what evil magic their souls were possessed, that at times his hate seemed almost theirs; the White Whale as much their insufferable foe as his; how all this came to be —what the White Whale was to them, or how to their unconscious understandings, also, in some dim, unsuspected way, he might have seemed the gliding great demon of the sea of life—all this to explain, would be to dive deeper than Ishmael can go. The subterranean miner that works in us all, how can one tell whither leads his shaft by the ever shifting muffled sound of his pick?" As for himself, Ishmael admits that he could not resist Ahab; "Who does not feel the irresistible arm drag? What skiff in tow of a seventy-four can stand still? For one, I gave myself up to the abandonment of the time and the place; but while yet all arush to encounter the whale could see naught in that brute but the deadliest ill."

5

"Tormented into desperation, Lear, the frantic king, tears off the mask, and speaks the same madness of vital truth." Melville made this observation in his essay on Hawthorne, when his own revela-

tions were shaping up for expression in *Moby Dick*. Ahab is a king
by natural right. Like Lear he is mad—with the madness of vital
truth. His madness is the final expression of his nobility. It is the
furthest thrust of his sea instinct. "Who's over me?" he rasps out
to Starbuck. "Truth hath no confines." The words follow in an aside
to Starbuck, in which Ahab explains himself at greater length than
he would with the crew. "Hark ye yet again,—the little lower layer.
All visible objects, man, are but as pasteboard masks. But in each
event—in the living act, the undoubted deed—there, some unknown
but still reasoning thing puts forth the mouldings of its features
from behind the unreasoning mask. If man will strike, strike through
the mask! How can the prisoner reach outside except by thrusting
through the wall? To me, the White Whale is that wall, shoved near
to me. Sometimes I think there's naught beyond. But 'tis enough. He
tasks me; he heaps me; I see in him outrageous strength with an
inscrutable malice sinewing it. That inscrutable thing is chiefly
what I hate; and be the White Whale agent, or be the White Whale
principal, I will wreak that hate upon him. Talk not to me of
blasphemy, man; I'd strike the sun if it insulted me." Ahab's madness
springs from an excess of humanity. The truth upon which he has
concentrated all his energies and sacrificed all that is kind to man's
mortality has a profound and universal import for man. The moral
and spiritual universe, all that is cherished and cherishable by
men, is at stake in it. Much thought about it will exasperate men
far more temperate than Ahab. It is so near, yet so illusive; so
hauntingly present, yet so inapprehensible! Ahab's great heart is
stretched to bursting under the ceaseless effort of his mind to lay
hold of it. He cries, "but Ahab never thinks; he only feels, feels,
feels; that's tingling enough for mortal man! . . . Thinking is, or
ought to be a coolness and a calmness, and our poor hearts throb
and our poor brains beat too much for that." When he first appears
on his quarterdeck he stands erect, "looking straight out beyond
the ship's ever pitching prow" with "an infinity of firmest fortitude
a determinate, unsurrenderable wilfulness . . . in the dedication of

is glance." If he resembles Prometheus it is not too much to say
at he resembles a far more poignant divinity, standing "with a
rucifixion in his face; in all the nameless regal overbearing dignity
: some mighty woe."

Ahab pursues the truth as the champion of man, leaving behind
im all traditional conclusions, all common assumptions, all codes
nd creeds and articles of faith. Although the universe of sea and
xy opens around him an appalling abyss, and although the abyss
eems the visible apprehension of his mind that the truth will prove
aat there is no truth, still he sails on. He will at any rate have the
niverse show its cards, so that a man may know how it stands with
im, whether or not there is anything beyond himself to which he
an entrust his dearest hopes, and then bear himself accordingly.
feel deadly faint," he says, "faint, bowed, and humped, as though
were Adam staggering beneath the piled centuries since Paradise."

Ahab is nobly mad. Yet there are ambiguities about his conduct
aat this madness does not explain. Something else must be taken
to account. We must discriminate in this matter of his madness.
Ie says himself, "They think me mad—Starbuck does; but I'm
emoniac, I am madness maddened!" That is just it. On his last
ip, as the result of his mutilation, he fell prey to a terrible mono-
nania. In all that he suffered in forty years of seafaring that injury
ffected him as nothing else. It was like Job's plague of boils that of
ll his humiliations touched nearest the quick. For "no turbanned
'urk, no hired Venetian or Malay" could have smitten Ahab with
nore seeming malice. "Small reason was there, to doubt then, that
ver since that almost fatal encounter, Ahab had cherished a wild
indictiveness against the Whale, all the more fell for that in his
rantic morbidness he at last came to identify with him, not only all
is bodily woes, but all his intellectual and spiritual exasperations.
'he White Whale swam before him as the monomaniac incarna-
ion of all those malicious agencies which some deep men feel
ating in them, till they are left living on with half a heart and half
lung. That intangible malignity which has been from the begin-

ning; to whose dominion even the modern Christians ascribe
half of the worlds; which the ancient Ophites of the East reverer
in their statue devil;—Ahab did not fall down and worship it
them; but, deliriously transferring its idea to the abhorred W
Whale, he pitted himself, all mutilated against it. All that r
maddens and torments; all that stirs up the lees of things; all t
with malice in it; all that cracks the sinews and cakes the brain
the subtle demonisms of life and thought; all evil, to crazy A
were visibly personified, and made practically assailable in M
Dick."

His monomania could hide itself, if necessary, to serve its
ends. His absence while the *Pequod* was preparing for the voy
did not trouble the owners. "I don't know exactly what's the ma
with him," says Peleg, "but he keeps close inside the house; a
of sick and yet he don't look so." But out at sea it would
manifested when "with glaring eyes Ahab would burst from
state-room, as though escaping from a bed that was on fire." W
Ahab slept, then, sometimes "the eternal living principle or
in him" would dissociate itself from Ahab's scorched mind, so
what seemed Ahab was divorced from "the common vitality
was for the time but a vacated thing, a formless, somnambul
being." His monomaniac's purpose "by its own sheer inveteracy
will" had fixed itself into a self-assumed, mechanical being of
own. "God help thee, old man, thy thoughts have created a creat
in thee; and he whose intense thinking thus makes him a Pro
theus; a vulture feeds upon that heart forever; that vulture the v
creature he creates."

Without impairing his strength of mind and purpose, Ah
monomania has all but possessed itself of Ahab. His noble madr
still has its own consciousness and ends in view. But it is horri
disfigured and perverted by his monomania which held it lik
vise. "Ahab's full lunacy subsided not, but deepeningly contract
. . . But as in his narrow-flowing monomania not one jot of Ah
broad madness had been left behind; so in that broad madness,

one jot of his great natural intellect had perished. That before living agent, now became the living instrument. If such a furious trope may stand, his special lunacy stormed his general sanity, and carried it, and turned all its concentrated cannon upon its own mad mark."

The White Whale is all evil to Ahab. Nevertheless it is wrong to say, as do almost all the critics of *Moby Dick,* that Melville intended him to represent evil. The White Whale has a tremendous power to do harm. But unless the word is so denatured as to be synonymous with harmful or dangerous, he cannot be called evil. If a man sees evil in him, then it is his own evil which is reflected back at him.

The chapter called "The Doubloon" makes Melville's meaning here perfectly clear. Ahab has had the great gold coin nailed to the main-mast, the reward for the first man who hails Moby Dick. "The ship's navel," Pip calls it. One day it happens that, one after another, Ahab, the three mates and members of the crew walk up to the coin and study the design of three mountain peaks stamped on the face of it. Each interprets it according to his own nature. For instance, Ahab makes out "three peaks as proud as Lucifer," while Starbuck makes out three "heaven-abiding peaks that almost seem the Trinity." Pip has been watching all this and when the last man has gone by he steals up to the coin. Now Pip has gone quite mad but "man's insanity is heaven's sense; and wandering from all mortal reason, man comes at last to that celestial thought, which, to reason, is absurd and frantic; and weal or woe, feels then uncompromised, indifferent as his God." Reflecting on what he has just seen, Pip speaks the wonderful indifference of heaven's sense. "I look, you look, he looks; we look, ye look, they look." The words, oddly remembered from Pip's negligible schooling, sound like gibberish, yet they sum up what has just transpired. The object is indifferent, the subject is all that is needed because the subject always sees himself. This is Pip's version of the solipsism of consciousness, a theme which Melville continually broaches in *Moby*

Dick. Here, for certain, is the clue to Melville's meaning with respect to the White Whale. He stands for the inscrutable mystery of creation, as he also stands for what man sees in creation of himself.

Ahab's noble madness sprang from an excess of humanity. His monomania on the contrary is identified with mutilation. Truly a monomania, wherever it looks it sees only itself. It sees its evil in the White Whale. And Ahab's hate does not rest there. Be the White Whale agent or be he principal, Ahab will wreak his hate upon him. It was hardly in his nature not to believe in a divine power above creation. There must be a creator beyond his creation. There, too, Ahab saw his own hate reflected back at him. His soul and his religious sense could not but believe in God. His monomania, intruding itself, revealed a Satanic god.

Ahab's monomania is evil. It demands the ruthless sacrifice of love and preys on his common humanity. It implicates Ahab in "the heartless voids and immensities of the universe." He has leagued himself with them. Or, to show the tragic aspect, which is so close to the aspect of evil in Ahab's case, we may put it this way: when Ahab thrust his harpoon into the flanks of Moby Dick, at that awful moment which came after nearly forty years of facing the interlinked wonders and terrors of the sea, just then the universe got its barbs into him. His human front broke down at last and the inscrutable inhumanity of the universe passed into him. Noble Ahab stood in mortal danger of being abased to the condition of such an insensate thing as the ship's carpenter, a human semblance to bedeck the inhuman voids.

While the story of Ahab's pursuit of Moby Dick goes forward to its end, a drama of inner conflict is unfolded. A victim of his own nature, a victim of the tragedy of mind, Ahab would have been torn asunder (like Babbalanja, as "by wild horses") under any circumstances. His tragedy is far more bitter and more terrible because, finally, his own hand is raised against himself. His monomania has all but possessed itself of his noble madness. Therefore his humanity is all but hideously perverted as well as otherwise

aimed. Viewed outwardly, Ahab is like a figure in an old morality
lay, standing between a good and a bad angel and each suing
or his soul. Starbuck is his good angel. His bad angel is Fedallah,
all and swart, with one white tooth evilly protruding." But the
rama of inner conflict I speak of is deeper; it is the struggle of
hab's humanity—stout even in this extremity—to free itself from
he fell clutches of his evil monomania.

Ahab's first words show the unkindness that his hate has wrought
n him. "Down, dog, and kennel," he says outrageously to Stubb. In
he great scene on the quarterdeck when he makes his purpose
nown he is in the image of his monomania. He clubs down
tarbuck's reluctance, elevates over Starbuck the pagan harpooners
nd binds the crew with satanic rites. But presently his humanity
peaks out. His anguish is profoundly human. "This lovely light, it
ghts not me; all loveliness is anguish to me." Pointed south, the
equod sails into milder weather; there "more than once did he put
orth the faint blossom of a look, which, in any other man, would
ave soon flowered out into a smile." The painful isolation to which
he mysterious laws of his being have brought him is driven home
y the desolation of the seas beyond Good Hope. A school of harm-
ss little fish has been following the Pequod. Ahab observes that
hey forsake the Pequod to follow in the wake of a passing vessel,
omeward bound. In a tone of deep and helpless sorrow Ahab
urmurs, "Swim away from me, do ye?" His is like King Lear's
nguish, "The little dogs and all, Tray, Blanch, and Sweet-heart, see,
hey bark at me." Another ship is hailed, " 'Well, now, that's cheer-
g,' " says Ahab, "while whole thunder clouds swept aside from
is brow." For some time the Pequod has been becalmed and now it
reported that the stranger ship brings a breeze with her. "Better
nd better," Ahab says; then, showing that the deepest fountains
f his being are not sealed up, "Would now St. Paul would come
long that way, and to my breezelessness bring his breeze!"

I have said that in spite of everything Ahab's noble madness
eeps its own ends in view. In the chapter "The Candles" we see

his titanic defiance. But we see more. His soul and his religiou
sense are equal to his defiance. "I own thy speechless, placeles
power," he shouts to the lightning that forks from the masts of hi
ship, "but to the last gasp of my earthquake life will dispute its un
conditional, unintegral mastery in me. In the midst of the personi
fied impersonal, a personality stands here. Though but a point a
best; whenceso'er I came; whereso'er I go; yet while I earthly live
the queenly personality lives in me, and feels her royal rights.
The whole strength of his being is coiled in words which canno
fail to recall the words of Job: "Though Thou slay me, yet shall
worship Thee, but I shall maintain my own ways before Thee.
Then at once we see the broader slopes of his humanity again: "Bu
war is pain, and hate is woe. Come in thy lowest form of love, an
I will kneel and kiss thee."

All this time the *Pequod* is in danger of immediate destruction
Starbuck has ordered the ends of the chains thrown into the se
so as to draw off the lightning. Ahab countermands the order
"Avast," he cries, "let's have fair play here, though we be th
weaker side . . . out on all privileges." And not only this; whil
condescending to it, in virtue of something superior in him, he als
pities the lightning. "There is some unsuffusing thing beyond thee
thou clear spirit, to whom all thy eternity is but time, all th
creativeness mechanical. . . . Oh, thou foundling fire, thou hermi
immemorial, thou too has thy incommunicable riddle, thy unpartici
pated grief . . . defyingly I worship thee." Like Prometheus, onc
more, Ahab scales the ramparts of inhuman heaven. Infuriate
courage carries him along, but it is as if he carried, to plant upo
those ramparts, a banner bearing the names of the highest emblem
of humanity—love, compassion, justice. However, such are th
paradoxes of human greatness in general and of Ahab's predica
ment in particular, that hardly has he reached this high pinnacl
than he falls as low.

In order to gauge this catastrophe we should refer to the last para
graph in *White Jacket*. "Oh, shipmates and world-mates, all round

e the people suffer many abuses. Our gun-deck is full of com-
aints." Vain to appeal from lieutenants to captains or—"while
board our world frigate"—to "the indefinite Navy Commissioners."
et the worst of our evils we blindly inflict upon ourselves. . . .
om the last ills no being can save another; therein each man must
his own saviour. For the rest, whatever befall us, let us never
in our murderous guns inboard; let us not mutiny with bloody
kes in our hands." There is much in the passage which bears on
ab. What is most pertinent at the moment is the earnest invoca-
n at the end, expressing the loyalty and highmindedness which
is the nature of Ahab's monomania to discard. That has been true
his monomania all along. Now the truth is borne out dramatically.
no uncertain terms Ahab trains murderous guns inboard. The
lestial, mechanical lightning now forks from Ahab's own harpoon,
which Starbuck raises his protesting voice. "God, God is against
ee, old man; forbear! 'tis an ill voyage," and he moves to bring
e ship about and point her homeward. The panic-stricken crew
stantly follows his lead. But Ahab interposes. He seizes his burn-
g harpoon and waves it among them, "swearing to transfix with
the first sailor that but cast loose a rope's end. Petrified by his
pect, and still more shrinking from the fiery dart that he held, the
n fell back in dismay, and Ahab again spoke," recalling them to
eir oath to hunt the White Whale—to the death.

The drama of Ahab's inner conflicts does not end there. It resumes
en, not long afterwards, Ahab begins to take notice of Pip. Be-
een him and Pip there is a bond of madness, the same in both,
hough they have come by it in opposite ways; the one from
ength, the other from weakness. At any rate, Ahab begins to feel
mpathy with and for Pip. If suffered to grow and ramify this
ling might cast out Ahab's hateful monomania and restore him to
humanity. Ahab sees the point. He says to Pip, "There is that
thee . . . which I feel too curing to my malady . . . and for this
nt my malady becomes my most desired health," and orders him
his own cabin.

"No, no, no!" Pip pleads, "ye have not a whole body, sir; do but use poor me for your one lost leg; only tread upon me, sir; I a no more, so I remain a part of ye." "Oh! spite of million villains, tł makes me a bigot in the fadeless fidelity of man!—and a black! a crazy!—but methinks like-cures-like applies to him too; he gro so sane again. . . . If thou speakest thus to me much more, Aha purpose keels up in him. I tell thee no; it cannot be."

The situation here is akin to that between King Lear and I fool in the storm scenes:

> *My wits begin to turn,*
> *Come on, my boy. How dost, my boy? Art cold?*
> *I am cold myself . . . Come, your hovel.*
> *Poor fool and knave, I have one part in my heart*
> *That's sorry yet for thee.*

His sympathy with his fool is like a cordial to keep his madne off. It takes his mind from his own exasperation, and leads him a broader fellow feeling with his kind.

The crisis in Ahab's spiritual drama follows in the chapter cal] "The Symphony" which occurs just before the White Whale sighted and the chase begins. For Ahab's salvation it is necessa that his sympathies, renewed by Pip, should reach out to embra the great community of men—the common continent of men represented in Starbuck. And for a moment this seems on the po of consummation. It is a lovely mild day; a day such as seems "t bridal of the earth and sky." The stepmother world, Melville writ which had so long been cruel, "now threw affectionate arms rou his stubborn neck, and did seem to joyously sob over him, as over one, that however wilful and erring, she could yet find it her heart to save and to bless." Ahab's mood relents, and Starbu observing this draws up to him. Then Ahab's sympathies flow for drawing him deeper and deeper into their common humani "Close! stand close to me, Starbuck; let me look into a human e it is better than to gaze into the sea or sky; better than to gaze up

God. By the green land, by the bright hearthstone! this is the magic glass, man; I see my wife and my child in thine eye." Starbuck abundantly rejoins, "Oh, my captain! my captain! noble soul! grand old heart, after all! . . . Away with me! let us fly these deadly waters! let us home! Wife and child, too, are Starbuck's—wife and child of his brotherly, sisterly, play-fellow youth; even as thine, sir, are the wife and child of thy loving, longing, paternal old age! Away! let us away!—this instant let me alter the course!" Ahab continues to mingle his sympathies with Starbuck's landward thoughts. But, of a sudden, his mind takes off in its endless speculation; the sea-instinct surges up in him, and, almost simultaneously, his maniacal hate bares its visage. "Look! see yon albicore! who put it into him to chase and fang that flying-fish? Where do murderers go, man? Who's to doom, when the judge himself is dragged to the bar?" He looks up for Starbuck's answer, but "blanched to a corpse's hue with despair, the mate had stolen away." Ahab "crossed the deck to gaze over on the other side; but started at two reflected, fixed eyes in the water there. Fedallah was motionlessly leaning over the same rail."

By separating himself from Starbuck, Ahab has cut himself off from the common continent of man. He is doomed. The whole inward truth is reflected in the outward circumstances of his death. His boats all smashed, the rest of his men, all save two, have managed to climb aboard the *Pequod*, and she, her sides stove in by the Whale, begins to sink. Ahab dies alone, cut off, as he says, "from the last fond pride of meanest shipwrecked captains." Long before he had said to Starbuck about Moby Dick, "He tasks me; he heaps me." In "The Symphony" he had said, "What is it, what nameless, inscrutable, unearthly thing is it; what cozening, hidden lord and master . . . commands me; that against all natural lovings and longings, I so keep pushing, and crowding, and jamming myself on all the time?" The whole inward truth, as I say, is reflected in the manner of his death. On the previous day, the second in the three-day battle, Fedallah had disappeared. On the third and last day his corpse reappeared lashed round and round to the Whale's back. Then Ahab, stabbing his harpoon into the Whale, at the same moment gets caught up in his own line and is dragged after him, with his last breath shouting, "Toward thee I roll, thou all-destroying but unconquering whale; to the last I grapple with thee . . . while chasing thee, though tied to thee, thou damned Whale! *Thus*, I give up the spear!"

Yet we have one more glimpse of him. "Oh, lonely death on lonely life! Oh, now I feel my topmost greatness lies in my topmost grief," he cries at the end. His nobility is reaffirmed in these words. He speaks here as the noble victim of the tragedy of mind.

He dies in the grip of his own evil, his heart racked by hate. His "most brain-battering fight" has availed him nothing. The problem of evil, the responsibility for suffering, these mysteries have eluded him in the end. "How can the prisoner reach outside except by thrusting through the wall? To me, the White Whale is that wall shoved near to me." "The dead blind wall butts all enquiring heads at last," says Ahab another time, hopeless of getting any answer to his final questions. The most terrifying aspect of Moby Dick in the last encounter is the featureless, wall-like countenance he presents to his assailants.

Still, defeated as he is in these respects, Ahab does not acknowledge defeat. So far as he can see he retains his sovereignty. Then by sheer strength of will he transcends all the considerations, which had driven him on, all the considerations arising from his "queenly personality," except its royalty.

In Ahab we come to feel the same tremendous act of will which is required for a tremendous act of forgiveness, although the act itself has another form than forgiveness. He accepts fate. "This whole act's immutably decreed. 'Twas rehearsed . . . a billion years before this ocean rolled." Yet this act has a more positive force than resignation. His is "a prouder, if a darker faith." He reverses himself to take his station in the eternal, impersonal order of things, which is beyond right or wrong, justice and injustice, and to which all the forces of which a man has outward knowledge are the obedient servants. If this is surrender or abdication, it is in terms of absolute equality with all the known forces of creation.

6

Only Ishmael survived. It so happened that on the last day he was asked to take the part of bowsman in Ahab's boat, left vacant when Fedallah disappeared the day before. In the commotion of the battle he was tossed and left floating on the margin of the final scene, where he just escaped being sucked in after the sinking *Pequod*. All that remained to him was his own lifebuoy and by that means Ishmael kept himself afloat, until picked up by a vessel that chanced to come his way.

This lifebuoy had been a coffin made for Queequeg when he thought himself dying. Upon his recovery Starbuck ordered the carpenter to make it over to serve in the opposite capacity. Observing the transformation, Ahab is given pause; "A life-buoy of a coffin! Does it go further? Can it be that in some spiritual sense the coffin is, after all, but an immortality preserver! I'll think of that. But no. So far gone am I in the dark side of earth, that its other side, the theoretic bright one, seems but uncertain twilight to me." Ishmael escaped then by means of the coffin life preserver which Ahab had rejected as a possible symbol of faith.

The truth we come at by way of Ishmael's story is the final truth about *Moby Dick*,—the truth, I might add, that made it whole. At the beginning, Ishmael explains that he is suffering one of his fits of hypochondria; "a damp, drizzly November" in his soul. His misanthropic hypos are getting the best of him. Therefore—his usual remedy for this condition—he decides to go to sea. That is his substitute for "pistol and ball. With a philosophical flourish Cato throws himself upon his sword; I quietly take to the ship. There is nothing surprising in this. If they but knew it, almost all men . . . some time or other, cherish very nearly the same feelings towards

the ocean with me." When, some days later, on the little boat th
takes him from New Bedford to Nantucket, he first catches sight
open water, his soul leaps up in him. "How I snuffed the Tartar a
—how I spurned the turnpike earth!—that common highway all ov
dented with the marks of slavish heels and hoofs; and turned me
admire the magnanimity of the sea which will permit no record
In Nantucket, Ishmael chooses the garish and outlandish *Pequod*
the ship for himself and Queequeg. What he gleans about Capta
Ahab when he goes on board to sign affects him deeply; "I felt
sympathy and a sorrow for him, but I don't know what, unless
was the cruel loss of his leg." It is worth noticing that Ishmael is t
only one of those who sailed with Ahab on the *Pequod* who caug
sight of shadowy Fedallah being sneaked on board. Of wh
he felt when Ahab announced his purpose we already know som
thing: "Who does not feel the irresistible arm drag?" "I, Ishmael, w
one of that crew; my shouts had gone up with the rest; my oa
had been welded with theirs; and stronger I shouted, and more d
I hammer and clinch my oath, because of the dread in my soul.
wild, mystical, sympathetical feeling was in me; Ahab's quenchle
feud seemed mine."

That is sufficient to show Ishmael's danger. His story turns
his mortal need to maintain himself against the strong drag he fee
towards Ahab.

Since there is nothing on which Melville digresses that does n
serve his meaning, Ishmael's jeopardy can be put in the picturesq
language of the fishery as Melville explains it under the heading
"Fast-Fish and Loose-Fish." A fast-fish is a whale who has bee
stuck and who, presumably, can be brought alongside and ma
fast to the ship whose harpoon has caught him. A loose-fish is st
fair game for anybody: he is still free for anybody to have, himse
first of all. Ahab is a fast-fish. The universe has got its barb in hi
His humanity is transfixed. Ishmael, on the contrary, is a loose-fis
Will he keep himself so? Or will he like Ahab impale himself
the exasperating inscrutability of things? Will he cease to star

up a "sovereign nature (in himself) amid the powers of heaven, hell and earth"? "If any of those powers choose to withhold certain secrets, let them; that does not impair my sovereignty in myself; that does not make me tributary." But that, directly and indirectly, is what did impair Ahab's sovereignty.

The chapter called "The Whiteness of the Whale" begins with Ishmael saying, "What the White Whale was to Ahab has been hinted; what, at times, he was to me, as yet remains unsaid. . . . It was the whiteness of the Whale that above all things appalled me."

Thereupon he proceeds to follow the meaning of whiteness, tracking it down through all its associations in man's mind from time out of mind—as they appear in pageantry, story and ritual. Whiteness enhances beauty. It is associated with royalty and with royal preëminence, the same in kings and which, among peoples, gives "the white man ideal mastership over every dusky tribe." Whiteness is associated with gladness, with innocence, with the holy of holies. Yet, for all these associations, there is an ambiguity about whiteness; the same ambiguity that in the connotations of the sea seem to identify death with glory, bleached bones and desecration with spirituality. "Is it," Ishmael asks, "that by its indefiniteness it shadows forth the voids and immensities of the universe, and then stabs us from behind with the thought of annihilation, when beholding the white depths of the Milky Way? Or is it, that as in essence whiteness is not so much a colour as the visible absence of colour, and at the same time the concrete of all colours; is it for these reasons that there is such a dumb blankness, full of meaning, in a wide landscape of snows—a colourless, all-colour of atheism from which we shrink? And when we consider that other theory of the natural philosophers, that all other earthly hues—every stately or lovely emblazoning—the sweet tinges of sunset skies and woods; yea, and the gilded velvets of butterflies, and the butterfly cheeks of young girls; all these are but subtle deceits, not actually inherent in substances, but only laid on from without; so that all deified Nature absolutely paints like a harlot, whose allurements cover nothing but the charnel-house within; and when we proceed further, and consider that the mystical cosmetic which produces every one of her hues, the great principle of light, forever remains white or colourless in itself, and if operating without medium upon matter, would touch all objects, even tulips and roses, with its own blank tinge—pondering all this, the palsied universe lies before us a leper; and like wilful travellers in Lapland, who refuse to wear coloured and colouring glasses upon their eyes, so the wretched infidel gazes himself blind at the monumental white shroud that wraps all the prospect around him."

Under the spell of Ahab, yet going his own way, Ishmael catches sight or, better, has a "sensational presentiment" of the cleavage in creation which sprang up an active principle, in Ahab. Not "the time is out of joint" but the very underpinning of creation. "Oh, cursed spite,"—there lies the source "of all those malicious agencies which some deep men feel eating in them. . . . That intangible malignity which has been from the beginning. . . . All that maddens and torments . . . all truth with malice in it" and, "the instinct of the knowledge of the demonism in the world."

The horror of whiteness, is it the soul's fear of death, the fear of extinction after death? Yes, but it goes beyond that. It is more fearful because more intimate. It is the soul's fear of itself. For in its own conscious self lies the seed of its destruction. The preoccupation with truth, with ideality, with "ideal mastership," with "spiritual things," nay, with the Deity itself, which are of the conscious soul, these are of the light principle, which "great principle of light, forever remains white or colourless in itself." In the white light of the soul's preoccupation with truth all its earthly satisfactions seem illusory—all stale, flat and unprofitable. The vital needs of its own earth born humanity are but "coloured and colouring glasses." Refusing to wear these kindly glasses, the soul finds itself in a void. It sees everywhere, as was seen in the White Whale, when he faced the staggering *Pequod,* its own featurelessness, its own colorlessness.

Ishmael felt himself on the verge of the abyss which he saw outwardly in Ahab's lurid light. In that extremity he felt within himself the source of all the tormenting ambiguities of life. What is life to one side of the soul is death to the other, and death at last to both.

Strong as his attachment to Ahab is, Ishmael is open to contrary influences. He is reluctant to share a bed with Queequeg at the inn at New Bedford, but the next morning brings a change. Ishmael is glad to accept Queequeg's offer of friendship and they share a pipe over it. Then Queequeg, according to the custom in his country, makes him a gift of half his possessions in silver and tobacco. Ishmael feels himself restored. He is in the position that Ahab is in, much later, with Pip. Ishmael, however, goes the full length of his more kindly emotions; "I began to be sensible of strange feelings. I felt a melting in me. No more my splintered heart and maddened hand were turned against the wolfish world. This soothing savage had redeemed it."

While Ahab's hunt for the hated White Whale gets hotter, Ishmael's land sense struggles to preserve itself. Whereas Ahab curses "that mortal inter-indebtedness" which makes a man dependent on his fellows, Ishmael submits to the fact that it is "a mutual, joint-stock world, in all meridians." Two thirds of the way through the book comes the chapter, "A Squeeze of the Hand." Ishmael describes the operation of squeezing down lumps of sperm into a delicious aromatic milk. The work is done in tubs, and since many hands are at work in each tub, they often squeeze each other by mistake. "Squeeze! squeeze! squeeze!" cries Ishmael, himself melting down again. "I declare to you, that for the time I lived as in a musky meadow; I forgot all about our horrible oath. . . . I felt divinely free from all ill-will, or petulance, or malice, of any sort whatsoever. . . . Would that I could keep squeezing that sperm forever! For now, since by many prolonged, repeated experiences, I have perceived that in all cases man must eventually lower, or at least shift, his conceit of attainable felicity; not placing it anywhere in the intellect or the fancy; but in the wife, the heart, the bed, the table, the saddle, the fireside, the country; now that I have perceived all this, I am ready to squeeze case eternally."

In the next chapter but one Ishmael's drama reaches its climax. It is night and he is taking his turn at the helm. The rest of the crew are employed in boiling blubber and have gathered around two vast cauldrons under which fires have been kindled. From his place in the stern Ishmael looks on, while "the wind howled on, and the sea leaped, and the ship groaned and dived, and yet steadfastly shot her red hell further and further into the blackness. . . ." While he was watching it came over Ishmael that "the rushing *Pequod,* freighted with savages, and laden with fire . . . and plunging into that blackness of darkness, seemed the material counterpart of her monomoniac commander's soul." Then something happens. There just fails of being a fiery welding between his soul and Ahab's. He is conscious that something is very wrong. He cannot see the compass. There is nothing in front of him but a pit of gloom, "now and then made ghastly by flashes of redness. Uppermost was the impression, that whatever swift, rushing thing I stood on was not so much bound to any haven ahead as rushing from all havens astern. A stark, bewildered feeling, as of death, came over me. . . . My God! what is the matter with me? thought I. Lo! in my brief sleep I had turned myself about. . . . In an instant I faced back, just in time to prevent the vessel from flying up into the wind, and very probably capsizing her. How glad and how grateful the relief from this unnatural hallucination of the night, and the fatal contingency of being brought by the lee!"

"Look not too long in the face of the fire, O man!" Fire is idiosyncratic. It has a capricious, distorting intensity. It is the light of personal feelings, that take the universal sorrow of life as personal grievance, and reason for personal rage. And "that way madness lies." "There is a wisdom that is woe; but there is a woe that is madness. And there is a Catskill eagle in some souls that can alike dive down into the blackest gorges, and soar out of them again and become invisible in the sunny spaces."

The freedom of spirit, alike to plunge and to soar. Here we come upon the significance of Ishmael's escape in the coffin life-preserver, which is more directly rendered when Ishmael, or rather Melville, taking a suggestion from the vapour that hangs about a whale's head "as you will sometimes see it—glorified by a rainbow, as if heaven itself had put its seal upon his thoughts"—writes, "And so through all the thick mists of the dim doubts in my mind, divine intuitions now and then shoot, enkindling my fog with a heavenly ray. And for this I thank God; for all have doubts; many deny; but doubts or denials, few along with them have intuitions. Doubts of all things earthly, and intuitions of some things heavenly; this combination makes neither believer nor infidel, but makes a man who regards them both with equal eye."

Against the strong attraction he feels for Ahab, Ishmael manages to keep his spiritual balance, his spiritual and intellectual freedom. Sharing Ahab's perceptions and feeling himself drawn to Ahab's desperate conclusions, he manages to so hold himself that he keeps in view the whole circle of life's possible issues. His soul, like Bulkington's, his sleeping partner, keeps "the open independence of her sea."

Ishmael escaped. Slowly the suction of the sunk ship reached him and he was slowly drawn towards the closing vortex. But when he reached it it had subsided. "Round and round, then, and ever contracting toward the button-like black bubble at the axis of that slowly wheeling circle, like another Ixion I did revolve. Till, gaining that vital centre, the black bubble burst upward . . . and, owing to its great buoyancy, rising with great force, the coffin life-buoy shot lengthwise from the sea, fell over, and floated by my side."

What are we to understand by Ishmael's escape? Between him and Ahab there is a divergency which repeats the divergency between Babbalanja and Taji at the end of *Mardi*. Babbalanja and Taji stood for opposite pulls in Melville's temperament. We can be more specific and say they stood for opposite exigencies in the religious consciousness which was paramount in Melville's nature.

Ahab's last act was like Taji's: "Now I am my own soul's emperor; and my first act is abdication." So saying, Taji, like Ahab after him, disappeared; "and then pursuers and pursued flew on over an endless sea." But while Ishmael is a foil for Ahab as Babbalanja is for Taji, we cannot go the full length and identify his escape with Babbalanja's conversion in Serenia. Indeed, any single conclusion drawn from his escape would be false. It is simply one episode among several that make up Ishmael's own story, the whole force of which, if it can be said to conclude at all, is to conclude against conclusions.

7

We must remember Ahab's scar, "slender, rod-like . . . lividly whitish," running from among his white hairs "down one side of his tawny scorched face and neck, till it disappeared in his clothing." The Gay-Head Indian's explanation of the scar, we already know; a different explanation was offered by an old man, a Manxman, who maintained that "if ever Captain Ahab should be tranquilly laid out,"—which was not likely—"then, whoever should do that last office for the dead would find a birth-mark on him from crown to soul." For the moment, it is only important to notice that the crew of the *Pequod*, which is pretty evenly divided between the white and dark races, divides on the question of Ahab's scar; no white sailor daring to contradict the old Manxman.

From this point on, and even before it, there is an all-ramifying dark-light antithesis in the symbolism of *Moby Dick*. I have spoken elsewhere of the other antithesis, of sea and land, in the book. The sea-land antithesis lies in man's moral consciousness, at any rate in the sphere of his conscious purposes, his sense of himself as a human being. The dark-light antithesis lies far beyond that. To relate the one to the other, I would say that the dark-light antithesis only begins to discover itself when a man, abandoning himself to his sea-instinct, has lost, or is in danger of losing, his land sense. It is a revelation which follows when a man goes to such an extreme of consciousness that his human equilibrium or sense of centre of gravity is lost. Thereupon the extremes of his being are locked in a terrible antagonism.

When Melville explains what the White Whale was to Ahab and tells how his monomania had usurped his intellectual and spiritual powers, without impairing them, he is careful to put the full sweep of these powers before us. "This is much;" he adds, "yet Ahab's larger, darker, deeper part remains unhinted. But vain to popularize profundities . . . winding far down from within the very heart of this spiked Hotel de Cluny where we here stand—however grand and wonderful, now quit it;—and take your way, ye nobler, sadder souls, to those vast Roman halls of Thermes; where far beneath the fantastic towers of man's upper earth, his root of grandeur, his whole awful essence sits in bearded state; an antique buried beneath antiquities, and throned on torsoes! So with a broken throne, the great gods mock that captive king, . . . that proud, sad king!"

This passage presents us with a full-length portrait of Ahab's inner man in repose. Only on one other occasion do we see him so comprehensively. Then he is in action. It is in the chapter "The Candles"—and Ahab stands his "whole high, broad form" against the lightning that threatens him with instant destruction. "I own thy speechless, placeless power; . . . Nor was it wrung from me. . . . Thou canst blind; but I can then grope. Thou canst consume; but I can then be ashes. Take the homage of these poor eyes, and shutter-hands. I would not take it. . . . Yet blindfold, yet will I talk to thee. Light though thou be, thou leapest out of darkness; but I am darkness leaping out of light, leaping out of thee!" The two principles or, better, the two extremities of Ahab's being, the light and the dark, are in action, the one setting off the other.

The dark-light antithesis comes out in the crew again in "Midnight, Forecastle." It is after Ahab has declared his feud with the White Whale. The sailors have shouted their assent and drinks have been passed around. Now in the late evening the sailors, still feeling their liquor, are amusing themselves. A Frenchman calls for a dance: "Jig it, men, I say, merry's the word; hurrah! Damn me, won't you dance?" *Dark Tashtego:* "That's a white man; he calls for fun: humph! I save my sweat." *Long Island sailor:* "Well, well, ye sulkies, there's plenty more of us. Hoe corn when you may, say I. . . . Ah! here comes the music; now for it!" Pip is about to play on a tambourine. *Dark Maltese sailor:* "Now would all the waves were women. There's naught so sweet on earth—heaven may not match it!" *Dark Sicilian:* "Tell me not of it! Hark ye, lad—fleet interlacings of the limbs—lithe swayings . . . lip! heart! hip! all graze: unceasing touch and go!"

In this group of the crew the dark portion is set off from the white by a kind of instinctive integrity. They abstain from the dancing which strikes them as a childish makeshift for the satisfaction of the sexual instinct. Those of the Southern or Mediterranean blood join with the dark, for whom a Tahitian sailor speaks out most clearly, "Hail, holy nakedness of our dancing girls!"

A storm comes up suddenly. Lightning flashes. The old Manxman takes thought as he sees it. "Our captain has his birthmark; look yonder, boys, there's another in the sky—lurid-like, ye see, all else pitch black." *Daggoo:* "What of that? Who's afraid of black's afraid of me! I'm quarried out of it!" A Spanish sailor says that it was not lightning they saw but "Daggoo showing his teeth." A fight is in the making. Daggoo says to the Spaniard, "Swallow thine, manikin! White skin, white liver!" *Spaniard:* "Knife thee heartily! big frame, small spirit." *All:* "A row! a row! a row!" *Old Manxman,* "Ready formed. There! the ringed horizon. In that ring Cain struck Abel. Sweet work, right work! No? Why then, God, mad'st thou the ring?" The squall breaks; the sailors scatter, leaving Pip with his tambourine: "Hold on hard! Jimmini, what a squall. . . . Oh, thou big white God aloft there somewhere in yon darkness, have mercy on this small black boy down here; preserve him from all men that have no bowels to feel fear!"

The old Manxman is crack-brained. His craziness is related to

Ahab's madness and he sees dimly by the same illumination. In the full glow of Ahab's lurid madness—lurid like a volcano, fire buried in earth—the conflict in which he is caught up reaches back to the beginning of things, when God created light to make war against primordial darkness. From there the ancient feud reaches throughout creation. No consciousness but bears some trace of it. Ahab, because of his heroic stature, shows it in the scar that runs his whole length of man. The conflict divides flesh from spirit. It goes deeper, dividing the soul itself. The light principle is akin to fire in all its manifestations. It is akin to whiteness. It reaches from the creator God to man's conscious and spiritual processes. The dark principle is in man's instinctive subterranean being. It lies in that far region where consciousness does not trouble to define itself, where it is closer to blood than brain.

The white principle in Ahab pursues the Whale as the symbol of that truth which underlies all man's conscious reflections, the truth which is man's noblest preoccupation. The whole spiritual and intellectual strength of his nature is wrapped up in the pursuit, in virtue of which he towers above his crew. But here is another paradox, the final paradox about Ahab. White Ahab pursues the ultimate truth. Dark Ahab joins as furiously in the hunt. But Dark Ahab has another quarry. It is no longer a question of his monomania. "Hark ye yet again,—the little lower layer." Dark Ahab does not rage against the inscrutable mystery that veils the truth but against his own mind and conscious soul. That tasks him, that heaps him! The darkness in Ahab storms against the light principle in creation, whose barbs it feels, those barbs being his own mind and conscious soul. In this pursuit the mates are brushed aside. The crew—those "Turkish cheeks of spotted tawn"—aboundingly responded. Instinctively they recognized Dark Ahab's hate as theirs and dimly surmised in the White Whale "the gliding great demon of the seas of life."

8

Ahab is a heroic creation. Writing some years after *Moby Dick*, Melville distinguished between characters in fiction who commonly pass for original and characters who are truly original, "original in the sense that Hamlet is, or Don Quixote or Milton's Satan." The lesser sort are "prevailingly local, or of an age." They are mirrors that catch the apparel, the conceits and the grimaces of their day; whereas "the original character, essentially such, is like a revolving Drummond light, raying away from itself all around it—everything is lit by it, everything starts up to it (mark how it is with Hamlet), so that, in certain minds, there follows upon the adequate conception of such a character, an effect, in its way, akin to that which in Genesis attends upon the beginnings of things." To produce such characters, "an author, beside other things, must have seen much, and seen through much; to produce but one original character, he must have had much luck." Between "this sort of phenomenon in fiction" and the lesser sort "there would seem but one point in common . . . it cannot be born in the author's imagination—it being true in literature as in zoology, that all life is from the egg."

An original character, then, is the product of an author's experience and observation—the egg—in conjunction with that which qualifies his experience and sees through it, namely, his genius—what Melville called his luck. If his words seem to light up Melville's aims and intentions with respect to Ahab; they also recall us to the primordial grounds of Ahab's existence, Melville's own deepest nature. Moreover, once we have taken the comparison of Ahab to a light "raying away from itself all around it," there is an occult truth to the further comparison of his effect to that "which in Genesis attends upon the beginning of things."

Ahab drew his being from Melville's knowledge of human nature, the best part of which was his knowledge of himself. Ahab was a projection of the strongest propensities in Melville's human make-up. His essential tragedy was an imaginative realization of a contingency which, being the man he was, Melville himself had to face. "For in all of us lodges the same fuel to light the same fire. And he who has never felt, momentarily, what madness is has but a mouthful of brains." Certainly, in the strength and diversity of his own human propensities there lay the same fuel to light the same fire as devastated Ahab.

The letters Melville wrote to Hawthorne while he was writing *Moby Dick* show him on the skirts of the vortex which his imagination was making terribly real in Ahab. They show him spiritually in the identical danger that Ishmael was in, floating "on the margin" of the scene of Ahab's disappearance and the sunk *Pequod*. Proposing for himself that ideal of being which he called "the usable truth," he himself was experiencing the same strains that tore Ahab asunder. His own intransigent idealism speaks loudest in the apostrophe to Bulkington of the "mortally intolerable truth" —that as "in landlessness alone resides the highest truth, shoreless, indefinite as God—so better is it to perish in the howling infinite" than "craven crawl to land." These words, so straightforward when we read them, take a different turn when we associate them, as it is hard not to do, with other passages. "Shoreless, indefinite as God," the words recur when we read of the "indefiniteness of whiteness" that "shadows forth the heartless immensities of the world." The same ambiguity is felt in the words "shoreless, indefinite as God" when we read "so man's insanity is heaven's sense; and wandering from all mortal reason, man comes at last to the celestial thought, which, to reason is absurd and frantic; and weal or woe, feels then uncompromised, indifferent as his god." It is not frantic or absurd to say that the ambiguity in question betrays the fact that Melville himself is seeing at cross purposes, just as, although immeasurably heightened, Ahab saw and acted at cross purposes. Melville's idealism responded to Ahab—was, of course, projected in Ahab. Yet he stopped short of Ahab. He stopped short of the point where idealism, embittered, turns against humanity, and where preoccupation with the ultimate truth breaks with those realities, apart from which it has no human significance. True to the considerations which prompted them in the first place, his idealism and preoccupation with truth remained not a negation but an affirmation of life. What is the truth? he asked in *Moby Dick,* the whole force of his nature bent to the question. The question, however, did not lead to a vanishing point. It was, to change the image, a lever applied with great force, that heaved up its own only possible answer, the truth of what it is to be alive. It is an act of being.

Moby Dick is a representation of life like *Hamlet* or *King Lear,* but with a difference. I have already mentioned one aspect of this difference, namely, the concentration of effort in *Moby Dick* on what Shakespeare left to random probings or inference.

To put it simply, Melville is more present and pressing in his masterpiece than Shakespeare is in any of his plays. His subjective being is constantly taking over, by identifying itself with, the forms of his objective seeing. Or, returning to a point of similarity between *Hamlet* and *Moby Dick,* in each the range and variety of vision depends essentially on an inward balance and the most inclusive and exacting self-possession on the part of their respective authors. But in *Hamlet* this balance and self-possession is something achieved outside the scope of the play. In *Moby Dick,* on the other hand, Melville's exertion to keep his balance, upon the loss of which his vision would crumble, goes on in the book. All that he discovers as he perseveres is felt like so many threats in as many contending directions to his keeping his all-important balance. It appears, then, that to call *Moby Dick* an act of being is not so much to praise it as to characterize it accurately.

A great act of being, like a great swirl of the sea, it churns up and beats together the terror and the glory of life. "Out of the bottomless profundities" the gigantic tail of leviathan "seems spasmodically snatching at the highest heaven. So in dreams have I seen majestic Satan thrusting forth his tormented colossal claw from the flame Baltic of Hell. But in gazing at such scenes, it is all in what mood you are in; if in the Dantean, the devils will occur to you; if in that of Isaiah, the archangels." "Oh God! that man should be a thing for immortal souls to sieve through!" cries Ahab, staring into the vacant eyes of terror-stricken Pip. "Oh, horrible vulturism of earth," in which a man's most heavenly soul is implicated. "Oh life!" cries Starbuck, "'tis now that I do feel the latent horror in thee! but 'tis not in me! that horror's out of me! and with the soft feeling of the human in me, yet will I try to fight ye, ye grim, phantom futures!" Two thirds of the way through *Moby Dick*, Ishmael exclaims, "But even so, amid the tornadoed Atlantic of my being, do I myself still forever centrally disport in mute calm; and while ponderous planets of unwaning woe revolve round me, deep down and deep inland there I still bathe me in eternal mildness of joy." When *Moby Dick* was finished, Melville wrote to Hawthorne: "I have written a wicked book, and feel spotless as the lamb. Ineffable socialities are in me."

Starbuck, too, is a part of Melville, and his words just quoted are apposite to the rest. The mention of Starbuck, however, calls attention to the weakness of *Moby Dick* as a representation of life, a weakness which is all the more apparent when we compare it with any one of Shakespeare's tragedies. In Starbuck we see where the wholeness of its humanity is wanting. He is simply a counterpiece. For when he described Starbuck Melville's imagination failed him, and it failed him because his sympathies did not lie in the direction of such characters. His failure, so apparent in Starbuck, was not confined to him. In the whole book only Queequeg is a lovable character, and that, in view of the effect that Melville aimed at, is a serious defect. Melville's failure even reaches to Ahab, where it is most serious. Ahab's heart struggles to restore itself to human ties, without which it must perish. We know this, but we seldom feel it. A character that in many respects can stand comparison with King Lear, Ahab is not poignant like King Lear. The "soft feeling of the human" is not there, at any rate not in the right proportion for his heroic stature. His tragedy inspires terror as does no work in the language outside of Shakespeare. But it fails to inspire pity.

9

The mind's effort to sustain and know itself, that is another way of describing *Moby Dick*. Its similes, metaphors, symbols, allegory—what are they but the effort of a mind to add its truth to the truth of external facts? The style follows from the same law that Melville represents now one way, now another, in the conduct of his story;—the mind lost in its own ends informs whatever thing it contemplates.

Yet more is in question here than the mind. It is as though Melville had determined to give nothing less than the whole truth of consciousness. But then, as Polonius said of madness, how define consciousness except by being conscious? That is what it comes to in *Moby Dick*. The consciousness which is organically present cannot be explained otherwise than by pointing to some of its effects. The book is a hodge-podge of adventure story, moral drama, mysticism, practical information, diatribe. Yet all these apparently ill assorted ingredients cling together. More than that, they are felt to flow into one another. Each is solvent to the rest. Porousness, fluidity, plasticity, by whatever name we choose to designate this reciprocity, it belongs to consciousness, and to the kind of consciousness that is something else and something more than mind.

Melville's symbols—those, at least, which are not, like the character of Starbuck, mere intellectual coinages—have a vitality from precisely the same source. On the level of story the White Whale is a whale, Ahab is a defined character, the sea is most certainly the sea. Wonderful as these creations are on the level of story, they are still more wonderful as symbols. They can be seen to line up and define themselves in a profound generalization about life. That is, they fall into an allegorical pattern, yet no statement as to their meaning can convey how vital, how meaningful these symbols are. Separately and in relation to each other they will not be held to any final definition or any fixed subject-object relationship. Ahab, the Whale, the sea, the light and the dark, they are all interrelated. Yet within their interrelationship they enjoy unlimited freedom of association. They are continually taking up new positions by themselves and toward one another and opening new vistas into the mystery of things. They have a profound ambiguity which baffles the mind, which is of consciousness, seeing all things in its own likeness, and its own image in all things, a process without beginning, middle or end.

There is this fluidity in *Moby Dick*. Yet it does not fall into what we call the stream of consciousness. For the consciousness in *Moby Dick* is in a state of exertion. It is trying to define or comprehend itself. Accordingly it does not relax and disintegrate on a stream of impressions. Against this stream it preserves the sense of itself and its own innermost rhythms—a sense of ebb and flow, of endless escape yet always return, infinite variety of mood and prospect, yet always identity; endless fluidity yet the sense of equilibrium somewhere, and with this, no matter how vague, a sense of centre and circumference. The consciousness in *Moby Dick* keeps this sense of itself. According to the last sense of it, it impresses itself more than it is impressed upon.

So the *Pequod* "rushed along, as if two antagonistic influences were struggling in her—one to mount direct to heaven, the other to drive yawingly to some horizontal goal." The White Whale breaches, lifts himself bodily out of the water or pecks his fluke at highest heaven, then plunges into bottomless profundities. Ahab, like the *Pequod*, is torn by antagonistic principles, stretching his whole stature to God on high yet trying to bind himself to horizontal man. Each is moulded to the likeness of the others and all to the likeness of a consciousness trying to complete itself.

The sea is the most inclusive symbol of all. Its presence crowds the book. It blends and fuses all in the sense of itself, its continual motion and change of aspect, its ubiquity, its everlasting identity. The sea is borne in upon us as leading off everywhere and returning in itself everywhere. It leads from Nantucket to the Pacific and equally from the Pacific to Nantucket. It rolls in the Pacific "the midmost waters of the world, the Indian Ocean and Atlantic being but its arms. The same waves wash the moles of the new-built Californian towns, but yesterday planted by the recentest race of men, and lave the faded but still gorgeous skirts of Asiatic lands, older than Abraham; while all between float milky ways of coral isles, and low-lying, endless, unknown archipelagoes and impenetrable Japans." "The sun hides not the ocean, which is the dark side of this earth, and which is two-thirds of this earth. So, therefore, that mortal man who hath more of joy than sorrow in him, that mortal man cannot be true—not true or undeveloped." In the sense or presence of the sea in *Moby Dick*, evil, the rapine of the sea, is associated with truth, truth with sadness, sadness with wisdom, and all with divinity. Of the sea in *Moby Dick* who shall say that it stands more for the truth of the ocean than for the truth of human consciousness, its evanescent, everlasting, bewildering, tormented self?

CHAPTER SIX

Pierre

MOBY DICK was published in 1851 and *Pierre* in the year following. There is a striking difference between the two books, the more remarkable because the one followed in the wake of the other. *Moby Dick* is a book of the sea. Not so *Pierre*, at least not at first sight. "There are some strange summer mornings in the country," Melville begins, "not a flower stirs; the trees forget to wave; . . . and all Nature, as if suddenly become conscious of her own profound mystery, and feeling no refuge from it but silence, sinks into this wonderful and indescribable repose." With the ocean-born commotion of *Moby Dick* still in our ears, the initial description in *Pierre* of a deep mid-summer hush over an inland countryside seems to show a complete about-face, in keeping with Melville's promise to Mrs. Hawthorne about his new book. In a letter in which he confessed that he had "some vague idea" while writing *Moby Dick* "that the whole book was susceptible of an allegorical construction," he added, "but, my Dear Lady, I shall not again send you a bowl of salt water. The next chalice I shall commend will be a rural bowl of milk."

In ostensible plan and setting, *Moby Dick* and *Pierre* are widely separated. If a novel at all, the former is of the mongrel breed in which the epic is seen to degenerate into the picaresque tale. Of *Pierre*, on the other hand, one can argue that it is a developed novel. It introduces us into the familiar world of society and manners. It has a recognizable novel plot in which a number of characters are involved. In *Moby Dick* one character dominates all. The others serve mainly as milestones to measure the extent of the action which lies with Ahab—which, for that matter, Ahab is. In *Pierre* all the important characters have a profound influence on one another and not one of them could be omitted without impairing the story as a whole.

Never mind for the moment that the turns which Melville give his story are melodramatic and that his own style, like the speech of his characters, is not infrequently rhetorical in a way that we have no stomach for today. The plot itself is sound; and if it is understood that Melville's theme is growth, the growth of a personality or psyche, many of the circumstances of the plot will appear to be well chosen. For one thing, sex plays a deservedly important part in the development. Moreover, there is present a kind of irony which has always been richly associated with imaginative realism. I mean the awareness of the tragic disproportion between a man's potentialities and the possibilities at his command for realizing them, which narrows to the realization that a man is never ready for any given crisis until he has passed through it. For it is the given crisis that confers the understanding and the ability to handle it. But the gift comes too late to avail a man and the crisis has not passed without leaving his life bent and, perhaps, irreparably destroyed. As Melville put in briefly, ". . . it is through the malice of this earthly air, that only by being guilty of Folly does mortal man in many cases arrive at the perception of Sense."

Melville's realism goes beyond the shaping of his plot to convey the theme of growth and its frustration. In his view of human motives, that they are to be traced back to where they betray a complex origin and admit of a manifold interpretation, he anticipates much of what recent psychology has contributed to the substance and technique of fiction. "For surely," Melville writes, "no mere mortal who has at all gone down into himself will ever pretend that his slightest thought or act solely originates in his own defined identity." Furthermore, after allowing for the characteristic violence of his presentation, one cannot discount the truth of his backgrounds whenever he takes the time to paint them in. There is a realism of materials in what he shows of the American environment in the 1830's and 1840's, with its social and literary pretentiousness, its spiritual refinement and eccentricity, the decline of the older aristocratic traditions and the coarse boisterousness of its new immigrant populations.

At the beginning the hero, Pierre Glendinning, has made the most of the happy circumstances of his character and upbringing. At nineteen he has always lived with his mother, a still beautiful and sumptuous widow, on his ancestral estates at Saddle Meadows. He is richly endowed by nature and good fortune. He has a strong and keen intelligence, a manly and generous heart, a splendid physique; and to all this "the golden humanities of religion" have been added. Pierre is like Hamlet as Ophelia remembered him before his father's death, "The courtiers', soldiers', scholars', eye, tongue, sword."

Yet something is wanting in Pierre's character. To use a common phrase which has been debilitated by vague usage, he has never faced reality. A reader of Dante and Shakespeare, he has himself had no "sensational presentiment" of "the infinite cliffs and gulfs of human mystery and misery," which Shakespeare and Dante opened to the eyes of his imagination. He has been kept within his mother's world of selfish exclusiveness where conventions and what it is pleasant to believe are substituted for the truth about life. Pierre has to confront that truth if he is to attain to manhood. His mother stands in the way. She would stunt his growth by possessing him entirely. Not satisfied to be his mother, still beautiful and youthful as she is, she would play sister to him. She would even preëmpt the role of his mistress or wife.

In spite of its enviable aspects then, Pierre's situation is precarious, and he is too innocent to be alive to his danger. True, he is engaged to marry, a step which might rescue him from bondage to his mother. But his fiancee, Lucy Tartan, is not likely to help him there. Herself a product of the same social and spiritual

environment, she does not seem the person to lead him into new
roads of development, a fact that Mrs. Glendinning is thoroughly
aware of—to her own sinister satisfaction. "His little wife, that is
to be," she tells herself, "will not estrange him from me; for she
too is docile. . . ."

Then, suddenly, the truth that a man ignores at the peril of his
manhood thrusts itself upon Pierre. It is revealed to him that he
has a sister, his father's illegitimate child before his marriage. Isabel
Banford, as the girl calls herself, has always lived in poverty and
distress, her privations standing in a perfect equilibrium with the
privileges which Pierre has always enjoyed. At this revelation he
staggers like a man who has been all but mortally stabbed. To
himself he groans that "the before undistrusted moral beauty of the
world is forever fled." His sacred father is no more a saint in his
eyes. "Now, now," he cries, "for the first time, Pierre, Truth rolls
a black billow through thy soul!"

Instinctively he knows that his mother will never acknowledge
Isabel's claims. So he must take up the challenge alone and mend
the injustice she has suffered by acknowledging his sister before
the world. Yet how to do this without dishonoring his father's
memory and torturing his mother? He hits on an expedient which
however odd, recommends itself because, as Pierre thinks, it will
put all the brunt and odium on his own shoulders. He decides to
pretend a secret marriage between Isabel and himself which he
announces to the world. Although inspired by the noblest motives
Pierre's action is disastrous. Not only does his mother disinherit him
on the instant, but innocent Lucy nearly dies from shock and in a
short time his mother does die of wounded pride. At the same time
there is a menacing change in the quality of his feeling for his new
found sister.

For all these misfortunes, however, we feel that something has
been gained. Shocking as it would be in the eyes of the world
Pierre's passion for Isabel has more strength in it than his attachment for Lucy. "Thou dost not pine for empty nominalness," he

ells Isabel, "but for vital realness." In her embraces the truth about
ife and about himself and a new impulse toward maturity is imparted to his entire being. In New York he tries to support himself
and Isabel by writing. Before this he had published in the magazines and been praised extravagantly for effusions such as his
sonnets, "The Tropical Summer," "Beauty: an Acrostic," "Life, an
Impromptu." Now, thoroughly ashamed of these jejune efforts, he
takes all on a really serious book, a book which should be "some
thoughtful thing of absolute Truth."

But very swiftly adversities begin to pile up upon him. The
anomaly of his relationship with Isabel becomes a source of torture
to him. His eyesight begins to fail and his vigorous health to
break down.

In the midst of his difficulties a letter from Lucy announces her
determination to join him and Isabel and help them as best she
can. Lucy is as good as her word, and in consequence she is cast
off by her mother, while a mortal enmity springs up between Pierre
on the one hand, and on the other Pierre's cousin, Glen Stanley,
also a suitor for Lucy's hand, and Lucy's brother. Pierre struggles to finish his book, but the odds are too heavy against him. His
publishers denounce him for a plagiarist and threaten action against
him. His cousin and Lucy's brother send him a letter denouncing him
for a liar. Desperate at last, Pierre takes leave of Isabel and Lucy
and goes out to meet his assailants, and he comes on them in a
crowded thoroughfare in the city. Glen strikes Pierre in the face
with a cowhide and Pierre promptly empties two pistols into him.
" 'Tis speechless sweet to murder thee," cries Pierre.

Taken to prison, he is visited by the two girls, neither of whom
has exact knowledge of the other's relationship to the man they
both share. Isabel cries out that she, not he, is a murderer: "thy
sister hath murdered thee, my brother, oh my brother!" At these
"wailed words" Lucy falls dead. Thereupon Isabel and Pierre drink
from a vial of poison which she has long concealed in her bosom.
She dies but a fraction of a second after him, "and her whole form

sloped side-ways, and she fell upon Pierre's heart, and her long hair ran over him, and arboured him in ebon vines."

Still overlooking the violent turns of the story, the plot, I repeat, is sound, and it is one which squares with the demands of psychological realism. Pierre is a creature of tragic irony. Throwing his lot in with Isabel, he spurns the false props which surrounded him in adolescence. But hardly has he begun his life anew in the city when he finds himself in a *cul-de-sac*. His feelings for Isabel cross and frustrate each other. Besides, although Isabel has endured distress and ignominy, and although she can bring him to realize the untruth of his mother's world, she is not the person, any more than Lucy was, to help him forward on the basis of a broad as well as truthful comprehension of life. Her great strength is passive, and she speaks the truth when she tells him, "This strange, mysterious, unexampled love between us, makes me all plastic in thy hand," and, again, "Thy hand is the caster's ladle, Pierre, which holds me entirely fluid. Into thy forms and slightest moods of thought, thou pourest me." Moreover, just like his mother, she wants to possess him wholly. Bitterly she protests, "Oh, I want none in the world but thee, my brother—but thee, but thee! . . . but all my life, all my full soul, contents not my brother." When Pierre speaks to her about Lucy, Isabel exclaims against Lucy, just as his mother had exclaimed against her: "that *she*, that *she*," she cries.

One ironical turn follows another. When Lucy reënters the story she is no longer the green girl whom Pierre has boyishly adored. Life has dealt with her, too, and she has grown in strength and insight. She, too, can defy the odium that Mrs. Glendinning's world heaps upon those who fling off its conventions. "Grief," she tells Pierre, "deep, unspeakable grief, hath made me this seer." She pleads with Pierre to let her help him with his book—and not, she says, in mere copying, "but in the original writing" as well. It is too late, however, for Pierre to avail himself of any help which Lucy can hold out. Partly because of Isabel's anomalous influence and, more, because of a drastic turn which his character has taken under the pressure of circumstances, Pierre cannot redress himself so as to escape from his *cul-de-sac*.

That is, stirred to life by Isabel's appeal, his idealism prompts him to sacrifice all his worldly riches. But when his idealism continues to meet with contumely and adversity, it hardens to fanaticism, and withdraws him from the reach of all human sympathy—from Isabel's quite as much as Lucy's sympathy. "Ye two pale ghosts," he calls them near the end, bidding them leave him forever, for, as he says, "Pierre is neuter now!"

Having shut himself off from other outlets, his idealism concentrates itself on his book. And here, too, it proves disastrous. The idea occurs to him that the wiser and profounder his book, the less likely will it be to furnish the needs of bodily existence; his wisdom is not exchangeable for bread and butter. Nevertheless, he can not compromise. Even if he wanted to, "he could not now be entertainingly and profitably shallow in some pellucid and merry romance." Lucy's offer, that she and Isabel assist him with his book, he refuses with scorn. His health broken, his very life and the lives of the two girls in jeopardy, still "the profound wilfulness in him would not give up."

The last irony of all, then, which gathers the beginning and end of Pierre's story in its folds, is that Pierre escapes the emasculating, hot-house domination of his mother only to immure himself in the arid stone of his own egoism. He has escaped her baleful pride of worldly possessions simply to fall victim to his disastrous pride of righteousness, truth and idealism.

The ironic vision, as Melville sees it, lends itself to many explications. Are men the playthings of an irresponsible deity, like flies to wanton boys? Are their aspirations overruled by an inscrutable Providence which has only its own secret ends in view? Are they predestined to good and evil, to happiness and misery? Or are they simply the victims of blind fate? Melville wrote in *Pierre,* that sucked within the maelstrom, man must go round. Strike at one end the longest conceivable row of billiard balls in close contact, and the furthermost ball will start forth, while all the rest stand still; and yet that last ball was not struck at all. So, through long previous generations, whether of births or thoughts, fate strikes the present man." Melville was in several minds about the questions which the ironic vision of life brings up. But at times, as in this passage, he was not so much a theologian or metaphysician as he was a realist, seeing fate not as an external force but simply as the dead weight of antecedent circumstances. He was in advance of his time and, in America, closer to the generation of Theodore Dreiser than the generation of William Dean Howells which succeeded his own. His position in this passage, which he approximates in other passages in *Pierre*, is the position of the psychological determinist. Yet, though this is obviously true, it touches only one aspect of this book, and that aspect, however interesting, stands to the book as a whole in the same proportion as the visible fraction of an iceberg to its submerged and invisible bulk.

2

Pierre was the only book of Melville's maturity as ambitious as *Moby Dick*. As if to intimate his real aims in *Pierre* and excuse the complications attendant on them, Melville wrote, "While the countless tribes of common novels laboriously spin veils of mystery only to complacently clear them up at last . . . yet the profounder emanations of the human mind, intended to illustrate all that can be known of human life, these never unravel their intricacies."

The truth is that *Pierre* aimed far beyond the scope of common novels and its complications defy any single resolution. Different as is the foreground of fact in *Pierre* from the foreground in its predecessor, the speculative background is much the same, and it was there, in the speculative background, that Melville's momentum, coming out of *Moby Dick,* drove him to place his main interest. Accordingly, for all the realistic notation of psychological truths in *Pierre,* another spirit so impregnates and usurps the characters and their actions that in the final impression of the book its realistic features are all but lost sight of. The characters and their actions are less human actualities than they are so many mathematical quantities used in psychological equations. If it had not been so it would have been no less than a miracle. If it were fair to judge *Pierre,* written in the wake of *Moby Dick,* primarily as a novel of psychological realism, it would be hardly less to wonder at than were it proved that the same man wrote the plays of Shakespeare and the works of Francis Bacon.

That critic was only half right who remarked that while one accepts Ahab as a demigod one cannot accept Pierre as a human being, "although Pierres are plentiful while one might dredge the five seas without bringing up the carcass of another Ahab." * The remark applies only to the illusion Melville created in the case of Ahab and failed to create in Pierre. For it is not acceptable to a realistic sense of things that a dewy American youth should change in a period of half a year into a figure as sered and bowed as the prophet Jeremiah. That is what happens to Pierre—a single circumstance which will show how far Melville was driven beyond all regard for actual psychological processes. But the critic's remark does not apply to Melville's intentions. For Melville intended Pierre to be as unique as Ahab, and unique in much the same titanic mould. This is made clear in the opening pages after Melville has described the noble proportions of his young hero's humanity. "Now," he wrote, "Pierre stands on this noble pedestal; we shall see if he keeps that fine footing . . . we shall see whether this wee little bit scrap of latinity be very far out of the way—*Nemo contra Deum nisi deus ipse.*"

There is one important feature in Pierre's character that distinguishes him from Ahab. Captain Ahab reminds us of Milton's Satan, of Prometheus, and thence, of Don Quixote. It cannot be said that he reminds us of Sir Galahad. Pierre, on the contrary, does remind us of Sir Galahad. He is, when he is introduced to us, a

* Lewis Mumford, *Herman Melville,* p. 207.

Christian gentleman, and his subsequent heroic action include
the pursuit of the absolute and Christlike righteousness as well a
absolute truth. But this does not prevent him from repeating Cap
tain Ahab's destiny, and if his virtue makes any difference at all
it is only to accentuate and accelerate the pace of his tragedy
Besides, for all his Christianity, Pierre like Ahab "declares himsel
a sovereign nature (in himself) amid the powers of heaven, hell
and earth." And he dies in the same tragic circumstances as Captair
Ahab. In more than one sense he destroys himself as he also bring
death on those who are closest to him. A little before the end we
read, "On either hand clung to by a girl who would have laid down
her life for him; Pierre, nevertheless, in his deepest, highest part
was utterly without sympathy from anything divine, human, brute
or vegetable. One in a city of hundreds of thousands of human
beings, Pierre was solitary as at the Pole." It was almost precisely
the same with Ahab. As he says of himself just before his end
"Ahab stands alone among the millions of the peopled earth, no
gods, nor men his neighbors! Cold, cold—I shiver!" Pierre's reckles
pursuit of virtue and truth led to just where Ahab's onslaught or
the truth of creation brought him. "The dead, blind wall butts al
inquiring heads at last," says Ahab. Pierre, just before he dies, with
the black walls of a prison around him, reflecting on the conse
quences of his devotion to truth and virtue, cries, "It is ambiguou
still."

Abstractly speaking, Pierre's tragedy was more bitter than Ahab's
and not only because he was so much younger. About to die, Ahab
exclaims, "Oh, now I feel my topmost greatness lies in my top
most grief." Pierre can feel no topmost greatness. Like Ahab he die
defiant, but unlike Ahab he does not thrust his spirit beyond the
goring vexations of the questions of good and evil. He dies in the
belief that he is damned, the only shred of his Christianity that
still clings to him, and Melville is not at any pains to correct hi
impression. "Had I been heartless now," Pierre reflects, "disowned
and spurningly portioned off the girl at Saddle Meadows, then

ad I been happy through a long life on earth, and perchance
hrough a long eternity in heaven! Now, 'tis merely hell in both
worlds. Well, be it hell. I will mould a trumpet of the flames, and,
with my breath of flame, breathe back my defiance!"

In *Pierre*, as in *Mardi* and *Moby Dick*, there is for theme a man's
ssumption of his full human consciousness. But whereas in *Moby
Dick* we are presented to Ahab only after he has taken on his full
urden of that consciousness, in *Mardi* and *Pierre* the theme is
aken up in its earlier phases so that we are present at the birth
nd growth of a soul. True, the tragic conclusion of Pierre's spiritual
rama overtakes him with overwhelming rapidity. As early in the
ory as his departure from Saddle Meadows he has fearful pre-
entiments. At that moment, with the thoughts of grief-stricken Lucy
nd his outraged mother gripping his heart, "Lo! I leave corpses
wherever I go!" groaned Pierre. "Can then my conduct be right?
o! by my conduct I seem threatened by the possibility of a sin
nomalous and accursed, so anomalous, it may well be the one for
hich Scripture says, there is never forgiveness. Corpses behind me,
nd the last sin before, how then can my conduct be right?" And
though in the tragic conclusion of his spiritual drama Pierre
ands alone like Ahab, nevertheless, as the action develops, there
e other characters or symbols that play a vital role in determin-
g his fate.

3

Even in their physical appearance there is a striking contrast
etween Lucy and Isabel. "Wondrous fair of face, blue-eyed, and
olden-haired, the bright blond, Lucy, was arrayed in colors har-
onious with the heavens." Isabel has dark olive cheeks, hair like
ony and dark, lustrous eyes. Good angel and bad angel, Pierre
lls Lucy and Isabel, taking leave of them at the end of the book.
nd Isabel, as it happens, proves to be Pierre's bad angel. But
e is not evil in herself. Similar as it is on the surface, the contrast
etween Lucy and Isabel is not the contrast between Yillah and

Hautia in *Mardi*. In *Pierre* the only bad character or symbol of evil is the mother. As Hautia stifled her heart with sensual lusts so Mrs. Glendinning has stifled hers with "the dreary heart-vacancie of conventional life." She represents spiritual death, and quite a important as the contrast between Lucy and Isabel is the fac that they are both united in opposition to Mrs. Glendinning. Lucy and Isabel represent principles or necessities equally vital to a man's soul.

When Pierre recognizes Isabel as his sister, out of that spiritua act his soul is born. After he has acted on his noble resolution and when he and Isabel are outcasts in the city, his soul continue to grow, which is to say it continues to acquire independence. The growth of his soul is identified with his effort to complete his grea book, "that which now absorbs the time and the life of Pierre, i not the book, but the primitive elementalizing of the strange stuf which in the act of attempting that book, has upheaved and up gushed in his soul. Two books are being writ; of which the worl shall only see one, and that the bungled one. The larger book, an the infinitely better, is for Pierre's own private shelf." A few page before, Melville had written, "when at Saddle Meadows, Pierr had wavered and trembled in those first wretched hours ensuin upon the receipt of Isabel's letter; then humanity had let go th hand of Pierre" (that is, when Pierre understood he could no count on his mother to help him fulfill his responsibilities) "an therefore his cry; but when at last inured to this, Pierre was seate at his book, willing that humanity should desert him, so long as h thought he felt a far higher support; then, ere long, he began t feel the utter loss of that other support, too; ay, even the paterna gods themselves did now desert Pierre; the toddler was too dling entirely alone, and not without shrieks." And Melville re turned to this image in the passage about Pierre's two books cite above; "Who shall tell all the thoughts and feelings of Pierre in tha desolate and shivering room. . . . But the devouring profunditie now opened up in him, consume all his vigour. . . . Now he see that with every accession of the personal divine to him, some great landslide of the general surrounding divineness slips from him, and falls crashing away. Said I not that the gods, as well as mankind, had unhanded themselves from this Pierre? So now in him you behold the baby toddler I spoke of; forced now to stand and toddle alone."

Pierre's soul struggles to fulfill itself—struggles to assume manhood and independence. But he fails to complete the book which is at once the symbol and simulacrum of his soul. And as we know, hardly has he put his heroic resolution into action, that is, when he is about to leave Saddle Meadows, than he has presentiments of spiritual catastrophe which do not wait long to be verified. Somewhere, then, after the birth of his soul, he has taken a wrong step or failed to take a right one. But where? In other words, where lies the middle and turning point of his spiritual drama?

The answer is found precisely in the middle of the book, where we read, "Though in some things he had unjuggled himself, and forced himself to eye the prospect as it was; yet, so far as Lucy was concerned, he was at bottom still a juggler. True, in his extraordinary scheme, Lucy was so intimately interwoven, that it seemed impossible for him at all to cast his future without some way having that heart's love in view. But ignorant of its quantity as yet, or fearful of ascertaining it; like an algebraist, for the real Lucy he, in his scheming thoughts, had substituted but a sign— some empty x—and in the ultimate solution of the problem that empty x still figured; not the real Lucy."

Ironically enough, Pierre, like his mother, miscalculated Lucy's strength. His mother knew herself to be "the essential opposite of Lucy" and believed herself essentially superior to her future daughter-in-law. "But here," Melville tells us, "Mrs. Glendinning was both right and wrong. So far as she here saw a difference between herself and Lucy Tartan, she did not err; but so far—and that was very far—as she thought she saw her innate superiority to her in the absolute scale of being, here she very widely and im-

measurably erred. For what may be artistically styled angelicalness, this is the highest essence compatible with created being; and
angelicalness hath no vulgar vigour in it." Mrs. Glendinning's mistake sprang from the worldling's contempt for the spiritually-
minded. Pierre's mistake about Lucy sprang from the directly
opposite point of view. His mistake, as it proved, was the idealist's
failure to gauge the human heart aright. He mistrusted and mis-
prized the power and might of human sympathy, and the resources
in the human heart for loving and heroic self-sacrifice. By associat-
ing Lucy with his mother in his mind he confounded the good and
the bad in mankind and he continued to err by acting as if Lucy
and his mother were equally blind, and equally opposed, to his
righteous conduct. Later when he has Lucy's letter assuring him
that she has recognized his nobility and announcing her determination to join him and Isabel, his mistake dawned on him and he
rejoiced. Here Melville writes: "When surrounded by the base and
mercenary crew, man, too long wonted to eye his race with a
suspicious disdain, suddenly is brushed by some angelical plume
of humanity, and the human accents of superhuman love, and the
human eyes of superhuman beauty and glory, suddenly burst on
his being; then how wonderful and fearful the shock! It is as if the
sky-cope were rent, and from the black valley of Jehoshaphat, he
caught upper glimpses of the seraphim in the visible act of ador-
ing." That is how it was with Pierre on learning that he still has
Lucy's sympathy and love. But it was too late now to recover
a place for Lucy and for what she represented of vital human
sympathies in his heart.

The symbolism of her amazing offer to help him write his book
should be plain by now. The individual cannot discard the common
ties that unite him to his kind; and more, men must depend on one
another in every great action, whether physical or intellectual
or spiritual. Pierre, however, is blind to this vital realization. Like
Ahab, he would curse the inter-indebtedness of men. He has sought
to fulfill himself in the opposite direction, that is, by way of absolute

independence or self-dependence. To Lucy's offer he replied, "Impossible! I fight a duel in which all seconds are forbid," and not long afterwards, taking leave of Lucy, Pierre says to her, "Dead embers of departed fires lie by thee, thou pale girl; with dead embers thou seekest to relume the flame of all extinguished love!"

Different as are the symbols themselves in *Pierre* from those in *Moby Dick*, the symbolical significance is much the same. The moral and spiritual contrast between Lucy and Isabel is the contrast between the sea and the land in *Moby Dick*. "Why is almost every robust healthy boy with a robust healthy soul in him, at some time or other crazy to go to sea?" Melville asks at the beginning of *Moby Dick*. Isabel, who has the same significance as the sea, at once appeals to the robust, healthy soul in Pierre—and he grows in spiritual stature. Nevertheless, according to the full symbolism of *Moby Dick*, for his salvation a man must check the sea instinct in his soul with his land sense of what is common and possible to human nature, upon the loss of which his human nature will be destroyed. That is what Pierre failed to do. Just before the passage in the middle of the book in which we are told that for the real Lucy Pierre "substituted but a sign"—just before that crucial passage Melville wrote: "There is a dark, mad mystery in some human hearts, which, sometimes, during the tyranny of a usurper mood, leads them to be all eagerness to cast off the most intense beloved bond, as a hindrance to the attachment of whatever transcendental object that usurper mood so tyrannically suggests. . . . We think we are not human; we become as immortal bachelors and gods; but again, like the Greek gods themselves, prone we descend to earth; glad to be uxorious once more; glad to hide these god-like heads within the bosoms made of too seducing clay."

Lucy's symbolical significance lies simultaneously in different categories. Partly her significance stems from Typee valley. In an orchestral prelude to the scene early in the book between the lovers Lucy and Pierre, Melville wrote: "All things that are sweet to see, or taste, or feel, or hear, all these things were made by Love; and none other things were made by Love. Love made not the Arctic zones." But her significance reaches to include the deeper affections of the human heart which Melville had realized in *Redburn* and *White Jacket*. In many respects she is like Starbuck, but heightened and rarefied. In her the outwardness of happy sensuous life has grown up to the outwardness of healthy human affections, and all this has been crowned by the outwardness of faith. She represents that spiritual submission of which the positive side is the acceptance of human actualities, apart from which even the best of hearts must shrivel up. When her mother disowns her, Lucy is very white and sits very still; but she does not flinch. "Helpings she had from unstirring arms; glimpses she caught of aid invisible; sustained she was by those high powers of immortal love, that once siding with the weakest reed which the utmost tempest tosses; then that utmost tempest shall be broken down before the irresistible resistings of that weakest reed." Heavenly as she appears to be, Lucy none the less is essentially human. She is a symbol of human growth, consummation, unity.

4

Isabel's significance, even vaguer than Lucy's, is broadly comprehended within the significance of the sea in *Moby Dick*. Under her influence Pierre, like the *Pequod*, as it seemed to Ishmael on one memorable occasion, left "all havens astern." And he comes to experience that extreme isolation from his kind whither thought, which will not compromise with man's human limitations, and idealism as uncompromising, must lead. Pierre severs himself from all common grounds of external experience and sensuous impressions to follow the infinite mazes of the implications of things. His case, as Melville states it under his central metaphor in the book, is this: "In those Hyperborean regions, to which enthusiastic Truth, and Earnestness, and Independence, will invariably lead a mind fitted by nature for profound and fearless thought, all objects are seen in a dubious, uncertain, and refracting light. Viewed through that rarefied atmosphere the most immemorially admitted maxims of men begin to slide and fluctuate, and finally become wholly inverted; the very heavens themselves being not innocent of producing this confounding effect, since it is mostly in the heavens themselves that these wonderful mirages are exhibited.

"But the example of many minds forever lost, like undiscoverable Arctic explorers, amid those treacherous regions, warns us entirely away from them; and we learn that it is not for man to follow the trail of truth too far, since by so doing he entirely loses the directing compass of his mind; for arrived at the Pole, to whose barrenness only it points, there, the needle indifferently respects all points of the horizon alike." Thither, into those polar regions, Pierre was fatally led under the spell of Isabel's influence, away from the middle earth with its "so rich a zone of torrid verdure" where Lucy's love would have held him.

Like Lucy's, Isabel's significance lies simultaneously in different categories. She is the eternally baffling object of human speculation, and she is also speculation itself, which, refusing all external guidance, collapses into introspection. She is the universal mysterious truth of creation in which his own soul shares and, accordingly, Pierre comes to feel her spell as "one with that Pantheistic masterspell, which eternally locks in mystery and in muteness the universal subject world." Her face, "vaguely historic and prophetic; backward, hinting of some irrevocable sin; forward, pointing to some inevitable ill," is one of those faces that seem "ever hovering between Tartarean misery and Paradisiac beauty"; and "compounded so of hell and heaven, overthrow in us all foregone persuasions, and make us wondering children in this world again." Not evil herself, Isabel is of the same dark mystery that includes the necessity for sin and suffering. Like the sea in *Moby Dick*, she is the dark, sad under-side of life, the side of un-faith; and the side that cannot articulate itself. Not to be identified with man's sensuous

nature, nevertheless she stands for instinctive depths in man's immemorial soul that are in contrast to, if not in actual conflict with,
his conscious intellectual and spiritual processes.

The incest between Pierre and Isabel has a multiplicity of meanings. It serves to illustrate Melville's thesis about the pursuit of
absolute truth and righteousness stated under the metaphor of the
traveller bound for the North Pole. It also illustrates another thesis
in the book, namely, that the purest conduct of which a man is
capable has some admixture of impurity to deface it. As Melville
exclaims, "Ah, if man were wholly made in heaven, why catch we
hell-glimpses? Why in the noblest marble pillar that stands beneath the all-comprising vault, ever should we descry the sinister
vein?"

Pierre's incestuous love for Isabel is also a symbol and as
such is not so simple to explain. In the first place, Isabel is Pierre's
soul's sister because his soul is partly of "the universal subject
world" eternally locked up in muteness and mystery. In this context, then, Lucy is an acquired attitude of the soul, a habit of poise
which it must assume. She represents faith and goodness which are
able to maintain themselves in the face of the dark mystery of sin
and suffering. Her faith and virtue are not like Mrs. Glendinning's,
wilful evasions and prevarications. Instinctively she knows that
Pierre did right to recognize Isabel as his sister and she promises
him that she, too, will recognize "the peculiar position of that
mysterious and ever sacred being." But instinctively she also knows
that Pierre cannot but at his greatest peril take Isabel for wife as
well as sister.

The middle part of Pierre's spiritual drama is this issue in his
soul between Isabel and Lucy. It was for him to check the sea instinct with the land sense. And Lucy, as we know, loses, and what
is more, she loses by default. When she reënters the story it is too
late for her to recover her place in Pierre's heart. He has given
himself wholly to Isabel. By taking her for wife he has put himself beside Ahab, who was so far gone "in the dark side of earth,"

that "its other side, the theoretic bright one," seemed but uncertain twilight to him. As we can see from the fragments given of Pierre's book, love, hope, faith and the beauty of the sunlit world have fled his heart. All is gloom, despair, hate; "I hate the world, and could trample all lungs of mankind as grapes, and heel them out of their breath, to think of the woe and the cant,—to think of the Truth and the Lie!"

Isabel, I repeat once more, is not evil in herself. It is that Pierre has allowed her to assume a position whereby she proves fatal to him and becomes his bad angel. When Lucy reënters his thoughts, Pierre between her and Isabel is like Ahab between Starbuck and Fedallah. Ahab in the chapter "The Symphony," after gazing into Starbuck's human eye,—"better than to gaze upon God," he had said,—"crossed the deck to gaze over on the other side; but started at two reflected, fixed eyes in the water there. Fedallah was motionlessly leaning over the same rail." So Pierre, reading Lucy's letter, "felt a vast, out-swelling triumphantness, that the girl whose rare merits his intuitive soul had once so clearly and passionately discerned, should indeed, in this most tremendous of all trials, have acquitted herself with such infinite majesty. Then again, he sank utterly down from her, as in a bottomless gulf, and ran shuddering through hideous galleries of despair, in pursuit of some vague, white shape, and lo! two unfathomable dark eyes met his, and Isabel stood mutely and mournfully, yet all-ravishingly before him."

5

Now that the common underlying drift of *Pierre* and *Moby Dick* is before us, I shall point out a significant difference of mood in the two books. In *Moby Dick* Melville wrote, "There are certain queer times and occasions in the strange mixed affair we call life when a man takes this whole universe for a vast practical joke, though the wit thereof he but dimly discerns, and more than suspects that the joke is at nobody's expense but his own. However, nothing dispirits, and nothing seems worth while disputing. He bolts down all events, all creeds, and beliefs, and persuasions, all hard things visible and invisible, never mind how knobby"; danger, disaster, death itself seem only sly, good-natured digs from "the unseen and unaccountable old joker. That odd sort of wayward mood I am speaking of, comes over a man only in some time of extreme tribulation; it comes in the very midst of his earnestness, so that what just before might have seemed to him a thing most momentous, now seems but a part of the general joke. There is nothing like the perils of whaling to breed this free-and-easy sort of genial, desperado philosophy."

In *Pierre* Melville wrote to much the same purpose, yet with a notable difference: "If fit opportunity offer in the hour of unusual affliction, minds of a certain temperament find a strange, hysterical relief, in a wild, perverse humorousness, the more alluring from its entire unsuitableness to the occasion. . . . The cool censoriousness of the mere philosopher would denominate such conduct as nothing short of temporary madness; and perhaps it is, since, in the inexorable and inhuman eye of mere undiluted reason, all grief, whether on our own account, or that of others, is the sheerest unreason and insanity."

In *Moby Dick* the "odd sort of wayward mood" that Ishmael puts on is the token of his detachment and sanity as against Ahab's transfixing madness. It shows the resilience of a consciousness in free and full possession of itself. In *Pierre,* on the contrary, the mood is not the means of holding off the madness of grief but a means of suppressing and concealing it. There is nothing genial in the desperate philosophy in *Pierre.* In contrast to *Moby Dick,* the mood has grown taut; it shows the constriction that comes from insecurity within; it is wild more than wayward. It becomes hysterical. We feel that it issues from intolerable tensions and uncertainties—that it is the expression of a grief-stricken man.

This is the mood at times of the hero, as when he has just taken action at the instigation of the painful truth about his father, divulged by Isabel. At this moment his words are like Hamlet's "wild and whirling words" after his father's ghost has pressed some home truths upon his heart. Yet the mood which I have described in *Pierre* is not merely sporadic; in its own way it is as pervasive as Ishmael's odd, wayward humor is in *Moby Dick*. Stemming from a memorable impression in *Typee*, of a dead warrior's effigy in a canoe, in the posture of a man pressing bravely forward into the infinite, while all the time in the prow of his canoe there faces him a mocking skull—stemming from this visual image and borrowing the inflections of Babbalanja's "merry" mad demon of truth in *Mardi*, there is in *Pierre* a death's-head mockery, a choked and terrible staccato laughter of self-derision which Melville was at little pains to disassociate from himself.

It is true that Melville cautions us not to take Pierre's views for his own. Nevertheless, the caution should be taken with as much reservation as his disavowal of allegory in *Moby Dick*. While Melville wrote about his young hero, a would-be author, in his turn Pierre was writing a book with a young hero-author whom he called Vivia. About to quote from Pierre's book, Melville tells us that "it is much to our purpose" for Pierre "seems to have directly plagiarized from his own experiences, to fill out the mood of his apparent author-hero." Melville has also assured us that he is more frank with Pierre "than the best men are with themselves. I am all unguarded and magnanimous with Pierre; therefore you see his weakness, and therefore only. In reserves men build imposing characters; not in revelations." As for himself Melville wrote, "It is impossible to talk or write without apparently throwing oneself hopelessly open; the Invulnerable Knight wears his visor down." Assuredly while he wrote *Pierre* Melville did not wear his visor down. Without other recourse than to the book itself it is self-evident that he too plagiarized from his own innermost experiences to fill out his hero's mood. Like the pelican mother he drew from his own tormented breast to give his offspring life.

Reverting to his central metaphor, Melville describes Pierre at his book, like a traveller bound north, where all familiarity and security, all that pertains to a man's common mortality, is lost to view. A "poor, frozen, blue-lipped, soul-shivering traveller . . . Ah! shivering thus day after day in his wrappers and cloaks, is this the warm lad that once sung to the world of the Tropical Summer?" From Pierre's "Tropical Summer" to his book about Vivia it is the same distance as from *Typee* to Melville's book about Pierre. In our turn, following the shadowy involutions of Melville's thought in *Pierre,* we cannot but exclaim with surprise that such a book should come from the same hand which imparted so much of luxuriance and exhilaration to *Typee*. The story which it tells simply keeps the direction of the whole book as it embodies Melville's own consciousness at the time of writing, and the whole book shows the shrinkage, the disintegration and collapse which follow when a man ignores his perception of that interior soundness and coherence; it shows that a man's self-possession depends on integration with the external world in which he finds himself. Melville recognized this truth and he was as fully aware of its psychological as of its moral and spiritual importance. He saw it, but he disregarded it. The consequences of his own disregard of it, forced upon him by his idealistic nature, might be shown in terms of psychological dislocation, as also in terms of spiritual and intellectual tragedy.

It is significant of Melville's point of departure in *Pierre,* and of his direction throughout the book, that its symbols are better explained according to the symbolism of *Moby Dick* than on any freshly broken ground of its own. The corollary to this is, as we can observe, that in *Pierre* fact as fact is developed by the symbolic significance it carries, and fact as symbol is overburdened. It is not for a moment that *Pierre* is more intellectual than *Moby Dick,* but that *Pierre* is more barely intellectual. There being no new integration with the visible world, the sphere at once of sensuous impressions, physical action and human wisdom, Melville's whole consciousness is not involved, and *Pierre* is not, like *Moby Dick,* a great act of being.

It is significant of this essential difference between the two books that whereas with Ahab thought has the body of action, with young Pierre action rapidly becomes thought. The same difference appears in the character of the symbols. Always holding on to his awareness of the outside world, the visible world of experience, Melville's symbols in *Moby Dick* have a rounded organic life of their own. In *Pierre*, on the other hand, the main symbols are felt as the coinages of Melville's mind, and instead of adding to each other's significance, they collide with and block one another, or collapse within themselves, frittering their force away in a multiplicity of intellectual refinements. Again, in the style of *Moby Dick*, as in the mood, there is the resilience of a consciousness in free and full possession of itself. Only about some of Ahab's speeches toward the end, when Melville's energies began to flag, do we feel something set and extrinsic, an attitudinizing that is set off from the spontaneous resources that made the book such an extraordinary whole. Admittedly, in *Pierre* Melville wrote in several different styles by intention, but there is not the same security on Melville's part with reference to his different intentions as there is in *Moby Dick* with reference to the whole. There are some very fine passages in the book, with a peculiar tenor and urgency of their own. But we virtually never feel the force of a consciousness that is constantly reviving and invigorating its inner sources by drawing on the outside world of tangible objects.

Melville cautions us that we are not to take Pierre's views for his own, and although this holds for certain particular views, Melville was identified with his youthful hero, and the identification lay deeper than the level on which a man's conscious views take shape. The middle part of Pierre's spiritual drama is obscure. That part, as we have seen, is Lucy's part, but it does not define itself proportionally to the earlier issue in Pierre's soul between his mother and Isabel or the conclusion in which he stands alone. In the light of other evidence this circumstance assumes a central significance. It stands for the fact that as in the story Pierre loses his hold of Lucy, so in the book Melville loses his hold of what Lucy represents. To show that Melville broke from Lucy will be to show him a tragic figure, and caught in his own tragic vision of life as he had depicted it in *Mardi* and *Moby Dick*. Of this vision the mainspring was his recognition of the dual nature of man, showing in man's finite needs and his infinite aspirations.

No man not among the saints loved virtue more vehemently than Herman Melville. Finding occasion in *Pierre* to mention the Sermon on the Mount, he calls it "that greatest real miracle of all religions." "From that divine mount, to all earnest loving youths, flows an inexhaustible soul-melting stream of tenderness and loving-kindness. . . . Such emotions as that sermon raises in the enthusiastic heart; such emotions all youthful hearts refuse to ascribe to humanity as their origin. This is of God, cries the heart, and in that cry ceases all inquisition."

Not long after this Melville introduces a lecture by one Plotinus Plinlimmon, which Pierre finds and reads in the coach that takes him from Saddle Meadows. The lecture turns out to be a dissertation on the difference between heavenly wisdom and worldly wisdom, which it designates, respectively, as horological time and chronometrical time. "Bacon's brains were mere watchmaker's brains; but Christ was a chronometer." Heavenly righteousness, that is, chronometrical time, was never meant for use in this world; "No, this conceit merely goes to show, that for the mass of men, the highest abstract heavenly righteousness is not only impossible, but would be entirely out of place, and positively wrong in a world like this. . . . A virtuous expediency, then, seems the highest desirable or attainable earthly excellence . . . that their Creator intended for them."

The Plinlimmon pamphlet is, of course, an admirable critique upon Pierre's conduct, who, acting in a wholly contrary way to Plinlimmon doctrine, rapidly became the victim of his moral idealism; he became, as he called himself, "the fool of Truth, the fool of Virtue."

But how did Melville regard the Plinlimmon pamphlet, which

afforded him grounds on which to take an independent position of Pierre? There are articles included under a "virtuous expediency" which were hot off Melville's heart;—as that a man shall take loving care of his wife and children, relations and friends; that he shall be "perfectly tolerant to all other men's opinions, whatever they may be" and "more especially" that he shall believe "that there is a God for infidels, as well as for believers," and shall act upon that belief. Plinlimmon's doctrine is not a materialistic negation of purely spiritual values. It declares that there is an absolute standard of righteousness which is of God. Only while affirming Heavenly Truth, it argues that a principle of relativity should also guide men's conduct and moral judgments in this world. The Plinlimmon pamphlet elaborates what Melville had long ago perceived, when he wrote in *Typee* that what is good practice for Americans may very well be bad practice for Polynesians and *vice versa;* and yet, as Melville wrote in *Typee,* there is an absolute standard of righteousness and justice for all. Plinlimmon's doctrine opens the doors of love and salvation to all kinds and conditions of men, to the cannibals of the South Seas and all the waifs and strays of the merchant marine, the whale fishery and the navy. It is the intellectual complement of the lesson of the heart, which centres on the unity of man under all different exteriors.

According to this wisdom of the heart all that withdraws men from men and puts barriers between them and obstructs the flow of vital sympathies, all that is evil. Virtue herself cannot afford to stand aloof. Virtue does not keep herself to herself on the quarterdeck but descends and fraternizes with the men in the forecastle— even like our Blessed Redeemer.

In *Pierre* he exactly reverses his judgment. "Thus in the Enthusiast to Duty," he writes, "the heaven-begotten Christ is born; and will not own a mortal parent, and spurns and rends all mortal bonds." Once he has come to a true perception of virtue on one hand and the nature of this world on the other, "then in the soul of the enthusiast youth two armies come to the shock; and unless he prove recreant, or unless he prove gullible, or unless he can find the talismanic secret, to reconcile this world with his own soul" [and there is no such secret] "then there is no peace for him, no slightest truce for him in this life." Between virtue and this world there is no compromise possible. So of Plinlimmon's dissertation Melville wrote: "I confess, that I myself can derive no conclusion which permanently satisfies those peculiar motions in my soul, to which that lecture seems more particularly addressed." A "thin, tattered, dried-fish-like thing"; and a "fried-fish-like, pamphlet-shaped rag" he calls the manuscript of the lecture. For all its good sense, its kindness and tolerance, in the frame of mind in which he wrote *Pierre,* Melville had no more stomach for Plinlimmon's doctrine than his youthful hero.

Between the lecture and Lucy there is a very close connection. Both of them acknowledge that human nature is finite. Lucy is virtuous, indeed; but her virtue is based on submission and the recognition that a man cannot be "a sovereign nature in himself." She represents the pity and the lecture represents the prudence which are simply different aspects of the same thing, the land-sense, which is acceptance of human nature within the limits of what human nature can be. Piety is the land-sense as it faces heaven, prudence is the land-sense as it faces the world. Not in themselves very lovely or excellent, perhaps; nevertheless, as Melville saw it, they make for what is lovely. For they confirm that acceptance of men and women as they are according to their common human nature,—on which the heart must build, and without which it is destroyed.

Lucy's part in Pierre's drama blurs because Melville's sympathies run counter to the perception that Lucy represents in common with the Plinlimmon pamphlet. What never blurs is the view that spiritual growth and independence are one and the same. "Truth, and Earnestness, and Independence," these are Melville's trinity, his three in one. The Calvinistic protestantism of his inheritance has overtaken him, and he cannot be satisfied with anything less than the absolute truth, to which, in the relationship of substance to form, stood absolute self-dependence of being—the same being the form of worship which his protestantism took. Spiritually, Melville refuses all human conditions of representing the truth, including the means of human existence, as unworthy of and demeaning to his ideals.

6

The time is out of joint;—Oh, cursed spite,
That ever I was born to set it right!

In the mood in which he wrote *Pierre*, that mood of self-derision, Melville read a profound and terrible significance in *Hamlet* which he incorporates into his own book. He designed his hero to be a Hamlet of the nineteenth century. Referring to Memnon, the young Egyptian king who appears in the *Iliad* on the Trojan side, Melville says, "with enthusiastic rashness," Memnon flung himself "on another's account into a rightful quarrel, fought hand to hand with his overmatch, and met his boyish and most dolorous death beneath the walls of Troy." "Herein," Melville adds, "lies an unsummed world of grief. For in this plaintive fable we find embodied the Hamletism of the antique world; the Hamletism of three thousand years ago: 'The flower of virtue cropped by a too rare mischance.' And the English tragedy is but Egyptian Memnon, Montaignised and modernised; for being but a mortal man Shakespeare had his fathers too." In *Pierre* Melville represents the tragedy of youthful virtue, as it is to be seen in the stories of King Memnon and Prince Hamlet, and once more represents human virtue dragged down to defeat and death in this world and flung, it would seem, so far as any other world is concerned, against an empty sky. Telling such a story would have been painful enough in all truth even if simply and directly told. But in *Pierre* there is the sweat of agonized flesh. There is also a dry anguish as of bones laid bare of flesh. Melville insists on exploring what he speaks of as "the hopeless gloom of its interior meaning." He intellectualizes and anatomizes Pierre's predicament so that it takes on the rigid insistence of a theorem. He insulates it from the purgative force of action and the sense of life's own recuperative resources which we feel at the end of *Hamlet* is a kind of compensation for the anguish we have been put to.

As Shakespeare (according to Melville) added Montaigne to the old story, Melville in his turn added to Shakespeare. The element of doubt which is so tragic in *Hamlet,* Melville enlarges on and deepens, instilling into it what he took to be the more conscious skepticism of the nineteenth century. His hero like Hamlet is destroyed in a righteous cause. Like Hamlet, too, he is troubled by doubts of the grounds on which he took action. "Be thou a spirit of health or goblin damn'd," so Hamlet questions the ghost whose revelations led him to disastrous consequences. The same tormenting doubt afflicts Melville's hero, who, even at the point of death, is not sure whether the mysterious being on whose word he sacrificed all he had for righteousness, as he believed, is "saint or fiend." Melville's hero, moreover, reaches the more painful stage of doubting his own motives. Were they really what he declared them to be to his own soul? Were they not, in reality, tainted? Pierre's story proves the truth of Plinlimmon's words that if a man tries to live in this world "according to the strict letter of the chronometricals," that is, after the example of Christ, he will find himself involved, in all probability, "in strange, *unique* follies and sins, unimagined before." From this dilemma there is no resort for the human mind, although some philosophers have pretended to the discovery of one. "That profound Silence, that only Voice of our God, which I before spoke of; from that divine thing without a name, those impostor philosophers pretend somehow to have got an answer; which is as absurd, as though they should say they had got water out of stone; for how can a man get a Voice out of Silence?"

Pierre is like Hamlet, the victim of truth and virtue. But Melville was not Shakespeare, to view the tragedy with an indifferent eye, and with all the possible issues of life rounding out his perspective. Melville has transfixed his own heart on the point of his tragic vision. In the light of the ideal of virtue, "the world seems to lie saturated and soaking with lies." The lover of virtue must appeal from men to God. So Pierre, taking his life and Lucy's and Isabel's in his hands for the sake of virtue, "On my strong faith in ye Invisibles, I stake three whole felicities, and three whole lives this day. If ye forsake me now,—farewell to Faith, farewell to Truth, farewell to God." Pierre, "naturally poetic, and therefore piercing as he was; how could he fail to acknowledge the existence of that all-controlling and all-permeating wonderfulness, which, when imperfectly and isolatedly recognised by the generality, is so significantly denominated The Finger of God? But it is not merely the Finger, it is the whole outspread Hand of God; for doth not Scripture intimate, that He holdeth all of us in the hollow of His hand?—a Hollow, truly!" "That inscrutable thing is chiefly what I hate," Ahab says about the White Whale. So it is with Melville in *Pierre.* When God appears in any guise except his hollowness, his silence, his inscrutability, it is in the image not of love but hate.

Near the end of the book, exhausted under the burden of his idealism, Pierre falls into a trance. In this trance he has a vision of a rocky mountainside, familiar to him as a boy, which formed a part of the beautiful distant prospect as seen from Saddle Meadows. The traveller thither would find among the scattered rocks a rock which bore a remarkable likeness to Enceladus the Titan.

" 'Enceladus! it is Enceladus!' Pierre cried out in his sleep. That moment the phantom faced him; and Pierre saw Enceladus no more." There, where the Titan's face should have been, Pierre saw his own face, but enormous, facing him "with prophetic discomfiture and woe. With trembling frame he started from his chair, and woke from that ideal horror to all his actual grief."

Pierre himself read his own damnation in this vision. But Melville dissents. Pierre "did not wilfully wrest some final comfort" from this vision and the ancient myth which it recalled. But Melville goes on to interpret them in a way which might have given Pierre some comfort. "Old Titan's self was the son of incestuous Coelus and Terra, the son of incestuous Heaven and Earth. And Titan married his mother Terra, another and accumulatively incestuous match. And thereof Enceladus was one issue. So Enceladus was both the son and grandson of an incest; and even thus, there had been born from the organic blended heavenliness and earthliness of Pierre, another mixed, uncertain, heaven-aspiring, but still not wholly earth-emancipated mood; which again, by its terrestrial taint held down to its terrestrial mother, generated there the present doubly incestuous Enceladus within him; so that the present mood of Pierre—that reckless sky-assaulting mood of his, was nevertheless on one side the grandson of the sky. For it is according to eternal fitness, that the precipitated Titan should still seek to regain his paternal birthright even by fierce escalade. Wherefore whoso storms the sky gives best proof he came from thither! But whatso crawls contented in the moat before that crystal fort, shows it was born within that slime, and there forever will abide."

Overlooking the details of Melville's symbolism in this genealogy as it relates to Pierre's mother and father, Isabel and, by inference anyway, to Lucy, I would point out that, except for the addition of the double incest, in this ultimate view of him Pierre's parentage is identical with Ahab's. In "The Candles" chapter Ahab addresses the lightning; "Oh, thou magnanimous! now do I glory in my genealogy. But thou art my fiery father; my sweet mother I know not." And he has just said, out of exactly the same mood as Pierre's, "Light though thou be, thou leapest out of darkness; but I am darkness leaping out of light, leaping out of thee!"

It turns out to be of little comparative significance that the youthful Pierre in the space of six months overtakes Ahab who has sailed the seas for forty long years. Pierre is but a shadow to Melville, and Melville, in the grip of his idealism, the upshot of his radical protestantism, has lost all communication with the visible world of experience, and its restorative perspectives in which men are united in physical action, in love, in worship and the pursuit of truth. "But even Solomon," he says, " 'the man that wandereth out of the way of understanding shall remain . . . in the congregation of the dead.' " Wandering from the ways of common understanding, love turns to hate, worship puts on its face of enmity. In those Hyperborean regions all the points of man's compass are reversed and confounded. Melville himself has become one with Ahab and like Ahab his humanity is wounded and like Ahab he trains murderous guns inboard. He hates the common human nature which he shares. Of all the paradoxes in which we see Melville caught up, the most terrible is this, that his love of virtue and truth—and of virtue as set forth in the New Testament—has brought him to Ahab's extremity. Such is his love of virtue that he hates men for being unworthy and abusing it, and his hate goes beyond men to the unscrutable laws of the universe for betraying virtue to the ignoble uses of men. Insisting on independence—on the sovereign right to treat with all the "Powers" of heaven, hell and earth "upon an equal basis"—and so seeking and giving himself no quarter in the form of faith from the inquisitions of his mind, he pits his humanity against the inhumanity of the world—the "horrible and inscrutable inhumanities"—and his humanity has broken before the inscrutable inhumanity of the universe. That is, while doubting all things earthly, he has lost hold of intuitions of some things heavenly. His human integrity has been wounded, the wound is hate, Ahab's quenchless feud is his.

Melville saw in *Hamlet* the tragedy of youthful idealism and he repeated it in *Pierre,* identifying himself with his hero and, at the same time, adding to its other aspect or other dimension, as Shakespeare had done before him, that other aspect or dimension being the tragedy of mind. This that I call the tragedy of Hamlet is the tragedy of idealism.

We may clarify the parallel between *Pierre* and *Hamlet* by saying that *Pierre* begins at the point of Melville's furthest vision in *Moby*

Dick. There is accordingly a presentiment in the book, the positive aspect of that loss of all external perspective which I have noticed, which gives *Pierre* a terror of tragic vision even greater than *Moby Dick*'s. Once this appears, one feels a terrible irony, not far removed from suicidal intentions, in its initial deep inland setting:— "all Nature, as if suddenly become conscious of her own profound mystery, and feeling no refuge from it but silence, sinks into this wonderful and indescribable repose."

On the first day of the chase in *Moby Dick* the White Whale has disappeared from sight, and Ahab, standing in his boat, can discover no sign of him in the sea. "But suddenly as he peered down and down into its depths, he profoundly saw a white living spot no bigger than a white weasel, with wonderful celerity uprising, and magnifying as it rose, till it turned, and then there were plainly revealed two long crooked rows of white, glistening teeth, floating up from the undiscoverable bottom. It was Moby Dick's open mouth and scrolled jaw; his vast, shadowed bulk still half blending with the blue of the sea." There is no passage in all the book with more frightful suggestion—the embodiment of a dream that is ever so familiar and still the most terrifying and elusive. But Ahab is spared the last tragic realization of the mind. Caught in the line of his own harpoon which he has driven into his adversary, he disappears from sight still chasing, as he says, though tied to, the damned Whale. But he does not see what is signified by the circumstances of his death, that it is himself, and always has been himself, or a part of himself, whom he pursues with fury.

The revelation that Ahab was spared overtakes Pierre on the threshold of young manhood. In the awakening which Isabel produces in him, he now glimpses a deeper meaning in the book to which he turns instinctively, and so terrible a meaning that he turns on this book. "Torn into a hundred shreds the printed pages of *Hell* and *Hamlet* lay at his feet. . . . Dante had taught him that he had bitter cause of quarrel. *Hamlet* taunted him with faltering in the fight." But, and worse, *Hamlet* also insinuated "that there was none to strike." To Hamlet man is the quintessence of dust. Pierre, expounding to Isabel the text he found in *Hamlet,* "Look:" he says, "a nothing is the substance, it casts one shadow one way, and another the other way; and these two shadows cast from one nothing; these, seems to me, are Virtue and Vice." "Then why torment thyself so, dearest Pierre?" "It is the law. . . . That a nothing should torment a nothing; for I am a nothing. It is all a dream —we dream that we dreamed we dream." In the name of Virtue we torment ourselves,—that is the law; we heap and task ourselves. Virtue and Vice are both shadows. That they fall in opposite directions does not distinguish better from worse. It only goes to show man's dual nature. What is shadow to one side is light to the other. Sin and death to one side are not sin and death to the other. Life to one is death to the other.

In the last view of *Pierre* the symbols are of little account, for it is with Melville as it was with Pierre, "I will be impious, for piety hath juggled me, and taught me to revere, where I should spurn. From all idols, I tear all veils; henceforth I will see the hidden things; and live right out in my own hidden life." Therefore we have the tragic thing itself, the bare substance,—what Melville called to Hawthorne, "a certain tragic phase of humanity," meaning "the tragedies of human thought in its own unbiassed, native, and profounder workings." The mind,—"We do it wrong, being so majestical." It is of the nobility of the mind to strip away "the thousand sweet illusions of Life" which are "purchased at the price of Life's Truth." But this same nobility is death. Man cannot live without illusions. To be happy, indeed to be human, a man's mind must not see that his oasis is a mirage. He must believe in the color and warmth that the sun gives, he must believe in human faces; to survive he must live in appearance, not in reality. But the mind is under a tragic necessity to show that the sunlit human world is a mirage. Ahab hunted down the inscrutable thing away off in the almost final waters of the Pacific, and there he was confronted by the White Whale's featureless features. A step further and one sees that once the mind has taken thought the same inscrutability is immediately at hand. In the place of solid, stubborn familiarity, ambiguous strangeness is all around. In the mood of thought, or what is the same thing, in the mood of Truth, the "inscrutable malice" that Ahab hated in Moby Dick, does not wait to be hunted down; it jumps out at one from behind the most familiar objects. There is no land at all, no place of mortal security; there is no solid ground under our feet. The sea invades all.

But while exposing the falsity of all that is to be seen and hoped for in the perspectives of the visible world of experience, while destroying all the illusions which are vital to man's mortal nature, the mind finds no grounds of its own on which to base a nobler security. "Appalling is the soul of a man! Better might one be pushed off into the material spaces beyond the uttermost orbit of our sun, than once feel himself fairly afloat in himself . . . Appallingly vacant as vast is the soul of a man."

It is of the tragedy of mind to obliterate "all that's kind to our mortalities." The tragedy goes further; the mind bent upon truth, its noblest preoccupation, comes to doubt its own instruments. "For the more and the more that he wrote, and the deeper and the deeper that he dived, Pierre saw the everlasting elusiveness of Truth; the universal lurking insincerity of even the greatest and purest written thoughts. Like knavish cards, the leaves of all great books were covertly packed." Melville has himself confessed before this, "that when a man is in a really profound mood, then all the many verbal or written profundities are unspeakably repulsive, and seem downright childish."

All is vanity; "we dream that we dreamed we dream." The shows of the world on which we feed our sensuous and material nature, these are illusions. But still the final truth is not told. The mind finds no higher reality. It is itself its only reality. In the last act of the tragedy the mind finds itself its own mortal enemy. Eternity, immortality, the infinite, all the noblest preoccupations of the mind, these are death. The hills around Saddle Meadows are lovely in the purple distance. They symbolize Pierre's noblest aspirations. But arrived at, those hills present another aspect. "Stark desolation; ruin, merciless and ceaseless; chills and gloom . . . Beaten off by such undreamed-of glooms and steeps, you now sadly retraced your steps, and, mayhap, went skirting the inferior sideway terraces of pastures; where the multiple and most sterile inodorous immortalness of the small, white flower furnished no aliment for the mild cow's meditative cud. But here and there you still might smell from far the sweet aromaticness of clumps of catnip, that dear farmhouse herb." You saw foundation stones and rotting timbers of houses long deserted, their desolation hidden by the clumps of catnip; "Illy-hid; for every spring the amaranthine and celestial flower gained on the mortal household herb; for every autumn the catnip died, but never an autumn made the amaranth to wane. The catnip and the amaranth!—man's earthly household peace, and the ever-encroaching appetite for God."

"To be, or not to be: that is the question." In that reflection, the expression of man's higher consciousness, lie the seeds of death.

> *And thus the native hue of resolution*
> *Is sicklied o'er with the pale cast of thought.*

In the mood of thought the world is "a sterile promontory." There is no truth, no reality outside the mind. The truth about thought, the act of the mind, is the truth that Melville surmised in the chapter in *Moby Dick* "The Whiteness of the Whale." All that is high and noble, even divinity itself, is expressed by whiteness, and yet there lurks "an elusive something in the innermost idea of this hue, which strikes more of panic to the soul than that redness which affrights in blood." Thought, the mind, the only reality is "the great principle of light" which "forever remains white or colorless in itself, and if operating without medium upon matter, would touch all objects, even tulips and roses, with its own blank tinge,"— and unless one consents to illusions and wears "colored and coloring glasses," then he "the wretched infidel gazes himself blind. . . ."

The last tragic realization of all is that the mind in the noble pursuit of truth comes only to a true sense of itself as the only reality, and that reality is the principle of destruction. That a nothing should torment and destroy itself, that is the law. We dream that we dreamed a dream. The element of doubt which he found in *Hamlet,* Melville pushed to the ultimate. But giving skepticism a new body, as it were, he could find no refuge in it. As long as it is intended for us to dream that we dream, there is no escape from the nightmare.

CHAPTER SEVEN

After Pierre

SUCH IS THE cataclysmic violence of *Pierre* that the reader who has seen into it might very easily doubt that it could have an echo or any sequel at all in the soul of the man who wrought it. There was a sequel, none the less, in a slow process of recuperation and rehabilitation. It was a very slow process to begin with, and so full of vacillations that it will be difficult to portray.

Mrs. Melville left a brief record of her husband's life in which she noted: "Published *White-Whale* in 1851—wrote *Pierre*, published 1852. We all felt anxious about the strain on his health in the spring of 1853." Melville himself has left a sketch of his state of mind in this year. In the preamble of his story *Cock-a-Doodle-Doo!* he describes himself early one morning as "too full of hypos to sleep" and setting out on a walk before breakfast. A mean, backward spring day, he buttons himself up tight against the cold,— "and spitefully thrusting my crab-stick into the oozy sod, bent my blue form to the steep ascent of the hill. This toiling posture brought my head pretty well earthward, as if I were in the act of butting it against the world. I marked the fact, but only grinned at it with a ghastly grin." Letting his eyes wander a moment over the wide, bare countryside, he thinks of "what a slight mark, after all, man makes in this huge great earth. Yet the earth makes a mark on him." Then he thinks of all the railroad accidents he has heard of lately; in one of them a score of noble hearts, a bride and her groom, and an innocent infant were hurled to death. "Yet what's the use of complaining? What justice of the peace will right this matter? Yea, what's the use of bothering the very heavens about it?" Since the heavens themselves ordain these things, do they not? "A miserable world! Who would take the trouble to make a fortune in it, when he knows not how long he can keep it, for the thousand villains and asses who have the management of railroads and steamboats, and innumerable other vital things in the world." A caricature, this? Yes, but like every good caricature it is based on the truth. It does not strain the point to say that it shows Melville in the grip of Ahab, just as Ahab had been in the grip of Fedallah. "Look! see yon albicore! who put it into him to chase and fang that flying fish? Where do murderers go, man? Who's to doom, when the judge himself is dragged to the bar?" So Ahab repulsed the mediations of Starbuck and saw the reflection of evil Fedallah in the water where Starbuck's human face had been a second before.

In 1853 Melville went to work to get a United States Consular post in the Pacific. Was it that in spite of his mood of Ahab he was ready to give up the fight, at any rate as he had fought it heretofore? Whatever may have been in Melville's mind to prompt him to this step, the heavens themselves would not consent to calling a truce. Like a plagiarism from *Pierre*, and as melodramatic as anything in the book, his publishers suffered a severe fire which destroyed the plates of all Melville's books and most of the copies then in stock. "Oh, what a quenchless feud is this, that Time hath with the sons of Men!" Melville had still to experience the full bitterness of this feud. He was to lose both his sons. One was to run away from home; the other was to die from a rifle wound which may have been suicide.

His intention to find some other means than literature to win a livelihood did not succeed until many years had passed, and he was obliged to keep on writing. How little heart he had for it we can read in *Clarel*:

> *Remaineth to me what? the pen?*
> *Dead feather of ethereal life!*

From 1853 to 1856 he contributed to the magazines. In 1855 he published his historical romance *Israel Potter*. The following year he republished some of his magazine stories and essays in *The Piazza Tales*. In 1857 *The Confidence Man* was published in New York. At the time Melville was in Europe on his way home from his pilgrimage to the Holy Land, out of which came, in 1876, his long narrative poem *Clarel*. A book of verse had preceded this by just a decade, the result of Melville's impressions of the Civil War, called *Battle Pieces*. In 1863 he gave up "Arrowhead," his house near Pittsfield, and moved with his family to New York. Here in 1865, fourteen years after *Pierre*, he succeeded in getting a different employment. For twenty years he had the inglorious position of an out-of-doors inspector of customs. After his resignation from this, in 1885, there were two late books of poems, *John Marr and Other Sailors* and *Timoleon*, both privately printed in very small numbers. In 1891, the year of his death, he finished *Billy Budd*, the book in which he came home to prose. In spite of the long lapse of time there is an extraordinary proximity between *Billy Budd* and *Typee, Redburn* and *White Jacket*; and something has also been added out of those obscure years which puts it in an integral relationship to *Moby Dick* and *Pierre*. *Billy Budd* had to wait for publication until 1924.

The period of Melville's life stretching from the publication of *Pierre*, or from within a short time of this event to his death, has been called by one of his biographers "The Long Quietus" and by another "The Long Seclusion." "He acted very much as if he were dead, so far as the business of literature was concerned," writes a third. In New York he shunned literary dinners and foregatherings. He did not give lectures. He declined all the means to publicity which to the run of authors then and now it would be incomprehensible not to cultivate. Even when approached by a rare individual with a true perception of his achievement, Melville refused to unfold himself. To a young man, a professor of English, who wrote him in 1889 that he believed Melville's books, especially the earlier ones, "the most thoroughly New World product in all American literature," and that in his opinion *Moby Dick* had never received its due of recognition, and who asked Melville for some

account of his life and "literary methods," Melville returned a polit
reply, but declined to oblige him. "I have," Melville explained
"lately come into possession of unobstructed leisure, but only jus
as, in the course of nature, my vigour sensibly declines. What littl
of it is left I husband for certain matters as yet incomplete, an
which indeed may never be completed." The result of his indifferenc
and his reticence was registered in an editorial in the *New Yor*
Times, occasioned by Melville's death: "There has died and bee
buried in this city, during the current week, at an advanced age,
man who is so little known, even by name, to the generation now i
the vigour of life, that only one newspaper contained an obituar
account of him, and this was of but three or four lines."

Why did Melville resolve to withdraw into this seclusion an
so far as the public was concerned, the unbroken silence of hi
later life? Many reasons suggest themselves, not one of which i
satisfactory by itself, though in some sort of combination and wit
due allowance for the passage of time they may furnish a satis
factory explanation.

That Melville was very hard up and his books could do little t
relieve him in this respect was a factor in 1853 and not less of
factor a decade later. There was his presentiment of waning power
revealed in *Pierre* and in his correspondence with Hawthorn
backed by the fact of his withering reputation. Also to be considere
is the honesty and terrible sincerity of a mind that found Solomon'
the wisest of all books and could not escape the conclusion tha
reputation and even the desire to speak truth were vanity. It ha
been argued that Melville was so stung by the slighting criticism o
Moby Dick that he conceived *Pierre* as a bomb to throw at th
critics and the public to which they pandered and so to have don
with them forever. According to this view what Melville wrot
for publication after *Pierre* was no more than a series of stop-gap
in the interim of finding different employment. There is a good dea
to justify this view of the case. One can point to the bitter satir
of the American literary world in *Pierre* and to Melville's ostenta

tious recklessness,—"I write precisely as I please,"—in support of it.
Yet, as it seems to me, the bitterness which provoked his satire on
critics and publishers and reading public is a small thing in comparison with the revulsion against all mankind, himself included,
which threatens to shiver the book to pieces from first to last.

If we would get to anything like a true idea of Melville in these
critical years we must be careful not to over-simplify. We must
keep in mind that, whatever else may have been true, his frame of
mind was not static. It is certain that he himself would have given
a different account of himself and his innermost feelings in 1863
from what he would have given, in equal sincerity, a decade earlier,
right after *Pierre,* and the same certainly holds for the remainder
of his life-time. We must distinguish, then, between his different
incentives and attitudes, some of which were uppermost at one
time, others at another time. While writing *Pierre* he was angry at
the critics and the course which his anger prompted him to take
was to turn his back on them. In *Pierre,* too, he had the miserable
sensation of falling far short of his ambitions, which made him want
nothing so much as escape into silence. Neither of these sensations
passed away at once, but with the passage of time they tended more
and more to lose their particularity. In *Pierre* we see an author in
arms against his critics; and we see a man struggling painfully
toward his goal against a growing awareness of incapacity and
failing strength. But including these two views, and more than
both combined, we see in *Pierre* a man in the coils of horrible self-
conflict. It was bound to take Melville a long time to recover from
the consequences of this self-conflict. The nervous strain which
worried his family did not last long. He recovered from it within a
few months, as the remarkable composure and his command of tone
and effect in his story *Bartleby,* written in 1853, sufficiently prove.
But other ravages remained to be repaired. For many years it was
with Melville as with Hamlet, ". . . thou wouldst not think how ill
all's here about my heart." In *The Confidence Man,* written in 1856,
we see him sick at heart and sick in soul. In the journal of his

travels in Palestine there is this unique flash of self-revelation in a welter of external observations, "Ride over mouldy plain to Dead Sea . . . foam on beach & pebbles like slaver of mad dog—smarting bitter of the water,—carried the bitter in my mouth all day—bitterness of life—thought of all bitter things—Bitter is it to be poor & bitter to be reviled, & Oh bitter are these waters of Death, though I." An author's wounded vanity was included, to be sure, but more than that is in question here, and much more than public recognition was needed to return Melville to the minimum of human wellbeing that it takes to make life tolerable.

If I can feel certain of anything about Melville in these years it is that after *Pierre* he needed silence and this from quite another compulsion than that of wanting to slam the door on the critics or to escape from his sense of personal failure. As we know, Melville was obliged to continue writing to support himself and his family. When the opportunity for other employment offered, he took it and put writing aside. His obscure existence as a customs inspector was the form which outward circumstances lent to an inner compulsion. Even in what he wrote in the interval between *Pierre* and the customs job his need for silence expressed itself. There is in these stories and sketches what for Melville was an extraordinary reserve, the nearest possible equivalent of silence. But behind this reserve we glimpse the compulsion that occasioned it. This was no other than the instinct, if not of self-preservation, at any rate of self-rehabilitation. For a long time this instinct continued to require silence. In much of what Melville wrote after *Pierre* to the day of his death there is what I cannot do better than call an element of silence. And this, we come to feel, more and more, was a saving element. But its end was not silence. Otherwise he would not have written *Clarel* or anything that came after *Clarel*. One can see the same instinct taking other directions; in his journals of his travels to the Holy Land and back, where it is seeking a perspective in which personal grief loses its finality; it shows itself otherwise in Melville's turning from prose to a new discipline of writing poetry. We see in

aking stock of itself and growing in conscious form and direction
n the gist and tenor of *Clarel*, far beyond the poetic form of that
work. We are to see it at last, wonderfully secure and composed,
and wonderfully consummated, I would say, in *Billy Budd*. But
Billy Budd is as yet a long way off.

In the writings after *Pierre* through *The Confidence Man* we
find ourselves in a sad, obscure, sequestered place. Here, as always,
Melville's innermost exigencies determined his choice of themes.
We catch a glimpse of him in the role of Shakespeare's Timon, maddened by the ingratitude of his fellow citizens of Athens, shaking
the dust of his city and repairing to the solitude of the woods:

> . . . *henceforth hated be*
> *Of Timon man and all humanity!*

Still, there are other incentives at work. We can see him groping his
way back from the terrible "sensational presentiments" which he
had experienced in *Pierre* and reaching out for a new integration
with life. He was exploring, but in new directions, the implications
of the fact that life has other aims to serve than such as can be
identified with the individual's consciousness. At the same time he
was experimenting with the discovery that changing circumstances
and changing aspects of life are constantly making new demands
on that consciousness; that it is continuously called upon to compound old attitudes and adopt new attitudes and new realizations
if it is to avail itself of the resources of life and survive.

2

For *Israel Potter* Melville borrowed from an old chapbook
"forlornly published" and "rescued by the merest chance from the
rag-pickers" purporting to recount the life and remarkable ad-
ventures of one Israel R. Potter of Cranston, R. I., who fought in
the American Revolution. Melville polished and revised and added
to the facts as he found them and produced what is in all truth a

brilliant historical novel. Melville's hero was born in a little tow
among the rocky and stone-walled Berkshire Hills. "The numbe
and length of these walls is not more surprising than the size c
the blocks comprising them. The very Titans seemed to have bee
at work. That so small an army as the first settlers must needs hav
been, should have taken such wonderful pains to enclose so ur
grateful a soil; that they should have accomplished such herculea
undertakings with so slight prospect of reward; this is a considera
tion which gives us a significant hint of the temper of the men c
the revolutionary era. Nor could a fitter country be found for th
birthplace of the devoted patriot, Israel Potter."

Israel fought at Bunker Hill and soon afterwards, falling int
the enemy's hands, was shipped a prisoner-of-war to England. H
escaped and made his way to Paris to serve as an agent of th
great Benjamin Franklin. Later he sailed with Paul Jones, took pa
in the raid upon Whitehaven and in the victory of the *Bon Homm
Richard* over the *Serapis*. Fortune, however, never favored him. H
was captured again and brought back to England. For forty yea:
Israel Potter was an exile in an alien land. At last, when old an
infirm, he returned to his native land and made his way back t
the hillside where he was born. A stranger was plowing where h
father's house had stood. His father's name and his own wa
forgotten.

"He was repulsed in efforts after a pension . . . His scars prove
his only medals. He dictated a little book, the record of his fortune
But long ago it faded out of print—himself out of being—his nam
out of memory. He died the same day that the oldest oak on h
native hills was blown down."

Remarkable is the skill with which Melville introduces historic:
background and the varied brilliance of its details. Nothing is be
ter of its kind than the sketch of Franklin,—a sketch curiousl
mixed in mood, being sympathetic and yet ironical, recalling th
description of the inhuman ship's carpenter on board the *Pequo*
"Printer, post-master, almanac maker, essayist, chemist, orato
tinker, statesman, humorist, **philosopher, parlour man, politic**

conomist, professor of housewifery, ambassador, projector, maxim-
monger, herb-doctor, wit: Jack of all trades, master of each and
mastered by none—the type and genius of his land. Franklin was
everything but a poet." Quite as good in its own kind is the descrip-
ion, too long to quote here, of the action between the *Richard* and
he *Serapis;* as good, this, as Walt Whitman's wonderful "old-time
ea-fight" in *Leaves of Grass.*

Melville adorned and refurbished the facts which he found in the
ld sleazy chapbook. But his appropriation went further than mere
lterations and additions of facts. For all its objective character as a
istorical romance, the story of Israel Potter became in his hands
n image of his own soul. Israel, uprooted and alone, was such a one
s Melville felt himself to be; one "afflicted, tossed with tempest
nd not comforted,"—not comforted, that is, except by a sort of
eroic stoicism, which is braver than all the recognized acts of
eroism in the world. Israel, shifting for himself as best he could,
und employment in a lime kiln outside London. "He," Melville
vrote, "whom love of country made a hater of her foes," found him-
elf "serving that very people as a slave, better succeeding in making
heir bricks than firing their ships . . . Poor Israel! well named—
ondsman in the English Egypt. But he drowned the thought by
till more recklessly spattering with his ladle: 'What signifies who
ve be, or where we are, or what we do?' Slap-dash! 'Kings as clowns
re codgers—who ain't a nobody?' Splash! 'All is vanity and clay.'"
n London, whither Israel gravitated, it became his habit to wander
n the most destitute, miserable and vice-ridden sections of the city.
Not that he was gloomy or morose by nature: "But hereby stoic in-
luences were at work, to fit him at a soon-coming day for enacting
 part in the last extremities here seen; when by sickness, destitu-
ion, each busy ill of exile, he was destined to experience a fate, un-
ommon even to luckless humanity—a fate whose crowning qualities
vere its remoteness from relief and its depth of obscurity."

There are other stories of the same period which group them-
elves around *Israel Potter.* There is the story of the clerk Bartleby,
ike Israel of the flotsam of luckless humanity. Bartleby's heroism is

even more obscure and his defeat and victory still harder to res
rect. To all his employer's requests to do this or that he repli
simply "I would prefer not to." His employer, who wished to b
friend him, felt obliged to take a high hand:

"'Will you tell me *anything* about yourself?'

"'I would prefer not to.'

"'But what reasonable objection can you have to speak to me?
feel friendly toward you.' . . . 'What is your answer, Bartleby?'

"'At present I prefer to give no answer.'"

A comic situation is sustained without jarring the delicate und
tones of wistfulness and pathos. Bartleby would not work and wh
threatened with dismissal he answered that he preferred not to
dismissed, then retreated to gaze out of a window at the blank w
of the building opposite. At last, in order to be rid of him, his e
ployer moved to another location and his former office was lock
against Bartleby. But Bartleby still haunted the old buildir
"generally, sitting upon the banisters of the stairs by day, and slee
ing in the entry by night." His former employer came to remonstra
with him. Did Bartleby know that he is a cause of tribulation
him? No answer.

"'Now one of two things must take place. Either you must
something, or something must be done to you. Now what sort
business would you like to engage in? Would you like to re-enga
in copying for someone?'

"'No, I would prefer not to make any change.'"

In due time the landlord of the building steps in and Bartleby
taken off to jail. His former employer comes to see him there a
finds him "standing all alone in the quietest of the yards, his fa
toward a high wall, while all around, from the narrow slits of t
jail windows, I thought I saw peering out upon him the eyes
murderers and thieves." Bartleby will explain nothing and asks
kindnesses. In *Pierre* Melville speaks of that "slumbering intelligen
visible in some recumbent beasts—beasts whose intelligence see
struck dumb in them by some sorrowful and inexplicable spel

Bartleby is like an injured animal who has withdrawn in obedience to some incommunicable necessity to repair its inexplicable hurt. Another day his friend comes to see him and finds him in the prison yard as before but this time "strangely huddled at the base of the wall." "The round face of the grub-man peered upon me now. 'His dinner is ready. Won't he dine today, either? Or does he live without dining?'

" 'Lives without dining,' said I, and closed the eyes.

" 'Eh!—He's asleep, ain't he?'

" 'With kings and counsellors,' murmured I."

Then there is the story of the wood sawyer, Merrymusk, from which I quoted Melville's sketch of his own state of mind in 1853. Poor Merrymusk has a wonderful rooster,—Melville named him Signor Beneventano. The more desperate the case of Merrymusk and his family with disease and poverty, so much the more bravely does the rooster crow. "He looked like a Spanish grandee caught in a shower, and standing under some peasant's shed . . . He irradiated the shanty; he glorified its meanness." Merrymusk, his wife and children, all die within a few hours of each other. "The cock shook his plumage over them. The cock crew. It was now like a Bravo! like a Hurrah! like a Three-times-three! . . . He strode out of the shanty. I followed. He flew upon the apex of the dwelling, spread wide his wings, sounded one supernatural note, and dropped at my feet. The cock was dead." On the solitary stone in the woods, which marks the spot where Merrymusk, his family and Signor Beneventano are buried, there is no skull and cross-bones chiselled but a lusty cock in the act of crowing, with the words beneath:

> *"O death, where is thy sting?*
> *O grave, where is thy victory?"*

And then there is the story of Hunilla. "I looked into her eyes but saw no tear. There was something which seemed strangely haughty in her air, and yet it was the air of woe. A Spanish and an Indian grief, which would not visibly lament. Pride's height in vain abased

to proneness on the rack; nature's pride subduing nature's torture."
Hunilla had been left on a desert island while her husband and
brother sailed to the mainland to sell their stores of tortoise oil.
They never returned alive. Her husband's body was washed up
on the beach, and Hunilla buried it in a shallow grave. Day after
day she watched the horizon for a sail. Strangers came, brutes of
men, who raped her and went away, leaving her to her solitude
and shame. Still Hunilla bore up with a kind of animal fortitude
and, at last, was rescued by friendly sailors and brought home to
the village on the mainland. But now,—"To Hunilla, pain seemed
so necessary, that pain in other beings, though by love and sympathy made her own, was unrepiningly to be borne. A heart of
yearning in a frame of steel. A heart of earthly yearning, frozen by
the frost which falleth from the sky."

"As mariners, tossed in tempest on some desolate ledge, patch
them a boat out of the remnants of their vessel's wreck, and launch
it in the self-same waves, see here Hunilla, this lone ship-wrecked
soul, out of treachery invoking trust. Humanity, thou strong thing,
I worship thee, not in the laurelled victor, but in this vanquished
one."

The conclusion is obvious; Melville was accepting failure and
the long, dreary consequences of failure. He was learning, as his
hero Pierre had not finally learned, catlike to walk in the dark
Obscurity and anonymity, these are his themes,—more particularly
the obscure anonymous heroism of life. It goes unnoticed in the
world. But then, on the other side of the proposition, as he was
beginning to see, who is to say what constitutes defeat, and where
the line really falls between defeat and victory? Not such a long
time before this he had written, in *Mardi*, "So, if after all these
fearful, fainting trances, the verdict be, the golden haven was not
gained;—yet in bold quest thereof, better to sink in boundless deeps
than float on vulgar shoals; and give me, ye gods, an utter wreck
if wreck I do."

Now, with *Moby Dick* and *Pierre* behind him, he knew that th worst fate which his youthful imagination could paint was reserved for him, to float on vulgar shoals. But his mature imagination came to his rescue. His imagination had the virility to see heroism in a wholly new perspective and to recognize it when divorced from all heroic events and circumstances. His imagination rescued him, I say; but then with Melville truth of soul and imaginative vision were the same. For this reason, and also because of the fortitude of his vision, Melville, the most masculine of American writers, who had chased whales and lived among cannibals,—this same Melville, now facing obscurity and seeking seclusion, resembled no one so much as a certain New England spinster, herself a recluse, Emily Dickinson. I might choose any one of several handfuls of her tiny poems to convey one whole span of Melville's experience. In view of the particular stories I have cited, I choose this one to serve me here:

We grow accustomed to the dark
When light is put away,
As when the neighbor hold the lamp
To witness her good-by.

A moment we uncertain step
For newness of the night,
Then fit our vision to the dark
And meet the road, erect!

And so of larger darknesses—
Those evenings of the brain
When not a moon disclose a sign,
Or star come out within.

The bravest grope a little
And sometimes hit a tree
Directly in the forehead—
But, as they learn to see,

Either the darkness alters—
Or something in the sight
Adjusts itself to midnight—
And life steps almost straight.

3

It is in the experience of everyone at some time or other to feel that his soul has nothing but its own courage to rely on. In the stories that followed *Pierre* we see Melville in the posture of that stoic courage, yet this is not all that we can discern about him in these stories. He is shifting to redress his balance and get his feet on some sort of solid footing. His problem,—always, I believe, his central problem,—is still more, how to come to terms with mankind. In *Moby Dick,* where he had full command of himself, one feels, as of the fundamental coherence and of the red life-blood of the book, Melville's compassion for man, "the thing itself," as Lear called Mad Tom: "thou art the thing itself; unaccommodated man is no more but such a poor, bare, forked animal as thou art." It is this compassion which is signalised by the rites and ties of friendship between Ishmael and Queequeg. It is this same compassion dramatized that gives Ahab his poignant humanity,—that keeps him in other words, within this reach of our sympathies. Ahab is a great champion of "unaccommodated man," therefore we follow him as Melville followed him before us. Although a battered and at last, a ruined, likeness, he still bears a likeness to Prometheus. In *Pierre,* on the other hand, Melville's sympathies are the other way round. They lie with the hero first and last. There, because he found men unworthy of the hero, instead of the compassion for man which held on in *Moby Dick* and held it together, there was little besides hatred and scorn. There lay the root of the moral collapse which took place in *Pierre.* Paralleling if not impelling Melville's determination to see all truth in the perspective of one individual it brought him to the "sensational presentiment" of the final abyss. In the stories after *Pierre* Melville was recovering his orientation. Israel Potter was not a hero as Melville conceived the hero in *Pierre*. He was "the thing itself"; so were Merrymusk, Bartleby and Hunilla. Melville was groping back to the centripetence which he had enjoyed in *Moby Dick*. In time, this release of his sympathies was to have an intellectual counterpart. In the period right after *Pierre* it was enough that he get hold of such a life-line as I have been describing. For the tempest that burst upon him in *Pierre* had not yet spent itself. It revived and burst on him again with malign vehemence when he wrote *The Confidence Man*.

With good reason it has been said that *The Confidence Man* marks the nadir of disillusionment and despair which Melville sank to in the aftermath of *Pierre*. In it Melville applied to the bases of human relations the same corrosive skepticism which he had applied to the consciousness of the individual and the ideas of a man's security within himself, his moral responsibility and his soul. All the horror which Melville felt about creation, the universe within and without, and the ambiguity of God, he concentrated on his fellow men, seeing them morally as such nasty little monstrosities as Breughel painted his devils. *The Confidence Man* is what Prospero called Caliban, a "thing of darkness."

Because it marks a crisis in Melville's spiritual life I do not imply that like some critics I consider it, from the literary point of view, an abortion. If anything, *The Confidence Man* is overdone,—not that its satire is exaggerated; on that score one might criticise the world's best satires,—rather it is over-elaborated; its ingenuity is too patent, so that it has the intellectual feel of a jigsaw puzzle. For all that, it has a strong, tough body of observed facts of human nature, and there is a strong, tough intellection at work in it. Because of these features, as also because of its ingenious plot and the strength of Melville's use of language, it has a gnarled and knotted strength, but not without the sap still running. It is like

Ben Jonson's comedies with which, according to *White Jacket*, Melville had long been familiar. It is like *Bartholomew Fair*, all compacted, as that comedy is, with quacks and quackery. For the intensity of its indignation, however, it is closer to *Volpone*.

We are on board a Mississippi steamboat, the *Fidele*, making the run from St. Louis to New Orleans. A man dressed in cream colors makes his way through the passengers who crowd around a placard on which a reward is offered for the detection of a mysterious impostor, recently arrived from the East. The man in cream colors produces a slate and writes on it for the benefit of all, "Charity thinketh no evil. Charity suffereth long and is kind. Charity endureth all things. Charity believeth all things. Charity never faileth." The man's conduct causes annoyance and provokes jeers and cuffs. He signals that he is deaf and dumb and withdraws. Presently there appears a new centre of interest in the form of a deformed negro, no taller than a big dog, who makes shift to shuffle about, "making music, such as it was," and causing all around him to smile. Soon he too raises suspicions and is accused of faking his deformity. Asked by someone if there is any person on board who will vouch for him, he says there are plenty, "God bless 'em," and describes them all. After this he disappears, but not before some kindly soul has given him a handful of money.

Thereafter appear one after the other all the "kind gimmen" to whom the darky has referred for a good report of himself. Each in turn proves a professor or practitioner of confidence, good faith and charity, and each makes converts to the faith, at the same time that he receives personal loans or takes contributions for such organized enterprises of confidence as the Omni-balsamic Reinvigorator Company, the Widow and Orphan Asylum for the Seminoles, the World Charity Joint Stock Company, the Philosophical Intelligence Office and the Black Rapids Coal Company. Of course it is the same confidence man, originally in cream colors, who appears in many disguises, and either brazenly or with careful cunning takes in everyone who is not of his spiritual kin,—that is, everyone who is not "on" to human nature. And the moral which is applied with exhaustive ingenuity is that goodness, kindliness, trust, serve for nothing but springes to catch woodcocks. They are the moral vacuum which human nature abhors and will not suffer to exist.

There is savage indignation and there is spiritual anguish at the book's core. "Ay," says the one honest man aboard the *Fidele*, "come from Maine or Georgia, you come from a slave state, and a slave pen, where the best breeds are to be bought up at any price from a livelihood to the Presidency. Abolitionism, ye gods, but expresses the fellow-feeling of slave for slave." We are presented to a world of familiar, stubborn facts, just as we are in *Bartholomew Fair*. Yet because of a spiritual intensity which has its own intense visual imagery, *The Confidence Man* is, finally, more nearly related to Dante's *Inferno* than to Jonson's mundane comedies. Take the description of a miser who has been cheated of a few dollars and goes in search of the man who cheated him. "A dried-up old man, with the stature of a boy of twelve, was tottering about . . . his ferret eyes blinking in the sunlight of the snowy boat, as imbecilely eager, and, at intervals, coughing, he peered hither and thither as if in alarmed search for his nurse. He presented the aspect of one who, bed-rid, has, through overruling excitement, like that of a fire, been stimulated to his feet."

Melville is in hell; and he is himself the devil who inflicts the most refined tortures. His apparent objectivity is directed at showing the utter groundlessness of everything which has made him cherish life. The self-derision of Pierre has become more horrible by assuming a staid and settled manner. It has borrowed the air of an anatomist in his dissecting room, slowly and conscientiously calling up all the live nerves and the live sensibilities that made Melville's idealism "a sensible, warm motion."

It is something after all to have arrived in hell, for then the worst is known, there are no longer any illusions to be plucked out; any change must be for the better. As Edgar says in *King Lear*,

Yet better thus, and known to be contemn'd,
Than still contemn'd and flattered. To be worst,
The lowest and most dejected thing of fortune,
Stands still in esperance, lives not in fear:
The lamentable change is from the best. . . .

There is interpolated in *The Confidence Man* a strange story, the point of which, I believe, has escaped notice. I refer to the story of Colonel Moredock, the Indian-hater, followed by a discussion of the genus "Indian-hater" and the metaphysics of Indian-hating. The allegory here is so transparent that it needs no comment. The point to which it leads is important; to my way of thinking it is the most important thing in the book.

Indian-hating still exists, we are assured, since every backwoodsman comes to it by birthright, and Indian-hating, "no doubt, will continue to exist, so long as Indians do." Your backwoodsman is a lonely man; and a thoughtful man. He is strong and unsophisticated and "not without some fineness to his nature." He is self-reliant "to the degree of standing by his own judgment, though it stand alone. . . . With few companions, solitude by necessity his lengthened lot, he stands the trial—no slight one, since, next to dying, solitude, rightly borne, is perhaps of fortitude the most rigorous test." If inclined to knowledge, as the backwoodsman usually is, "he hears little from his schoolmasters, the old chroniclers of the forest, but histories of Indian lying, Indian theft, Indian double-dealing, Indian fraud and perfidy, Indian want of conscience, Indian bloodthirstiness, Indian diabolism—histories which, though of wild woods, are almost as full of things unangelic as the Newgate calendar or the Annals of Europe." The charitable man will think that he does the Redskins injustice: "Certain it is, the Indians themselves think so; quite unanimously, too." It is to be noticed, however, that when an Indian becomes a genuine proselyte to Christianity, a thing very rare, "he will not in that case conceal his enlightened conviction, that the race's portion by nature is total depravity."

Every backwoodsman comes to Indian-hating by birthright; "When to his due share of this the backwoodsman adds his private passion, we have then the stock out of which is formed, if formed at all, the Indian-hater *par excellence*." That is to say, the Indian-hater *par excellence* is one "who, having with his mother's milk drank in small love for red men, in youth or early manhood, ere the sensibilities become osseous, receives at their hands some signal outrage, or, which in effect is much the same, some of kin have, or some friend." Now nature all around him by her solitudes bidding him to muse upon this grief, "he accordingly does so, till the thought develops such attraction, that much as straggling vapours troop from all sides to a storm-cloud, so straggling thoughts of other outrages troop to the nucleus thought, assimilate with it, and swell it."

Colonel Moredock's mother was thrice widowed by the toma-hawk. Then she and all her children, he alone excepted, were treacherously murdered by Redskins; and this disaster overtook him just as he was entering upon manhood. It would seem, there-fore, that young Moredock was destined to be an Indian-hater *par excellence*. Not so, however. Colonel Moredock left a story, whereas the Indian-hater *par excellence* leaves no record behind him. It is evident, writes Melville, "that in strict speech there can be no biography of an Indian-hater *par excellence*, any more than one of a swordfish, or other deep-sea denizen; or, which is still less imaginable, one of a dead man. The career of the Indian-hater *par excellence* has the impenetrability of the fate of a lost steamer." It happens, "luckily for the curious," that "there is a species of diluted Indian-hater, one whose heart proves not so steely as his brain. Soft enticements . . . often draw him from the ascetic trail. . . . Like a mariner, too, though much abroad, he may have a wife and family in some green harbour which he does not forget." Such a one was Colonel Moredock. He was "an example of some-thing apparently self-contradicting, certainly curious, but, at the same time, undeniable; namely, that nearly all Indian-haters have at bottom loving hearts; at any rate, hearts, if anything, more generous than the average."

The story of Colonel Moredock is told by a man described as "a stranger,"—he is the Confidence Man, again—and he simply repeats the story which was told him in good faith to a garish individual, called "the cosmopolitan." Neither one puts any stock in the story. Colonel Moredock is called a man of questionable morality, deserving the questionable esteem of Doctor Johnson, "that eminent English moralist, who said he liked a good hater." "That story," says the cosmopolitan, "strikes me with even more incredulity than wonder. To me some parts don't hang together. If the man of hate, how could John Moredock be also the man of love?" Apart from this paradox, misanthropy is as unintelligible to him as infidelity. The stranger confesses to the same sanguine sentiments; so far as his experience goes, either mankind is worthy one's best love, or else he has been singularly lucky. Mankind has been a bridge that has supported him. Shall he not praise it? "Man is a noble fellow, and in an age of satirists," says the cosmopolitan, "I am not displeased to find one who has confidence in him, and bravely stands up for him." So they shake hands on it and go off to have a drink together.

The reader's mind, however, cannot be so ready to let the story drop. He has felt the truth that feels like an earthquake. According to the metaphor in *Pierre*, he has been precipitated with Melville into those "Hyperborean regions" where "all objects are seen in a dubious, uncertain and refracting light." At the same time, he has had the novel presentiment that Melville's feet were somehow firmly planted and his moral compass true. The man of hate is the man of love. He hates precisely because he loves. The angry satirist and not the man who blandly dismisses him is the true believer in his kind. It is he who is rooted in his kind,—who is rooted in the reality of life. The man who blandly professes hope, confidence and charity, who has no experience of bitterness and hate, that man has no grounds of existence at all, because neither

on the other hand, has he any experience of love. He is neither loving nor truthful. Colonel Moredock was both. A diluted Indian-
hater, he combined in the language of *Moby Dick*, the sea instinct
with the land sense. The ties that make up the land sense still
held in him. The truth behind the paradox of Colonel Moredock,
that truth Melville recognized in himself. And with this recognition—here, at the nadir of his disillusionment and despair—he
turned a dark corner. In *Pierre* he had uncovered hate masquerad-
ing in the forms of love. Now he had advanced to the discovery
that the reality of hate is of love. Love is the primal reality. All
that is is of love and all that is not has lost hold of love, and so
of the clue of existence. It appears that to say Melville had reached
hell when he wrote *The Confidence Man* is not accurate after all.
He had stopped just short of that gate on which Dante read
"Through me is the way among the lost people." He had not been
abandoned by the hope which can restore all hopes.

> *The lamentable change is from the best;*
> *The worst returns to laughter.*

It was still a long and devious return that lay ahead of him. At
the end, as we shall see, was not laughter in the sense of boisterous
spirits but the muted laughter of a deeply secured serenity.

4

Melville's sketch called "I and My Chimney" will be more familiar
than *The Confidence Man* or the other pieces which preceded it.
It has an easy-going, sunny quaintness about it that recalls Washington Irving. Nevertheless, essentially it is Melville's very own.
The chimney is the same which still stands at "Arrowhead." "From
the exact middle of the mansion it soars from the cellar, right up
through each successive floor, till, four feet square, it breaks water
from the ridge-pole of the roof, like an anvil-headed whale through
the crest of the billow."

A stranger who drops by looks at it critically, then measures it where it begins in the cellar, an enormity. "Twelve feet square: one hundred and forty-four square feet! Sir, this house would appear to have been built simply for the accommodation of your chimney."

" 'Yes, my chimney and me.' "

His wife, whom Melville pictures as a volatile and termagant Benjamin Franklin, objects to the chimney as old-fashioned and awkward; not at all to the cut of up-to-the-moment ideas of good taste and economy. She is always talking of running entries and partitions through it, and even of having it removed altogether. She works up a public sentiment against it among the neighbors, and once in her husband's absence she has the workmen in to start taking it down. Besides objecting to its awkward amplitude, she pleads that a chimney of this size must have a secret closet in it and such a closet presupposes buried treasure. After wavering before her demands, her husband turns obdurate for once; "Yes, wife, here, for once, I must say my say. Infinite sad mischief has resulted from the profane bursting open of secret recesses." Now he will take no more chances: he will not stir from home. "My city friends all wonder why I don't come to see them, as in former times. They think I am getting sour and unsocial. Some say that I have become a sort of mossy old misanthrope, while all the time the fact is, I am simply standing guard over my mossy old chimney; for it is resolved between me and my chimney, that I and my chimney will never surrender."

One dislikes to probe into the interior of this almost wholly charming piece. One feels Melville's reserve in it, which one feels called upon to respect. Yet Melville's reserve was never more transparent. Willy-nilly, shapes of significance emerge, one above the rest a familiar bulk and outline. The old chimney "excavated on each floor for certain curious out-of-the-way cupboards and closets, of all sorts and sizes," identifies itself with the White Jacket in an earlier story, which was provided, "with a great variety of pockets, pantries, clothes-presses and cupboards." Is it a symbol, then, of Melville's crotchety ego,—and the eternal Ishmael in him? Yes, and of more than that. "But this feeling," he wrote in *White Jacket*, "this feeling of the innate dignity remaining untouched, though outwardly the body be scarred for the whole term of the natural life, is one of the hushed things buried among the holiest privacies of the soul." Of the time when he has just escaped a flogging, White Jacket says "I felt my man's manhood so bottomless within me, that no word, no blow, no scourge of Captain Claret could cut me deep enough for that. I but swung to an instinct in me—the instinct diffused through all animated nature, the same that prompts even a worm to turn under the heel." The chimney looms up a symbol of Melville's importunate integrity and of the innate dignity which was his, but his in common with all humanity; the same that held its head erect in Israel Potter and, yes, even in Bartleby; the same that he depicted in Signor Beneventano and apostrophised in Hunilla; "Humanity, thou strong thing." The chimney is the symbol of what he otherwise represented in *Moby Dick;* now "take your way, ye nobler, sadder souls, to those vast Roman halls of Thermes; where far beneath the fantastic towers of man's upper earth, his root of grandeur, his whole awful essence sits in bearded state."

The symbolism here has no fixed outlines but revolves in a cloud of nuances and delicate extensions. One might call it a sacramental act of recognition and acceptance. The old chimney, "solitary and alone . . . like his sacred majesty of Russia, a unit of an auto-crat," stands for life and, also, for the silence which, being strong, life can demand for itself. It stands for life beyond the limits of human nature,—all life that shares in the profound mystery of nature, in which birth and growth and decay, and youth and age, and death and resurrection, all mingle,—all indissolubly mingle. His wife in the story just "doesn't believe in old age." But, as for himself, "I take to oldness in things," he says, and loves old Mon-taigne and "high above all," his "high-mantled old chimney" which his wife "out of that infatuate juvenility of hers" misprizes so. "I place every dependence on my chimney. As for its settling, I like it. I, too, am settling, you know, in my gait. I and my chimney are settling together, and shall keep settling, too, till, as in a great featherbed, we shall both have settled away clean out of sight."

In this same sketch Melville observed that "of all artists of the picturesque, decay wears the palm." A far more profound recognition, however, was beginning to emerge behind this observation, briefly set forth on the fly-leaf of a batch of his late poems, "Yes, decay is often a gardener." By relaxing the necessity the human mind is under to force a conclusion from life, decay leads to the acceptance of life, the only soil out of which a multitude of human satisfactions can ever flower. Hence decay is often a gardener. The acceptance of life which he envisaged in the process of decay, Melville expressed in his poem "The Lake." He describes himself walking in the woods and meditating on the transitoriness of all beauty and all forms of truth; or, to borrow from his own words in *Pierre*, "pondering on the inevitable evanescence of all earthly loveliness; which makes the sweetest things of life only food for ever-devouring and omniverous melancholy." His thoughts are interrupted by a lovely apparition who chides him and leaves him thrilling with new sensations and new presentiments.

> " 'Since light and shade are equal set,
> And all revolves, no more ye know;
> Ah, why should tears the pale cheek fret
> For ought that waneth here below.
> Let go, let go!'

> "With that, her warm lips thrilled me through,
> She kissed me, while her chaplet cold
> Its rootlets brushed against my brow,
> With all her humid, clinging mould.
> She vanished, leaving fragrant breath
> And warmth and chill of wedded life and death."

What accounts for the full, warm contours of the "Chimney" sketch is that here—although this is never so delicately intimated— Melville was beginning to comprehend the needs of life as it composes itself to old age, and old age itself, as among the hushed and "holiest privacies of the soul," as it rounds out the full compass of the mystery of life. Decay is a consecration and confirmation of the strength of life, restoring life to itself and its own mysterious resources. "Yes, decay is often a gardener." It is because it just anticipates this remark which was to stand for a profound reconciliation on Melville's part that "I and My Chimney," written in the same year as *The Confidence Man,* seems steeped in sunlight, like the old chimney itself, taking the full broad sunlight of a long summer afternoon.

CHAPTER EIGHT

Clarel

I N 1856 Melville took ship once more. He spent ten days in
England, where he visited Hawthorne. Both men recorded
this last meeting between them in their journals. I have already
quoted from Hawthorne's remarks. Melville wrote for Wednesday,
November 12th, 1856, "At Southport. An agreeable day. Took a long
walk by the sea. Sands & grass. Wild & desolate. Good talk . . ." He
added that Hawthorne remained the whole day in Southport on
his account. A week later Melville embarked for the Mediterranean.

His first destination was Constantinople, where he passed several
days crowded with impressions which he did not so much write
down as transliterate in his journal. From Constantinople he sailed
to Egypt, stopping at Smyrna on the way. From Egypt he proceeded
eastward to Palestine.

I have referred to this episode in his life as his pilgrimage to the
Holy Land. This designation may sound dramatic,—altogether too
dramatic for a journey undertaken for the benefit of a man's physical
health, which was Melville's ostensible reason for taking it. Yet
I shall let this designation stand. Every step which Melville took
which was important to him was dramatic, and this journey of his
to the Holy Land was important. Given his temperament, it was
the normal expression of his life-long emotional susceptibility to
Christianity at the core of which was an emotional attachment to
the person of Jesus Christ. This susceptibility, this emotional tenderness, spoke in the lovely gravity of his description of Serenia
in *Mardi*. It reappeared in *Clarel* in different guises, according to

different contexts, but with the same earnestness. Back in 1849, on his way to talk business with his publishers in London, Melville had toyed with the idea of going to the East, even then with the thought of visiting Jerusalem uppermost in his mind.

Melville's journey to the Holy Land was a pilgrimage to the place of origin of Christianity. This aspect of the truth blends with another aspect which can be identified with a recurring idea in *Clarel*.

> *The Past, the Past is half of time,*
> *The proven half.*

Behind the invertebrate nineteenth century (as Melville saw it in *Clarel*), behind Luther and the Reformation, even behind Rome, stands

> *The Crag of Sinai. Here then plant*
> *Thyself secure: 'tis adamant.*

The idea here, which keeps recurring in *Clarel*, is that the further East one goes the further he gropes his way back to the mysterious sources of truth.

This view of his journey, that it was a pilgrimage to the past, brings up another consideration. When he set out, Melville had not recovered yet from the crisis which he had undergone in *Pierre*. As we know, this crisis was sprung upon him by his Protestant inheritance, with its introspective insistence on the moral responsibility and moral autonomy of the individual. In *Pierre* his subjectivism running a desperate course had left him dangerously off centre. A glance almost anywhere in the journals of his travels will show him in the act of redressing his balance. He was, so to speak, practising extroversion. The flood of external impressions which he put down in his journals are so free of the processes of thought and reflection that many of them are not even cast into sentence form.

I quote from what he wrote on Saturday, December 13th, 1856, after spending a few days in Constantinople. "To the bazaar, a wilderness of traffic. . . . Immense crowds. Georgians, Armenians, Greeks, Jews & Turks are the merchants. Magnificent embroidered silk & gilt sabres & caparisons for horses. You lose yourself & are bewildered and confounded with the labyrinth, the din, the barbaric confusion of the whole,—went to Watch Tower. . . . From the top, my God, what a view! Surpassing everything. The Propontis, the Bosphorus, the Golden Horn, the domes, the minarets, the bridges, the men-of-war, the cypresses.—Indescribable. . . . The Mosque is a sort of marble mosque of which the minarets (four or six) are the stakes. In fact when inside it struck me that the idea of this kind of edifice was borrowed from the tent. . . . Off shoes and went in. This custom more sensible than taking off hat. Muddy shoes; but never muddy head. . . . Went down to the Golden Horn. Crossed bridge of pontoons. Stood in the middle and not a cloud in the sky. Deep blue and clear. Delightful elastic atmosphere, although December. A kind of English June cooled and tempered sherbet-like with an American October. . . . Armenian funerals winding through the streets. Coffin covered with flowers borne on a bier. Wax candles burn on each side in daylight. Boys & men chanting alternately. . . . Saw a burial. Armenian. Juggling & incantations of the priests—making signs, etc.—Nearby, saw a woman over a new grave—no grass on it yet. Such abandonment of misery! Called to the dead, put her head down as close to it as possible, as if calling down a hatchway, a cellar; besought—'Why don't you speak to me? My God!—It is I! Ah,—speak—but one word!'—All deaf—so much for consolation—This woman & her cries haunt me horribly.— . . . These Constantinople bridges exceed London bridges for picturesqueness. Contrast between London Bridge & these. Kayacks darting under the wooden arches. . . . Guide boys on the bridge. Greeks. beautiful faces, lively loquacious. . . . Cedar and Cypress the only trees about the capital. The Cypress a green minaret, & blends with the stone ones. Minaret perhaps derived from cypress shape. The intermingling of the dark tree with the bright spire expressive of the intermingling of life &

death. . . . Coming back from Bospherus, stood on the First Bridge. Curious to stand amid these millions of fellow beings, some of whom seem not unwilling to accept our civilization, but with one consent rejecting much of our morality & all of our religion. Aspect of the Bridge like that of a Grand Fancy Ball. (An immense Persian Rug.)"

The journals run on in this way from first to last. If they were not Melville's, one might conclude simply that the writer, like any other man, was enjoying new sights and making the most of his freedom from the restraints of domestic and professional life. However, that does not cover the case for Melville. In more senses than one his journals were a preliminary to *Clarel*. They show Melville in the initial stages of a reorientation in his consciousness which we shall not understand until we can set *Clarel* side by side with *Pierre*. On his Eastern travels Melville was reaching out for counterpoise to the inner world of consciousness which had opened underneath him in *Pierre*. He was reaching for the "sensational presentiment" of something the opposite to what he experienced in *Pierre*, a principle, like the law of gravity itself, to counterpoise the anarchy and disintegration of the individual's consciousness when left to its own centrifugence. The first step was to secure a different perspective from his perspective in *Pierre*, in which all objects and all relationships decompose before the frightful imminence of an empty infinity. The only alternative to oppose to that perspective was the concrete of history. And where could history be viewed better than in the eastern Mediterranean? On his travels Melville was incorporating himself into the perspective of history. What we come to feel in reading his travel journals through is that Melville was putting himself to a personal and sensational experience of the antiquity, the multitudinous variety and the continuity of history. There are some lines near the beginning of *Clarel* which show that in the perspective of history he had found what he needed,—a principle, perhaps an organic unity in life, to set against the chaos of the individual's consciousness by itself. His young hero, Clarel, who has lately arrived in Jerusalem, is moved to reflect on the bewildering multiplicity of different religions and different shrines all over the world. Thereupon a new realization breaks in on him:

> . . . *What profound*
> *Impulsion makes these tribes to range?*
> *Stable in time's incessant change*
> *Now first he marks, now awed he heeds*
> *The intersympathy of creeds,*
> *Alien or hostile tho' they seem—*
> *Exalted thought or grovelling dream.*

Clarel is a poem. Moreover, it is written mostly in short, four-beat lines, strung in rhymed couplets, of all metrical forms the most removed and antipathetic to the best prose in *Moby Dick* and *Pierre*. The choice of this metrical form seems madness at first sight; yet there is a deep-seated logic in the very fact that it was antithetical to Melville's most characteristic prose. By reversing his perspective Melville had jacked himself above the chaotic eddies and fluidities which had all but engulfed him in *Pierre*. His use of a medium of expression the opposite to what he had used before was forced on him if he was to confirm himself in his new perspective. The form of *Clarel* was a prop or support to his new state of consciousness, in which his spontaneous ego or self-consciousness no longer played an all-commanding role.

Clarel was published in 1876. Melville did not even get started on it until ten long years had lapsed since his Eastern travels. But that does not brush aside my contention that there is a logic of inner necessity between the journals and his verse form in *Clarel*. Melville had played with versifying at the time of *Mardi*. When did he pick it up again? In a letter to her mother, in 1859, Mrs. Melville wrote, "Herman has taken to writing poetry. You need not tell anyone, for you know how such things get around." What she meant in the last words, or what they mean about her and her relations with Herman, I cannot stop to inquire. The next year, Melville had a whole book of poems ready for publication, and it is only fair to add that his wife took it upon herself to find a publisher. She did not succeed. Of the poems in question those which Melville kept were not published until 1891, when they appeared in the *Timoleon* volume, some of them separately entitled *Fruit of Travel Long Ago*. The most notable of these poems can be referred to specific observations in his journals, and they may be said to establish the connection between Melville's travels and his recourse to metrical form. It is not too much to say that they represent a new impulse or nudge which his travels imparted to his mind. *Clarel*, which belongs with them in point of ostensible subject matter and date of inception, simply marks a more advanced stage of the same impulse. When he wrote *Clarel* Melville had secured such a command of metrical expression that he could make what on its face was a most unsuitable form serve to convey his strength of mind and the deviousness of his thought. Simultaneously in *Clarel* he commanded a comprehensive view of the experience whose initial phases he had long since recorded in his journals. A reorientation I have called this completed experience. It was all of that. It was a counter revolution in his consciousness.

2

Ostensibly *Clarel* is a revised guide book with a slight romantic story added on. The hero, a young American, formerly a student of divinity, goes on a pilgrimage to the Holy Land. In Jerusalem he falls in love with a maiden, Ruth, whose American father adopted both the religion and land of the Jews. Ruth's father is killed on his farm by marauding Arabs. Clarel would comfort her, but by the rites of her religion she is forbidden during her mourning to converse with strangers.

Clarel joins a company of pilgrims and tourists and continues his travels. They ride slowly through the mountainous and desert country, stopping at all places of Biblical renown and eventually return to Jerusalem by way of Bethlehem. In Jerusalem Clarel finds that Ruth has died in his absence. All alone now, Clarel must bear his sorrow as best he can. The last we see of him, he is in the vast motley of people who crowd along the Via Crucis at the heart of the Holy City. So ends the story, which is no more than a straw to show the deeper drift of Melville's thought in this voluminous work.

With here and there a patch of vegetation, of green grass and green trees growing amidst the desert wastes, Palestine is an image of the tragic dualism of life which served for theme in *Mardi, Moby Dick* and *Pierre*. But another symbolic value is superimposed on this. In the terrible calm that overtook the *Pequod* on the further side of Good Hope Ahab cried out "Would now St. Paul would come along . . . and to my breezelessness bring his breeze!"—his breeze of faith. In *Clarel* a dusty and breathless languor pervades all.

> . . . And here and there
> In flaws the languid evening air
> Stirs the dull weeds adust. . . .

> . . . By dry airs fanned
> The languid hyssop waveth slow,
> Dusty, on stones by ruin rent.

Finally there is the calm of the Dead Sea, by whose shores an old man, the one divine believer among these pilgrims, dies and is buried.

> No more the languid waters lave;
> Not now they wander in and out
> Of those void chambers walled about—
> So dull the calm, so dead the wave.

The lines recall Poe's poem on a doomed city, "The City in the Sea,"

> *No swellings tell that winds may be*
> *Upon some far-off happier sea—*
> *No heavings hint that winds have been*
> *On seas less hideously serene.*

In *Clarel,* Palestine is an image of the modern consciousness, parched by lack of faith and wasted by too much cerebration.

There are a few individuals in the company who take life as it comes and have the animal simplicity of Queequeg, or who wear a more lacquered hedonism. There is the soldier of fine physique who recked "naught . . . of wisest book" and stared down all creeds with solid indifference. There is the Levantine banker, "in florid opulence preserved," who considers it ill-bred to speak of death. There is the young prodigal from Lyons, with a head of chestnut hair, "like to a Polynesian girl's," who is irked by Clarel's intellectual and spiritual importunities. Drop it, he tells Clarel;

> *Come, look at straight things more in line,*
> *Blue eyes or black, which like you best?*

These are the lighthearted few; but for the most part the characters are like the hero, seekers after spiritual refreshment. They carry "thought's burden" and share Clarel's "complex passion," born of a necessity to believe and a necessity of the mind to call all things in doubt. With different degrees of courage, or mental obliquity, they broach, as Melville says,

> *All questions on that primal ground*
> *Laid bare by faith's receding wave.*

The best of them, while they speak with reverence of the Gospel story and the doctrine and example of Jesus, still

> *No further went they, nor could fill*
> *Faith's measure—scarce her dwindled gill*
> *Now standard.*

With one notable exception the more serious characters are stamped with a likeness to some aspect of Melville. The exception is Vine. Vine holds himself aloof, as if cherishing a secluded sanctuary in himself. He is polite, but half-hearted; he never responds generously.

> *Nor sided he with anything:*
> *By fits, indeed, he wakeful looked;*
> *But, in the main, how ill he brooked*
> *That weary length of arguing—*

I am convinced that for Vine Melville drew on his impressions, by no means wholly sympathetic now, of Hawthorne. Set against Vine, as a foil, is Rolfe. He has been a sailor and can quote "pure nature at his need." Rolfe,

> *Though given to study, as might seem*
> *Was no scholastic partisan*
> *Or euphonist of Academe,*
> *But supplemented Plato's theme*
> *With daedal life in boats and tents,*
> *A messmate of the elements.*

Rolfe treasures memories of an Eden "isled" in distant seas; whither long ago, "a truant ship-boy," he escaped, the first white man to appear there. He was welcomed by the natives "as a descended god," and implored of priests and people to abide with them:

> *Abide for peace is here:*
> *Behold, nor hear nor cold we fear*
> *Nor any dearth; one happy tide—*
> *A dance, a garland of the year:*
> *Abide!*

These sylvan reveries returned to charm and reproach him. He remembers ruefully his compunctions that made him renounce the island, "abjure the simple joy," and hurry "over the briny world away."

In Rolfe there is a broader span of Melville's experience,—nothing less than what he had set forth in *Typee* and *Mardi*,—and more of his complex make-up than there is in any of the other characters in the narrative. Rolfe, too, is Melville as we know him in his letters to Hawthorne. Vine recoils from his impetuous discourse. Young Clarel, who reverts to a younger and shyer Melville, is disturbed by his uncircumspect expression and revelations. Yet, as he saw,

> . . . *Rolfe is sterling, though not less*
> *At variance with that parlor-strain*
> *Which counts each thought that borders pain*
> *A social treason. Sterling—yes,*
> *Despite illogical wild range*
> *Of brain and heart's impulsive counterchange.*

Melville's pilgrims are assembled and introduced in much the same way as Chaucer's pilgrims in the *Canterbury Tales*. Among Melville's pilgrims there is one Derwent, a clergyman of the Church of England, who is the 19th Century counterpart of Chaucer's Monk, who was

> *A manly man, to been an abbot able* . . .
> *This ilke Monk leet olde thynges pace,*
> *And heeld after the newe world the space.*

It is certain that Derwent enjoyed his Browning just as he enjoyed roast beef and port wine. He shows his stubborn Anglo-Saxon prejudices as in the case of the delicate and ascetic young Franciscan who serves as guide in the church in Bethlehem. Derwent acknowledges his "love, devotion, ardor, fine" yet complains, "unmanly seems he." The monk is not a healthy young man. Derwent himself has plenty of physical health. He is a broad churchman and proud of it. Like a turkey he struts about and fans his liberal-

ism and optimism, the same that beguiled so many of his generation in England and America. Profoundly antipathetic to Melville in many respects, he nevertheless has a certain soundness at
heart and can speak the truth on occasions. He represents one
beat anyway in the complex of strophes and antistrophes in the
composition of Melville's consciousness.

Set against Derwent there is the Swede Mortmain, a disen-
chanted and embittered revolutionary idealist, and when Mortmain
has dropped out, a self-exiled American, Ungar, takes his place and
embodies the same strain. I shall let Mortmain and Ungar speak
for themselves. As Rolfe represents Melville's breadth they represent his depth. If we look upon *Clarel* as the sequel to *Pierre*, then
these two, Mortmain and Ungar, may be represented as tremors
in the bowels of the earth, continuing in new directions long after
the convulsion which produced them has passed.

3

Behind the panoramic view of Palestine in *Clarel* we are presented to a panoramic view of history deploying into the nineteenth
century. It is a sombre view, very much like Carlyle's—"in the
wild, dim-lighted chaos all stars of Heaven gone out. No star of
Heaven visible, hardly now to any man; the pestiferous fogs, and
foul exhalations grown continual, have, except on the highest mountain tops, blotted out all stars: will-o-wisps, of various course and
color, take the place of stars. Over the wild-surging chaos, in the
leaden air, are only sudden glares of revolutionary lightning; then
mere darkness, with philanthropic phosphorescences, empty mete-
oric lights." The vaunted progress of the age is nothing more than
capitalistic exploitation. A brazen materialism lords it everywhere.
The old oracles are dead, which used to give hope and joy to the
spirit of man. Upstart oracles take the place of the old ones and
repeat like so many Calliopes the vainglorious incantation,

> *Lodged in power, enlarged in all,*
> *Man achieves his last exemption—*
> *Hopes no heaven, but fears no fall,*
> *King in time, nor needs redemption.*

In spite of all that is claimed for it, science adds no new light; "Man's ignorant state" it only deepens and enlarges. Science only gives instruments to the sub-human materialism of the age. Says Ungar,

> *Your arts advance in faith's decay:*
> *You are but drilling the new Hun*
> *Whose growl even now can some dismay;*
> *Vindictive in his heart of hearts,*
> *He schools him in your minds and marts—*
> *A skilled destroyer.*

With the light of faith, the light of poetry has gone out, and the light of old legends;—

> *The abbot and the palmer rest:*
> *The legends follow them and die—*
> *Those legends which, be it confessed,*
> *Did nearer bring to them the sky—*
> *Did nearer woo it to their hope*
> *Of all that seers and saints avow—*
> *Than Galileo's telescope*
> *Can bid it unto prosing Science now.*

Of the decade (more or less) which ended in the revolutionary flare-ups of 1848, Melville wrote,

> *Europe was in a decade dim:*
> *Upon the future's trembling rim*
> *The comet hovered.*

Mortmain had put himself in the van of the revolution. An idealist, like Shelley,

> *. . . that uncreated Good*
> *He sought, whose absence is the cause*
> *Of creeds and Atheist, mobs and laws.*

He had hoped to open up "new prospects . . . to Adam's kind," and fame "had trumped him far and free";—now he is disillusioned and embittered.

> *Man's vicious: snaffle him with kings;*
> *Or, if kings cease to curb, devise*
> *Severer bit.*

To him America is

> *. . . that vainglorious land*
> *Where human nature they enthrone*
> *Displacing the divine.*

Mortmain wants nothing for himself but kindly oblivion, and this last wish is granted. He dies and is buried in a nameless grave in the desert of Palestine. Thereupon Ungar appears and continues his vitriolic strain. The French Revolution which had promised so much, had only opened the way, says Ungar, to greater degradation among men. Impiety and materialism had followed hand in hand. In 1789 the Parisian mob still revered the cross. But what of their offspring? Only the other day in Paris the mob made a hat rack of the cross. The shallows of the Revolution showed as ugly as the rapids. Of old, poverty was esteemed by saints and seers alike. Now in "Mammon's English pen" poverty is pauperism and punishable by law as a misdemeanor. As for America, suppose that it is founded on the assumption that men are good when left to their natural intentions: and suppose that the New World is given as the stage on which to act this assumption out,—

> *. . . Know,*
> *Whatever happen in the end*
> *Be sure 'twill yield to one and all*
> *New confirmation of the fall*
> *Of Adam.*

The optimism of the age is hardly less repellent than the re-
dundant forms of its gross materialism; the optimism, that is, of
those whom Melville had called the "yes-gentry" to Hawthorne,
who, as he wrote in *Clarel*, play "the fine progressive part," and
find a flattering audience on all sides;

> *Who bold can harmonize for all*
> *Moses and Comte, Renan and Paul:*
> *'Tis the robustious circus-man,*
> *With legs astride the dappled span*
> *Elate he drives white, black, before:*
> *The small apprentices adore.*

Derwent is such a one. In the future right at hand he sees "the
object clear: belief revised"; men liberated and made equal; "no
mystery, just none at all; plain sailing." "True reform goes on by
nature; doing, never done." Earlier Derwent has said of Christ,

> *I do avow He still doth seem*
> *Pontiff of optimists supreme.*

At this Mortmain turned upon him; lay off, he seems to say;

> *'Twas Shaftsbury first assumed your tone,*
> *Trying to cheerfulize Christ's moan.*

Rolfe aside mutters (about Derwent),

> *Things all diverse he would unite:*
> *His idol's a hermaphrodite.*

As Melville surveys it from his several vantage points in *Clarel,*
the nineteenth century is invertebrate, amorphous. Its good and bad,
its idealism and materialism are not real opposites. Nothing stands,

> *Opinion eats; all crumbles down:*
> *Where stretched an isthmus, rolls a strait:*
> *Cut off, cut off! Canst feel elate*
> *While all the depths of Being moan . . . ?*

Mortmain speaks here, but Rolfe has anticipated him:

> *Yes, doubt attends. Doubt's heavy hand*
> *Is set against us; and his brand*
> *Still warreth for his natural lord—*
> *King Common-Place—whose rule abhorred*
> *Yearly extends in vulgar sway,*
> *Absorbs Atlantis and Cathay . . .*

The Reformation started this process of disfiguration and, afterwards,
of disintegration. Now the work is carried on by the revolutionary
idealism of the age. This idealism is simply Protestantism turned
secular.

> *. . . Ay, Democracy*
> *Lops, lops; but where's her planted bed?*
> *The future, what is that to her*
> *Who vaunts she's no inheritor?*
> *'Tis in her mouth, not in her heart.*
> *The Past she spurns, though 'tis the Past*
> *From which she gets her saving part—*
> *That Good which lets her Evil last.*

In contrast to the featurelessness of the present, the past presents
a gracious and human countenance. Men were bound together in
a living whole then. They were bound by the bonds of tradition,
legend, poetry, religious faith.

Religion then was the good guest,
First served, and last, in every gate . . .
She every human venture shared . . .
The church was like a bonfire warm:
All ranks were gathered in her charm.

In the disintegration and decay that assails humanity on all sides, the Church of Rome is the last great stronghold of the old organic law of life. Hardly one of the pilgrims but asserts to the strength of Rome. The pert young scientist has his ribald song about her, "patcher of the rotten cloth." Derwent proclaims that he will never be drawn in "by her enticing arts." To Rolfe, who recognizes her strength and affirms that regardless of superficial changes, "man's heart is what it used to be," Derwent rejoins—with a weight of meaning he is too little rooted to be aware of—"I don't know that." "But Rome does, though," Rolfe replies, "and hence her stout persistency." A moment before this exchange between Rolfe and Derwent a young Dominican has argued the case for the Church with force and adroitness. About to take his leave, he says:

> *. . . Methinks ye hold*
> *Reserved objections. I'll unfold*
> *But one:—Rome being fixed in form,*
> *Unyielding there, how may she keep*
> *Adjustment with new times? But deep*
> *Below rigidities of form*
> *The invisible nerves and tissues change*
> *Adaptively. As men that range*
> *From clime to clime, frome zone to zone,*
> *(Say Russian hosts that menace Ind)*
> *Through all vicissitudes still find*
> *The body acclimate itself*
> *While form and function hold their own . . .*
> > *Well, you are wise;*
> *Enough—you can analogize*
> *And take my meaning.*

English Derwent does not get his meaning. But Rolfe, an American, does.

The issue lies between Rome and religion on one hand and atheism and the "Red Republic" on the other. No third alternative can stand between these mighty opposites. So the young Dominican has argued. After he has gone Rolfe enlarges on his argument to Derwent. Whole nations now philosophize to their undoing. Who has gained by "all the sacrifice of Europe's revolutions?" The Protestant? The Liberal? Not at all:

> *Rome and the Atheist have gained:*
> *These two shall fight it out—these two;*
> *Protestantism being retained*
> *For base of operations sly*
> *By Atheism.*

4

By reason of the troubled mood, begotten of Melville's consciousness of the contemporary conflict between science and religion, *Clarel* aligns itself with the poetry of Tennyson, Arnold and Clough. Does it not also betray the same nostalgic mediaevalism which colored English poetry in the middle decades of the last century? Certainly there is a strong bias in the poem in favor of the Church of Rome as the great stronghold of the Middle Ages; and it would seem that if Melville was not actually on the point of conversion to Roman Catholicism, he was at any rate turning away from the baleful realities of his world and seeking asylum in a romantic ideal of the past. The truth, however, is just the other way round. Between *Pierre* and *Clarel* the shift is not from realism to romanticism, as the text books would say, but from romanticism to realism. Melville, to begin with, was addressing himself to precisely the same realities which he had envisaged in *Mardi, Moby Dick* and *Pierre.* But his perspective is different in *Clarel.* It is not the perspective of a romantic ideal of the individual, such as he had portrayed in Taji, Captain Ahab and Pierre. His perspective now is the perspective of history, of an age; of things as they are. The mind of man aspires to a superhuman ideal. It seeks, like the revolutionary idealism in France and America, an "uncreated good," a good of its own dreaming. The boundless idealism of the human mind is a reality. It is equally a reality that the only conditions under which human nature can grow and fulfill itself in organic human forms are finite. In an individual or a country or an epoch there is the same ineluctable law; whereby, if unchecked, the mind's idealism will only lead to disaster or to greater degradation. This is the tragedy of mind. In the perspective of the noble individual it shows with tragic dignity. There, as we have seen in *Mardi, Moby Dick* and *Pierre,* the conclusion is a great mind made desolate and a great heart riven in twain. In the perspective of things as they are, the conclusion is the spectacle of a people enervated in spirit and sunk in an oblivion of materialistic exploitation. Nevertheless, the conclusion is the same essentially in either perspective. Pierre, at the end of his tragedy, drained dry of emotional and spiritual life, calls himself neuter. Melville's criticism of the nineteenth century was just that; it was neuter. Neither in its beliefs or unbeliefs did it show any visceral strength of human nature.

There is still more to say about this difference of perspective between *Pierre* and *Clarel.* In the perspective of the noble individual one of the tragic circumstances of life is that goodness cannot exist without some admixture of evil. In *Clarel* Melville has his eyes on the same reality from which this tragic circumstance must follow. But in his broader perspective he sees all round the reality. If the tragedy of mind loses its tragic dignity in the broader perspective, so, also, does it lose its tragic finality. Now, as Melville has come to see, if good cannot exist without some evil, neither does evil exist without good.

It comes again to the opposite of what he had seen in *Pierre,* where good and evil were two shadows cast by a single nothing. Now he sees good and evil inextricably involved in a single reality. In the light of this realization, his criticism of the nineteenth century may be restated thus: in its materialism it denied the good; in its idealism it denied the evil. In either case it denied the reality of life, and, denying this reality, humanity withered on all sides like an uprooted forest. The nineteenth century was a waste land, as sterile as the sands and rocky mountains of Palestine.

In *Mardi* Melville had written, putting the words into Babbalanja's mouth, "All round me, my fellow-men are new-grafting their vines, and dwelling in flourishing arbours; while I am forever pruning mine, till it is become but a stump. Yet in this pruning will I persist; I will not add, I will diminish; I will train myself down to the standard of what is unchangeably true." We do not miss the nobility of mind in these words, which, but for a change of voice, might just as well have been spoken through the mouth of Pierre. In *Clarel*, on the other hand, this very same action of the mind which he had prized in the individual he condemns in a generation. "Democracy lops, lops." Democracy—taking it to typify the revolutionary idealism of the age—would cut itself free from the common environment of life as it grows out of the past:

> The Past she spurns, though 'tis the Past
> From which she gets her saving part—
> That Good which lets her Evil last.

In *Clarel* Melville is as much preoccupied with truth as ever. But he no longer apprehends truth as lying somewhere "over the future's trembling rim." Truth lies with the body of creation. It is one with the organic reality of life in which good and evil are inextricably joined, and in virtue of which you cannot deny one without denying the other. Therefore, not by cutting one's self free from the common environment and clearing a free, untrammeled prospect of one's own, does one get a view of the truth. Not by denying life, but by affirming what is most characteristic about life, namely, its organic processes, does one put himself in the way of truth. To fail to perceive this, and to proceed on the opposite tack, is, for an individual, or a nation, or an age, to wander out of the way of truth as, also, out of the way of life.

Melville was drawn to Catholicism and repelled by Protestantism because he found in the one and failed to find in the other the perception of truth. "Man's heart is what it used to be"; Rome knows this, "and hence her stout persistency." Rome affirms the universal dualism of good and evil, of flesh and spirit, in human nature, at the same time that she affirms the organic antiquity and unity of men, transcending and binding all individuals and generations. The mystery of evil is ineradicable, being organic. But faith, too, is ineradicable, being organic. Regardless of intellectual content, in the slow growth of her rites and dogmas Melville recognized an affirmation of the organic processes of life. Between Protestantism and Catholicism Melville saw in history the same crux which had concerned him before in the individual,

> *The head rejects; so much the more*
> *The heart embraces . . . . .*
>
> *Though much we knew in desert late,*
> *Beneath no kind auspicious star,*
> *Of lifted minds in poised debate—*
> *'Twas of the brain. Consult the heart! . . .*
> *Does she renounce the trust divine?*
> *Hide it she may, but scarce resign;*
> *Like to a casket buried deep*
> *Which, in a fine and fibrous throng,*
> *The rootlets of the forest keep—*
> *'Tis tangled in her meshes strong.*

Between Protestantism and Catholicism he recognized the old antithesis of mind and heart. Protestantism followed the mind. Like Babbalanja it was forever pruning, till it was become but a stump.

At the end of *Clarel* Melville faces this mystery of human nature:

> *Yea, ape and angel, strife and old debate—* . . .
> *The running battle of the star and clod* . . .

In spite of materialism and rationalism, in spite of science and satire, the old mystery remains and one way or the other the individual must confront it:

> *Unmoved by all the claims our times avow,*
> *The ancient Sphinx still keeps the porch of shade*
> *And comes Despair, whom not her calm may cow,*
> *And coldly on that adamantine brow*
> *Scrawls undeterred his bitter pasquinade.*
> *But Faith (who from the scrawl indignant turns),*
> *With blood warm oozing from her wounded trust,*
> *Inscribes even on her shards of broken urns*
> *The sign o' the cross*—the spirit above the dust!

The old sphinx mystery remains, and there are two ways of seeking a resolution of its burden. From the opening chapters of *Moby Dick* we remember the intimate association of the two antithetical postures of worship and antagonistic attack. The mind stands outside the mystery; its way is frontal attack. That was Ahab's way and Pierre's. It had become Melville's. Where is one to find a better brief description of *Pierre,* the book, than in Melville's words just quoted? *Pierre* is a "bitter pasquinade." But there is the other way, the heart's way. Long since Melville had looked this way only to turn in the opposite direction. We are to remember Bulkington, Ishmael's partner on board the *Pequod,* but, as Melville was at pains to point out, Ishmael's sleeping partner. Bulkington's way was not, like Ahab's, frontal attack, but faith grounded on the truthful acceptance of the tragic mystery of life. "Terrors of the terrible! is all this agony in vain? Take heart, take heart, O Bulkington! . . . Up from the spray of thy ocean-perishing—straight up, leaps thy apotheosis!" At the end of *Clarel,* likewise, Melville takes leave of his hero in words which convey the only conclusion to the whole matter, which neither ignores the tragic facts nor closes the door to hope and faith:

> Then keep thy heart, though yet but ill-resigned—
> Clarel, thy heart, the issues there but mind;
> That like a crocus budding through the snow—
> That like a swimmer rising from the deep—
> Emerge thou mayst from the last whelming sea,
> And prove that death but routs life into victory.

The Christianity in *Clarel* is not final and fundamental. It does, however, blend with what is final and fundamental in it. For *Clarel* is a religious poem. It represents a religious act on Melville's part, namely, the religious conversion of himself to life. But first of all, in order to put himself in a position for this conversion, he had to make a recantation. Melville's recantation back of *Clarel* is almost identical with Mortmain's in the foreground of the poem. Mortmain, it will be remembered, had sought an uncreated good; he had hoped to throw new prospects open to his kind; he, too, had striven to enthrone human nature, replacing the divine. It requires no great divination to see that Mortmain's heresies were identical with the aims of Melville's idealism which had been the driving power to his imagination in *Mardi, Moby Dick* and *Pierre*. In *Clarel* Melville has recanted his mind's Promethean role. What is the same thing, but in terms more germane to Melville, he has recanted his radical Protestantism. In *Pierre*, to look back again for a moment, according to the central metaphor, Melville's hero followed into "those Hyperborean regions, to which enthusiastic Truth, and Earnestness, and Independence, will invariably lead a mind fitted by nature for profound and fearless thought." Truth, Earnestness (that is, Virtue) and Independence,—these had been the trinity of Melville's importunate worship in *Pierre*. In *Clarel* he is as devoted as ever to Truth and Earnestness but, and this is crucial, he has dropped Independence from his trinity. *Clarel* is religious because it takes the opposite direction to Melville's radical Protestantism.

"Appallingly vacant as vast is the soul of a man," Melville wrote in *Pierre*. His hero, pushed by his Protestantism to its last extremity, had found in himself the same inhuman void which confronted Ahab in the ultimate aspect of the universe; and thither, into this void, Melville had preceded his hero; "Better might one be pushed off into the material spaces beyond the uttermost orbit of our sun, *than once feel himself fairly afloat in himself.*" Like a flash-back upon Melville himself in *Pierre,* are the lines in *Clarel,* where Melville depicts the world of Europe and America in the last extremity of Protestantism,—

> *Where stretched an isthmus, rolls a strait:*
> *Cut off, cut off! Canst feel elate*
> *While all the depths of Being moan . . .*

The poem does not, however, subscribe to a set of dogmas about God and the hereafter. The aching void in Melville's religious consciousness in the narrow sense, that state waited to be repaired. But the appalling vacancy in his larger consciousness, at once more immediate and reaching to the depths of his being, this had been replenished out of a catholic sense of life, in which the whole is larger than the sum of its parts, and in which the parts, by subordinating themselves to the whole, find an unspeakable depth of security.

Almost any number of contexts might serve to give the weight and measure of Melville's reorientation of himself in *Clarel*. To take only one, there is his self-portraiture in the description of Rolfe which I have already quoted. Rolfe, we are told, "supplemented Plato's theme with daedal life in boats and tents." Here, very briefly, we have the two principles of consciousness which Melville identified sometimes with the mind and the heart and sometimes in the masculine or father principle and the feminine or mother principle. The masculine, taking Plato's theme, seeks the ultimate truth, the unity in life under its bewildering variety. The feminine principle or heart is receptive to the daedal variety of life. It acts for its own sake, this receptive principle, and also, because of a law of being, represented in the body by the systole and diastole of the heart, this receptivity is necessary to invigorate the opposite principle. "But thou art my fiery father," Ahab cried to the lightning, "my sweet mother I know not." Pierre's genealogy was the same as Ahab's, as he proved by "his heaven-aspiring, but still not wholly earth-emancipated mood . . . that reckless sky-assaulting mood of his." Under the momentum which took head in Ahab, Melville so identified himself with the masculine principle as to cut himself off from all the satisfactions of the feminine. In *Clarel* Melville is restoring himself to the feminine principle in his consciousness. He is renewing an umbilical relation to life.

"Ripeness is all," Melville knew this profoundly from Shakespeare. In *Pierre* he had the premonition that he would miss ripeness. Still like Babbalanja he would persist; he would not add, he would diminish. Behind *Clarel* lies the recognition that for ripeness, there must be receptivity: that from the point of view of the total consciousness it is not more blessed to give than to receive. One receives in order to be received into life and fulfilled by life. Somewhere, sometime behind *Clarel* one can conceive an act comparable to Ahab's last act which was the same as Taji's at the end of *Mardi;* "Now I am my own soul's emperor: and my first act is abdication." Ahab renounced all considerations growing out of his "queenly personality," to take his place among the maturing physical forces of this universe. Melville's act, as we may conceive, was a similar act of sovereign self-renunciation. But it aimed in exactly the opposite direction to Ahab's. Melville's act was toward humanity, not away from it. He renounced all the prerogatives of individuality in order to enter into the destiny which binds all human beings in one great spiritual and emotional organism. He abdicated his independence so as to be incorporated into the mystical body of humanity.

At the end of Shakespeare's last play, *The Two Noble Kinsmen,* Theseus is addressing the gods. "Let us be thankful," he says

For that which is, and with you leave dispute
That are above our question.

5

The real substance of *Clarel* is Melville's reorientation of himself after *Pierre*, which I have referred to just now as his religious conversion to life. The initial impulse stemmed from Melville's Eastern travels back in 1856 and 1857. Yet, as it seems to me, this reorientation would never have rounded itself out as it did had it not been for another event which had a tremendous impact on Melville's life. For a long time, now, the critics have agreed that the Civil War played a decisive role in Walt Whitman's spiritual development. I am not sure that it did not play as decisive a role in Melville's.

His more immediate response to the Civil War was in the poems called *Battle Pieces* published in 1866, ten years before *Clarel*. According to Melville's statement, these poems originated in an impulse imparted by the fall of Richmond in April, 1865, "They were composed without reference to collective arrangement, but, being brought together in review, naturally fall into the order assumed. . . . The aspects which the strife as a memory assumes are as manifold as are the moods of involuntary meditation—moods variable, and at times widely at variance." There is a kind of elation in these poems; and there are the declamatory statements common in war poetry about the "Cause" and the certain triumph of "Right." For a man like Melville, with strong spiritual and emotional needs but balked in the satisfaction of these needs by intellectual reservations equally strong, the illusory simplification of things that war invariably brings forth, afforded an unaccustomed harmony of being. We can also sense in these poems the relief from "thoughts burdened" which Melville experienced through a vicarious participation in existing physical action.

Nevertheless, there are deeper strains in *Battle Pieces*, rising out of Melville's most rooted realizations about life. In the first of the *Pieces* he wrote,

> *I muse upon my country's ills—*
> *The tempest bursting from the waste of Time*
> *On the world's fairest hope linked with man's foulest crime.*

The war was a terrible visitation. Perhaps it was required to lay bare the foundation of things, whereon to build anew and rear "the final empire and the happier world." In another poem Melville imagines his country lying in a horrible dream, her features distorted by pain and terror, then waking with the look of a transfiguration that speaks of

> *Power dedicate, and hope grown wise,*
> *And youth matured for age's seat—*

There are these gleams of hope in the *Battle Pieces*. There are also dark apprehensions for his country. The world's fairest hope is linked to man's foulest crime. Might it not prove that in taking the sword to sever the one from the other the hope was excised with the crime? In the poem "The Conflict of Opinions," Melville wrote,

> *Power unanointed may come—*
> *Dominion (unsought by the free)*
> *And the Iron Dome,*
> *Stronger for stress and strain,*
> *Fling her huge shadow athwart the main;*
> *But the Founders' dream shall flee . . .*

Regardless of where the ostensible victory lay, would not Mammon prove the only real victor in the end?

> *The People spread like a weedy grass,*
> *The thing they will they bring to pass,*
> *And prosper to the apoplex.*

Such were Melville's apprehensions for his country when he wrote the *Battle Pieces*. When he wrote *Clarel* he saw these apprehensions on the point of being realized. His countrymen appeared to revel and grub in a Saturnalia of animal materialism.

> *How of the teeming Prairie-Land?*
> *There shall the plenitude expand*
> *Unthinned, unawed? . . .*

Myriads playing pygmy parts—
Debased into equality:
In glut of all material arts
A civic barbarism may be:
Man disennobled—brutalised
By popular science—atheized
Into a smatterer . . .
Dead level of rank commonplace
An Anglo-Saxon China, see,
May on your vast plains shame the race
In the Dark Ages of Democracy.

The *Battle Pieces* represent Melville's more immediate response to the Civil War. When he wrote *Clarel* the force of its impact had not subsided. A casual comparison of the two works will show a profound continuity between them. Even if we leave *Battle Pieces* out of consideration here, and judge solely by what *Clarel* has to say about the Civil War, we cannot doubt that the momentum of Melville's mind in *Clarel* derived in large measure from the emotional and spiritual agitations which he had experienced from it.

A man of Melville's patriotism was bound to be deeply affected by the Civil War in whatever light he regarded it. Melville saw in the conflict still another instance of the universal tragedy of mind, with his country as present victim. And there were still other nerves and sensibilities in Melville through which the Civil War affected him. To "analogize" was the ingrained habit of his mind, and there is no question but that he saw in the Civil War just such an internal convulsion as he had himself experienced. Among the characters in *Clarel*, Rolfe, as I have said, represents Melville's breadth; Mortmain and Ungar his depth. Through Ungar we see at once Melville's more comprehensive view of the war and his most deeply personal response to it.

Ungar, a Southerner, is a voluntary exile from his country after the war, doing military service for the Turks. Rolfe, who is drawn to Ungar, reflects,

> *Ah me, poor Freedom, can it be*
> *A countryman's a refugee?*
> *What maketh him abroad to roam,*
> *Sharing with infidels a home?*
> *Is it the immense charred solitudes*
> *Once farms? And chimney stacks that reign*
> *War-burnt upon the houseless plain*
> *Of hearthstones without neighborhoods?*

At once we are reminded of the "charred landscape" in Pierre's soul, and of the desolation in Pierre's vision of Enceladus; "Stark desolation; ruin, merciless and ceaseless," "old foundation stones and rotting timbers"; the household herb, the catnip, still clustered around the ruins, but yearly giving way to the white "amaranthine and celestial flower" of Pierre's disastrous idealism. Pierre's soul, the reflection of Melville's, was the image in anticipation of the desolation wrought on the country, by the Civil War; itself, precipitated from the same sources as those which precipitated the convulsion in Pierre.

Ungar's ancestors had been among Lord Baltimore's colonists in Maryland who sought in the New World an asylum "from the nonconformists' zeal or bite" which had oppressed them in the motherland;

> *The New World's fairer flowers and dews*
> *Welcomed the English Catholic.*

Before the war, Ungar, a Southerner, had been outspoken in his denunciation of slavery. The institution was an iniquity; but at this point Ungar made a distinction. It was an iniquity in those who planted it,

> *While for inheritors—alas,*
> Who knows? *And let the problem pass.*

Now, after the war, Ungar is the "self-exiled one"; he is "too stead-fast." He would not share, as he might now, "the spoilers' seat and thrive." He would not "renounce conviction in defeat." What conviction? The conviction that although directed against an evil the Civil War was itself an evil; it was a recrudescence of the same destroying zeal which had driven his ancestors out of England in the Seventeenth Century. It was that "evil day, black in the New World's calendar . . . true Bridge of Sighs . . . between contrasted eras the span of fate," when touching construction of a pact, "a paper pact," with points abstruse "as theologic ones" and "profuse in matter for an honest doubt," the "country's pick and flower of sons" were called upon to act for life and death; and the stubborn knot of contention between North and South was cut— "but with the sword";

> . . . *that day*
> *With its decision yet could sway*
> *Ungar, and plunging thoughts excite.*

Melville felt about the Civil War just as Ungar did. But the impact of the war on Melville took the opposite direction from what it took in Ungar. Presently Ungar takes leave of the pilgrims to pursue the tangential course on which the Civil War had started him. The force of the Civil War on Melville was to bring him back to centre and restore him to himself.

We are to notice in the first place that in *Clarel* Melville was expressing after the Civil War precisely the same views which he had expressed on slavery and, in anticipation of the event, on the Civil War twelve years before its outbreak, in *Mardi*. When King Medea and his companions visit in the south of Vivenza,—that is, the Southern states,—the fact of slavery transfixes them. They all agree that it is an evil, a horrible evil; they are all equally at a loss to propose a way of eradicating the evil. Then Babbalanja sums the matter up: "Humanity cries out against this vast enormity:— not one man knows a prudent remedy. Blame not, then, the North;

and wisely judge the South. Ere, as a nation, they became responsible, this thing was planted in their midst. Such roots strike
deep . . . Easy it is to stand afar and rail . . . Whoso is free from
crime, let him cross himself—but hold his cross upon his lips. That
he is not bad, is not of him. Potter's clay and wax are all moulded
by hands invisible. The soil decides the man . . . These Southern
tribes have grown up with this thing . . ." And if to every man
"conscience be the awarder of its own doom," then of these Southern
men "many shall be found exempted from the least penalty of
this sin. But sin it is, no less;—a blot, foul as a crater-pool of hell;
it puts out the sun at noon; it parches all fertility . . . The future is
all hieroglyphics. Who may read . . . Time—all-healing Time—
Time, great philanthropist! Time must befriend these thralls."

To these words I must add a paragraph from the preceding
chapter in *Mardi*, in which, in anticipation of the event, Melville
spoke his mind on the Civil War: "Now, though far and wide, to
keep equal pace with the times, great reforms, of a verity, be needed;
nowhere are bloody revolutions required. Though it may be the
most certain of remedies, no prudent invalid opens his veins to let
out his disease with his life. And though all evils may be assuaged;
all evils cannot be done away. For evil is the chronic malady of
the universe; and checked in one place, breaks forth in another."

This identity of views upon the Civil War and its origin in slavery
in *Mardi* and *Clarel* is interesting, surely; but it only broaches the
main point of interest which lies between *Mardi*, the Civil War and,
ultimately, *Clarel*. In *Mardi*, Melville's radical Protestantism first
showed itself in an identifiable form. In *Mardi*, nonetheless, there is,
as ballast to this Protestantism, a principle of consciousness the exact
opposite to it. In the chapter called "Time and Templer," Melville
wrote, "It is not the Pyramids that are ancient, but the eternal granite
whereof they are made; which had been equally ancient though yet
in the quarry. For to make an eternity we must build with eternities;
whence, the vanity of the cry for anything alike durable and new;
and the folly of the reproach—Your granite hath come from the

old-fashioned hills." It was out of this consciousness of the organic antiquity and unity of mankind, to which the individual must subordinate himself, that Melville's views of slavery were expressed in *Mardi*. The force of the impact of the war as a present reality and in retrospect was to restore Melville to this catholic and religious consciousness of life, from which his radical Protestantism had cut him adrift.

Even in the *Battle Pieces* we feel the reservations of this consciousness set against the easy and partial affirmations of patriotism and partisan conflict. In the prose supplement which he added to *Battle Pieces,* in which we find his most comprehensive statement about the Civil War, the religious consciousness I speak of is in full possession, and illustrates itself in every line. In this prose supplement, added, so Melville tells us, from patriotic compunctions which in such critical times must be allowed to over-rule all literary scruples, Melville pleaded for charity and understanding from the victors toward the vanquished, so that, as he put it elsewhere, the flushed North from its own victory might be saved.

"It is enough for all practical purposes," Melville wrote, "if the South have been taught by the terrors of the Civil War to feel that Secession, like Slavery, is against Destiny . . . Patriotism is not baseness, neither is it inhumanity . . ." Those who mourn for their soldier dead in the South are "as sacred in the eye of Heaven" as the mourners of the North. "Zeal is not of necessity religion, neither is it always of the same essence with poetry or patriotism." It is right to rejoice over the triumph of the North only "so far as it may justly imply an advance for our whole country and for humanity." Why is there still so much uneasiness, now that more than a year has passed since the cessation of armed hostility? "Do we dread lest the repose may be deceptive? In the recent convulsion has the crater but shifted? Let us revere that sacred uncertainty which forever impends over men and nations." The perversion of victory into oppression will only lead to further disunion. "But this path of thought leads toward those waters of bitterness from which one can only turn aside and be silent." "Let us pray that the terrible historic tragedy of our time may not have been enacted without instructing our whole beloved country through terror and pity; and may fulfillment verify in the end those expectations which kindle the bards of Progress and Humanity."

In these prose statements about the war, we have, in esoteric terms, the right-mindedness of Starbuck illuminated by the angelical insight of Lucy. That is to say, we have common sense, but common sense transfigured. It may be, as Melville thought, that the prose supplement detracts from the symmetry of the book of poems to which it was appended. However that may be, it cannot fail in our eyes to add to Melville's proportions as a man. For its common sense and its elevation above common sense, it strikes a note as familiar in our ears as it is unique among all public utterances about the Civil War. There is only one other quarter in which to look for this particular note. "With malice toward none; with charity for all; with firmness in the right, as God gives us to see the right,—let us strive on to finish the work we are in: to bind up the nation's wounds, to care for him who shall have borne the battle, and for his widow and his orphan; to do all which may achieve and cherish a just and lasting peace among ourselves and with all nations." To my knowledge, it is only in Lincoln's Second Inaugural that we find the same sense about the War, with the same spiritual timbre and profoundly quiet elevation that distinguishes Melville's supplement to his *Battle Pieces*.

In the history of his country the Civil War seemed to Melville a Bridge of Sighs,—

> *Sad arch between contrasted eras;*
> *The span of fate.*

In his own life it played the opposite part. It served as a span between his abrupt and precipitous young manhood and the steady, broad-shouldered decline of his life. It baptised his spirit anew. By stirring him to the depths of his being it awoke in him that religious consciousness which was his mainstay in *Mardi* and *Moby Dick*. Moreover, out of the Civil War he was provided with just the right symbol for this religious consciousness. In the Civil War he saw an externalization of the terrible self-conflict which had racked him in *Pierre*, and which had left him in a lethal spiritual isolation. The Union which was at stake in the War became his symbol of the harmony and wholeness which should obtain in the individual's consciousness.

Near the end of *Clarel*, when the full realization of what it is to be a human being is closing round him, the impulse takes the young hero to escape his human destiny. Is there not some simple sensuous existence, unclouded by man's spiritual consciousness that he can fly to? But at once, facing the inexorable truth, he checks this impulse:

> *But whither now, my heart? wouldst fly*
> *Each thing that keepeth not the pace*
> *Of common uninquiring life?*
> *What! fall back on clay commonplace?*
> *Yearnest for peace so? . . .*

> *Now live*
> *At all, if once a fugitive*
> *From thy own nobler part, though pain*
> *Be portion inwrought with the grain?*

In *Clarel* fate is not apprehended as an external force of obstruction, like a prison wall, but as one with the organic reality and organic law of human beings. It is the way of growth, the way to more sorrowful, but, at the same time, to more significant life. Melville has accepted the tragedy implicit in human nature, because he has identified it with a positive and a universal necessity.

CHAPTER NINE

Billy Budd

I N THE CHAPTER on *Moby Dick*, I pointed out the parallel between King Lear and Captain Ahab. This parallel breaks off abruptly. As one follows Melville in his last books, rounding out his experience of life, the presentiment comes home that a deeper and more significant parallel is to be found between King Lear and Melville himself. It will not do to insist on this parallel too literally, but an awareness of it will add a depth to what I have still to say, which prose statement lacks and without which I cannot hope to convey the truth which remains to be told. In the "Chimney" sketch in which Melville composed himself to his old age, he spoke of himself as going about his fields, "a sort of lazy, happy-go-lucky" and "loafing old Lear." If this description was a mere whim, it was a remarkably prescient one.

In *King Lear*, in the storm scene on the heath, Lear thinks terribly upon his personal injuries and the revenge he will take: "but I will punish home." Then, almost immediately, he checks himself; that is, he checks his concentration upon his personal anguish,

> *O! that way madness lies; let me shun that;*
> *No more of that . . .*

His mind turns from himself and runs out to houseless, homeless humanity—"Poor naked wretches, wheresoe'er you are. . . ." For a moment his mind is out of the way of madness, but his grief is too immediate and overwhelming for him to escape and almost at once he staggers back and breaks out in vindictive abuse. In the Fifth Act he emerges once more. Somehow under all that he has endured he has recovered the clue to sanity and something more than sanity. He is possessed of a wisdom that seems heavenly. But it is a heavenly wisdom of this world, is of life in this world. He and Cordelia are prisoners: what matter? Come, he says to her,

> Come, let's away to prison;
> We two alone will sing like birds i' the cage:
> > . . . so we'll live,
> And pray, and sing, and tell old tales, and laugh
> At gilded butterflies, and hear poor rogues
> Talk of court news; and we'll talk with them too,
> Who loses and who wins; who's in, who's out;
> And take upon's the mystery of things,
> As if we were God's spies.

The effect of the scene in which Lear speaks these most wonderful of all Shakespeare's words is like sunlight suddenly streaming through a momentary rift in a storm; then darkness again. In the late Melville there is the same effect of contrast with a difference. Here the sunlight slowly makes its way against the clouds and, in the last view we have, the sunlight is still in possession of the sky and on the face of the land. Yet the same poignancy is here, because we feel all along that the sunlight has made its way among the clouds which never quite cease to threaten to blot it out. But the parallel with which I am concerned lies between Melville and King Lear, the man, not the drama.

One might choose to be particular and claim a correspondence between the storm and its effect on Lear and the impact of the Civil War on Melville. Letting this pass, there is a parallel between the transitions I have just looked at in Lear and the transitions from *The Confidence Man* to *Clarel* and from *Clarel* to *Billy Budd*. In *The Confidence Man* Melville was like Lear tearing at his own heart: "O! that way madness lies." In *Clarel* the dangerous vehemence from the sense of irremediable and unwarrantable personal injuries has subsided. There is the calm of an impersonal acceptance of the universal tragedy implied in human nature. The last we see of the hero he is losing himself in the motley throng along the Via Crucis, of all men of all nations:

> *In varied forms of fate they wend—*
> *Or animal or man, 'tis one:*
> *Cross-bearers all, alike they tend*
> *And follow, slowly follow on.*

Melville has accepted the sorrowful mystery of life, "the burthen of the mystery," as Wordsworth called it. He has accepted it because it is universal. That was the initial step, and taking it Melville was poised to participate in and partake of life more fully. From *Clarel* to *Billy Budd* the transition is far less abrupt than the earlier one from *The Confidence Man* to *Clarel*. In *Billy Budd* he has simply gone farther along the paths that are beginning to open for him in *Clarel*. In *Billy Budd* there is the same acceptance of the tragedy implicit in human nature. But in still other ways he has, like Lear, taken upon himself the mystery of things as if he were God's spy. That is, his acceptance of life has reached beyond the human lot of suffering and has discovered the mysterious reserves of life which go a long way to mitigate the tragedy which is inseparable from human consciousness.

Melville had poised himself for this in *Clarel*. He had recovered the prerequisite freedom and balance; the freedom and balance which Ahab, transfixed and paralysed by his vindictive hate, had lost and which Ishmael, in spite of the painful drag of his sympathy with Ahab, managed to hold on to: "Doubts of all things earthly, and intuitions of some things heavenly; this combination makes neither believer nor infidel, but makes a man who regards them both with equal eye."

It is right and true to call *Billy Budd* Melville's "testament of acceptance"; but we must be careful not to understand either too much or too little by the word acceptance. Melville's "acceptance" was not based on any denial of the tragic facts of life or any ignorance of the inexorable logic of these facts. The world which we are shown in his last book is figuratively—as he had called it long before in *White Jacket*—and literally, a man-of-war world, and the story of *Billy Budd* is as stark a tragedy as an American writer even to this day has ever penned.

The scene is an English man-of-war, the *Indomitable*, near the close of the eighteenth century, when conservative England and revolutionary France were locked in mortal combat. The hero, a young English sailor, is hanged for an act which his superiors, bound by the articles of war, have to adjudge a crime for which hanging was the only commensurate punishment, but which, in reality, far from being evil, was like the swift retributive stroke of an indignant angel.

Billy is the handsome sailor—guileless, good-natured, loving and beloved. Opposite him, like the bad angel against the good angel in an old morality, is the ship's police officer or master-of-arms, John Claggart. Out of apparently motiveless malice, Claggart is down on Billy and trumps up a charge against him. In the captain's cabin, in the presence of the captain, he accuses Billy of trying to incite the crew to mutiny. Now Billy has one deformity; he stammers. Bewildered and outraged, he cannot find the words to defend himself and repel Claggart's accusation. His whole being rises and, since words fail him, he takes other means to express himself. Quick as a flash and with the force of a cannon shot, he drives his right fist at Claggart's jaw and floors him. A few moments later the ship's surgeon pronounces the master-at-arms dead. "It is the divine judgment of Ananias," Captain Vere exclaims to the astonished surgeon; but again starting, he vehemently exclaimed "Struck dead by an angel of God. Yet the angel must hang." From this point on the interest centers in Captain Vere as he faces the dilemma which flashed upon him in these words.

Of the captain's character something more should be told. He is an excellent officer; there are few better than he in His Majesty's service. While always mindful of the welfare of his men, he will not tolerate any infraction of discipline. He is "intrepid to the verge of temerity, though never injudiciously so." He is a man of strong common sense. A great reader, he prefers wisely, for one of his profession, "books treating of actual men and events, no matter of what era . . . and unconventional writers who free from cant and convention, like Montaigne, honestly, and in the spirit of common sense, philosophize about realities." For all this solid base to his character, there is a hint of unworldliness in Captain Vere, recognized by his fellow officers in the nickname they gave him, "Starry Vere." Being the man he is in the position he occupies, Captain Vere acts promptly in the emergency which has taken place before his eyes. He immediately summons his lieutenants to sit in court martial on Billy Budd. Captain Vere's directions to his court martial cannot be overlooked. They bring out a point of special urgency as they also show his character in action. Of Claggart's inexplicable malice, which provoked Billy to strike him, the captain says, "Ay, there is a mystery; but to use a Scriptural phrase, it is 'a mystery of iniquity'; a matter for psychological theologians to discuss. But what has a military court to do with it?" Nor is the question of Billy's intent or non-intent pertinent. "The prisoner's deed, with that alone we have to do." Neither the speculative mind nor the heart has any business here; "the heart is the feminine in man and hard though it be, she must here be ruled out." Captain Vere understands the compunctions that his fellow officers must feel, and he reviews them; "In natural justice is nothing but the prisoner's overt act to be considered? Now can we adjudge to summary and shameful death a fellow-creature innocent before God and whom we feel to be so?—Does that state it aright? You sign sad assent. Well, I too feel that, the full force of that. It is Nature. But do these buttons that we wear attest that our allegiance is to Nature? No, to the King. Though the ocean, which is inviolate Nature primeval, though this be the element where we move and have our being as sailors, yet as the King's officers lies our duty in a sphere correspondingly natural?" No, for "in receiving our commissions we in the most important regards ceased to be natural free agents. When war is declared, are we the commissioned fighters previously consulted? We fight at command. . . . So now, would it be so much we ourselves that would condemn as it would be martial law operating through us? For that law and the rigor of it, we are not responsible. Our vowed responsibility is in this: that however pitilessly that law may operate, we nevertheless adhere to it and administer it . . . But while, put to it by those anxieties in you which I cannot but respect, I only repeat myself—while thus strangely we prolong proceedings which should be summary, the enemy may be sighted and an engagement result. We must do; and one of two things must we do—condemn or let go."

Captain Vere reminds the court of the larger situation which they must keep in mind. Their country is at war with another power; conservative England is threatened from without and from within. The sparks from the French Revolution have crossed the Channel. Mutinies have flared up in the English navy—there has been the mutiny at the Nore, the so-called Great Mutiny—and, although quelled, these outbreaks might be repeated at any moment. Hence, more than ever, His Majesty's officers are bound to insist on all points of discipline. A clement sentence in the case of Billy Budd might be construed as timidity and encourage insurrection. Says Captain Vere, turning the case over to his subordinates, "You see then whither, prompted by duty and the law, I steadfastly drive. But I beseech you, my friends, do not take me amiss."

The other officers "hardly had the inclination to gainsay one whom they felt to be an earnest man, one, too, not less their superior in mind than in naval rank." Billy is convicted and sentenced to hanging at the yard arm in the early morning watch, it now being night. The next morning, just at daybreak, the sentence was carried out.

In *Billy Budd* Melville returned to the situation he had represented in *Redburn* between his younger self and the sailor Jackson, and abstracted its essential and universal significance. Of all the

ship's company only Captain Vere and Claggart were "intellectually capable of adequately appreciating the moral phenomenon
presented in Billy Budd." As for Claggart, as Captain Vere had the
insight to discern, in him there was the opposite mystery to Billy's,
"the mystery of iniquity." What, Melville asks, "can more partake of
the mysterious than the antipathy spontaneous and profound such
as is invoked in certain exceptional mortals by the mere aspect of
some other mortal, however harmless he be?—if not called forth
by that harmlessness itself." Normal human nature affords no explanation of such a one as Claggart, who is at once an object of
pity and of the profoundest loathing. He and his kind are free
of vulgar vices. He is, says Melville, borrowing a definition attributed to Plato, a case of "Natural Depravity; a depravity according to nature." Melville explains that this is not the same as
Calvin's total depravity, because it does not apply to all mankind,
but only to certain individuals. This much Melville has to say about
the origin of evil. But his interest in his last book is not primarily
speculative or metaphysical. It is enough for him that the mysterious facts are confronted—are confronted honestly and honorably.

Melville distinguishes between nature and the world. Primeval
nature is good. The world is not under nature's rule. Not nature,
not love, but necessity, or fate, rules the world. It is a man-of-war's
world and we all fight at command. Idealism which would throw
off this yoke of necessity only leads to more misery for man. Of
the last decade of the eighteenth century, when the story takes
place, Melville wrote, "The opening proposition made by the Spirit
of that Age involved the rectification of the Old World's hereditary
wrongs. In France, to some extent, this was bloodily effected. But
what then? Straightway the Revolution itself became a wrong-
doer, one more oppressive than the kings. Under Napoleon it en-
throned upstart kings, and initiated that prolonged agony of continual war whose final throe was Waterloo." However unintelligible and arbitrary, there is an organic necessity in the world and
it cannot be disregarded. A principle of limitation, it is, neverthe-

less, also a principle of self-preservation. Even where it allows some latitude for choice, men are wise to conform with it by supplementing it with forms and definitions of their own. Captain Vere only repeats Melville's own, now settled conviction, "With mankind . . . forms, measured forms, are everything; and that is the import couched in the story of Orpheus with his lyre spellbinding the wild denizens of the woods." And "this he once applied to the disruption of forms going on across the Channel and the consequences thereof."

This is a far cry from Melville's state of mind in *Pierre,* when in spite of himself he could not bring himself to accept the clamorous moral of his own story; "For it is only the miraculous vanity of man," he wrote in *Pierre,* "which ever persuades him, that even for the most richly gifted mind, there ever arrives an earthly period, where it can truly say to itself, I have come to the Ultimate of Human Speculative Knowledge; hereafter, at this present point I will abide. Sudden onsets of a new truth will assail him, and overturn him as the Tartars did China: for there is no China wall that man can build in his soul which shall permanently stay the irruptions of those barbarous hordes which Truth ever nourishes in the loins of her frozen, yet teeming North; so that the Empire of Human Knowledge can never be lasting in any dynasty, since Truth still gives new Emperors to the earth." In *Billy Budd* Melville has completely reversed himself, so that what had been vanity before, to build a Chinese wall in one's soul, is now the part of wisdom. The fruit of Captain Vere's serious reading of books "treating of actual men and events" had been the ripening "of his own more reserved thoughts . . . so that as touching most fundamental topics, there had got to be established in him some positive convictions which he felt would abide in him essentially unmodified so long as his intelligent part remained unimpaired." He was opposed to the revolutionary ideals coming out of France. Unlike so many of his friends and kindred, he opposed them not because they threatened to sweep away the privileges of his class, but because "they seemed to him incapable of embodiment in lasting institutions" and were, he believed, "at war with the world and the peace of mankind." He had established certain fundamental assumptions, and "in view of the humbled period in which his lot was cast, this was well for him. His settled convictions were as a dyke against those invading waters of novel opinion, social, political, and otherwise, which carried away as in a torrent no few minds in those days, minds by nature not inferior to his own."

It is not that Captain Vere (or Melville) has capitulated in the sense of abdicating his speculative mind and his idealism. The conservatism here is not retreat. It is the same as it was in *Clarel*, the expression of Melville's religious consciousness of the organic unity of man. In substituting common sense for the speculative and idealistic view of the situation which confronted him, Captain Vere was implementing this religious consciousness. As he saw here and saw beyond the immediate situation, what is demanded for the ordering of this world is worldly common sense. He obeyed the dictates of common sense not for his own worldly advantage but for the good of all,—for the good of that organic whole which is society.

As an index to Melville's "acceptance," Captain Vere is still more interesting as he faces his own soul. He is obliged by the exigencies of this man-of-war world to disregard all considerations of the absolute good and the ultimate truth. But he does not therefore deny the existence of the absolute good and the ultimate truth. He is the first to recognize Billy's angelic innocence. In the present emergency his innocence cannot excuse the consequences of his act: "We proceed under the law of the Mutiny Act." But he has said, "At the Last Assizes it shall acquit." In his dilemma Captain Vere does not arraign God as a devil-god; nor does he conclude, according to *Pierre*, "that whatever other worlds God may be Lord of, he is not the Lord of this." The words occur in the Plinlimmon pamphlet, and in *Pierre* Melville could not bring himself to accept Plinlimmon's relativistic doctrine of virtue in this world. Like his hero, he would have all or nothing and, like his hero, he got nothing; or, because his imagination could not picture nothing, he got worse than nothing: "Now, 'tis merely hell in both worlds."

As Plinlimmon wrote, "What man who carries a heavenly soul in him, has not groaned to perceive, that unless he committed a sort of suicide as to the practical things of this world, he can never hope to regulate his earthly conduct by the same heavenly soul? And yet by an infallible instinct he knows, that that monitor cannot be wrong in itself." So it was with Captain Vere. As for Melville, it can be said that he has accepted the human predicament,— which follows inevitably from the dualism of human nature. Melville began to take account of it, and to chafe under it, in *Mardi;* he pressed into it further and wrestled with it in *Moby Dick.* In *Pierre* he refused to accept it. Now he sees that because a man acts under a worldly necessity he does not therefore debase his humanity: his soul, be it immortal or not, is not soiled thereby. And because a man has accepted the limitations of his nature he is not therefore lacking in human strength and dignity, and is not to be relegated, as we feel that Melville, in the presence of Ahab could not but relegate Starbuck, on the score of "the incompetence of mere unaided virtue or right-mindedness." Further than this he sees that it is possible to be in this world and not of it; that because a man has taken on the burden of human consciousness, with its sad knowledge of good and evil, he is not therefore excommunicated from primal goodness.

Between Billy's instinctive rectitude, that of an upright barbarian, and such as Adam's might have been "ere the urbane Serpent wriggled himself into his company," and Captain Vere's conscious human rectitude there is no estrangement. Far from that, there is a profound reciprocal understanding between the two.

> *Fair encounter*
> *Of two most rare affections! Heavens rain grace*
> *On that which breeds between them!*

It was Captain Vere who, of his own motion, communicated the death sentence to Billy. As to what transpired then, between these two, "each radically sharing in the rarer qualities of one nature," Melville would no more than hint. Captain Vere was old enough to have been Billy's father. "The austere devotee of military duty, letting himself melt back into what remains primeval in our formalized humanity, may in the end have caught Billy to his heart, even as Abraham may have caught young Isaac on the brink of resolutely offering him up in obedience to the exacting behest. But there is no telling the sacrament . . . wherever under circumstances at all akin to those here attempted to be set forth— two of great Nature's nobler order embrace." The next morning when Billy stood up for execution before the crew, his last words were "God bless Captain Vere." Not long afterward Captain Vere, dying of a wound received in an engagement with the enemy, was heard to murmur words inexplicable to his attendant, "Billy Budd, Billy Budd."

It is possible to see in these intimations the reflection of a heavenly mystery, in which the idea of divine love, as attributed to Christ, is reconciled with the known facts of the rough justice which overrules the world. There is a suggestion of such a reconciliation in terms of Christianity inasmuch as it is just hinted that Billy Budd, a foundling, was in truth, the son of Captain Vere. It should be mentioned, too, since no fact in the story is without some symbolical significance, that the enemy's ship which Captain Vere engaged and overcame, at the cost of his life, formerly named the *St. Louis,* had, by the revolutionary government of France, been re-christened the *Athéiste.* Furthermore, it is impossible not to see in Billy's execution a resemblance to the Crucifixion. Long after his death, his comrades "recalled the fresh young image of the Handsome Sailor, that face never deformed by a sneer or subtler vile freak of the heart within! This impression of him was doubtless deepened by the fact that he was gone, and in a measure mysteriously gone." The spar from which he was hanged was reverently

kept track of even long after it had been discarded. To those who
had known Billy "a chip of it was as a piece of the Cross." At the
moment of his death before the assembled crew, "it chanced that
the vapory fleece hanging low in the east, was shot through with
a soft glory as of the fleece of the Lamb of God seen in mystical
vision, and simultaneously therewith, watched by the wedged mass
of upturned faces, Billy ascended; and ascending, took the full
rose of the dawn."

It may be that the visitations of man's best nature signify a more
than human reality. It may be that such innocence and goodness
as blazed in Billy's heart have a sanction from a higher quarter
than the tribunals of this world. Melville does not say. "Doubts
of all things earthly,"—that is, doubts of all earthly beliefs and conclusions,—and "intuitions of some things heavenly,"—that was Melville's state of mind in his last book; a state of suspended belief
and unbelief, in which, as I quoted Keats as saying, there is no
"irritable reaching after facts and reason."

For the rest, in the "testament of acceptance," Melville ascribes
a constitutional soundness to humanity. Insofar as it was provoked
by wilful idealists, the French Revolution led to worse oppression
than before. But taking a long view of it and seeing it as an in-
fection coming to a head in a frame so constitutionally sound as
to be able to throw it off, it had a salutary effect which "not the
wisest could have foreseen" at the time. In a way "analogous to the
operation of the Revolution at large, the Great Mutiny, though by
Englishmen naturally deemed monstrous at the time, doubtless
gave the first latent prompting to most important reforms in the
British navy." Moreover, there is that in the foreground of the
story which attests the constitutional soundness of humanity. Between normal human nature and a being like Claggart there is a
gap, a "deadly space between." The sailors instinctively distrust
him and are repelled by him. Whereas to Billy they respond spon-
taneously. They are drawn together around him as around a bonfire on a cold day and are stirred to acts of good nature by his
cordial influence.

2

The mind of man is under a tragic necessity to grasp an ideal of life and, concurrently, by following the implications of things as they are, in the interest of truth, to see them as far less fair than they appear and as affording far less security than they appear to offer. That, of course, was what happened to Pierre. Under Isabel's influence he spurned the actual and possible for his ideal of the truthful and virtuous life. At the same time, the world as he had known it, so sure and solid in appearance, seemed to dissolve in fathomless mysteries and terrifying ambiguities. Pierre's experience was Melville's, who reached the conclusion that life is illusory and truth which destroys illusions, also destroys life; in the impulses of human growth the seed of death is planted. It has been affirmed that in identifying himself with his youthful hero, Melville reverted to adolescence. I would not altogether deny that this was so. On the other hand, it cannot be gainsaid that it is implicit in the mature mind to be aware, on one hand, of the discrepancy between the ideal and the actual and, on the other, between the appearance of things and the reality. His realization of these discrepancies was of the substance of Shakespeare's thought in *Hamlet* and *King Lear* and, it would seem certain, throughout the period of his life which produced his greatest tragedies along with such things as *Troilus and Cressida* and *Measure for Measure*. Moreover, wonderful as is Shakespeare's command of objectivity, it is impossible not to feel, in the works which I have just named, the strain on Shakespeare of these realizations. With a little less command, Shakespeare might have turned against life, "the thing itself," just as Melville turned against it in *Pierre*. As it is, Shakespeare betrays a distinct revulsion against no less a principle of life than sexual desire, which is far more than a moral condemnation on his part of sexual promiscuity. Melville did not have at hand, like Shakespeare, an artistic tradition and the artistic conventions for the objective representation of life. Besides, there was that in his inheritance, what I have called his radical Protestantism, which always threatened to turn him (as it did in *Pierre*) against the means as well as the substance of such representation. A cynical generation may identify Melville's radical Protestantism with arrested development. But unless one is prepared to maintain that strong feelings have no place in man's speculations on what it is only human to speculate upon—that a man should think not as a man but as a machine—then one cannot dismiss Melville as an idiosyncrasy of the past, whose intensity is no longer intelligible, or as a case of retarded adolescence. Not at all: "For in all of us lodges the same fuel to light the same fire." Moreover, the sequel to the crisis provoked by Melville's idealism, as we find it in Melville's "acceptance" in *Billy Budd* shows his span of experience to have been typically human. Only the accentuation and timing are peculiar to him—as an individual, conditioned by his inheritance and the time and country in which he lived. In *Billy Budd* we see a mind stabilizing itself on a lower level than that at which it had aimed before, the possible and the actual instead of the impossible ideal.

3

The character of Melville's prose in *Billy Budd*, expositive rather than declamatory, and matter-of-fact rather than nervously incisive, —as it is in parts of *Pierre*,—is in keeping with the idea of "acceptance." Yet there is, in this last book, an element of present and lyrical experience which the word "acceptance" is inadequate to convey. It stems from the stories written immediately after *Pierre* and is the final and most rare flowering of what lay behind Melville's reserve in these stories. His reserve there, in which we first discern the element of silence in Melville's later writings, wears an expression which we have all seen in human faces, mostly in those of adolescents and old people, from which we barely guess that they have some primary business of their own which they must be about, of growth and reconciliation, of renunciation and repair, which requires inviolable silence and privacy and, in the side toward themselves, the protection of shadowy recesses of being against the "infinite wakefulness" which threatens in the conscious soul. "All profound things and emotions of things," Melville had written, "are preceded and attended by Silence. What a Silence is that with which the pale bride precedes the responsive 'I will,' to the priest's solemn question, 'Wilt thou have this man for thy husband?' In silence, too, the wedded hands are clasped. Yea, in silence the child Christ was born into the world. Silence is the general consecration of the universe. Silence is the invisible laying on of the Divine Pontiff's hands upon the world. Silence is at once the most harmless and the most awful thing in all nature. It speaks of the Reserved Forces of Fate. Silence is the only Voice of our God." In *Pierre*, where Melville wrote these words, the silence of the voice of God is rendered with terrible consequences. What else there is of silence in this book, as that of Pierre's adolescence and his adolescent love for Lucy, is like the deadly calm at sea before the fatal storm. The silence I speak of in Melville's later writings has quite other connotations. It recalls (but with no echo of the irony which reechoes the words when we go back to them at once after finishing the book) the silence described on the first page of *Pierre*, of "strange summer mornings in the country" when "all nature, as if suddenly become conscious of her own profound mystery, and feeling no refuge from it but silence, sinks into this wonderful and indescribable repose." It speaks, this silence, in Melville's last writings, not of "the Reserved Forces of Fate," but of life's own inalienable and indestructible resources.

Billy Budd is a bloom from the same root as Melville's late flower poems which, in the last year of his life, he dedicated to his wife, reminding her of the flowers which he used to bring her from the meadows above "Arrowhead,"—"that farmhouse, long ago shorn by the urbane barbarian succeeding us in the proprietorship." Now he presents her with "these 'Weeds and Wildings,' thriftless children of quite another and yet later spontaneous aftergrowth." He regards the flowers which he described in these poems, with the same open-mindedness with which he regards his young hero in *Billy Budd*. This perennial growth of earthly loveliness, may it not be the symbol of resurrection into life eternal? These roses of earthly bloom, do they not prefigure Dante's Rose of Paradise? It may be. But in any case, in the patent fact that such loveliness can be at all, there is cause for deep and serene rejoicing. In *Billy Budd* Melville faced the tragic necessities of life. But that life could produce such warmth and radiance as glowed in Billy's heart, which could call forth something of its own warmth and radiance in the most callous and hard-hearted and melt down the barriers between worldly superiority and inferiority; that life has within itself such fuel to light such a glorious flame—this is felt as more than equal compensation for the tragic necessities that human life is under.

4

Once more the parallel between Melville and Shakespeare comes to the front. For *Billy Budd* stands in the same light to *Moby Dick* and *Pierre* that Shakespeare's last plays—*Pericles, The Winter's Tale, Cymbeline* and *The Tempest*—stand to the great tragedies. Of Shakespeare in these plays it is often said, as of Melville in *Billy Budd*, that he came to accept life. But if there is any basis for the remark in Shakespeare's case, then, as in Melville's, the word "acceptance" is inadequate. It is too blunt and too passive. In its place I would use the combination of words, recognition, restoration and return. Marina is restored to her father in *Pericles*, Posthumus, in *Cymbeline*, returns from banishment to his native land, and his wife, Imogen, is restored to him as he to her. Perdita's identity is recognized in *The Winter's Tale*; she is restored to her mother, as her mother is restored to her husband, and her husband to his own better nature. In *The Tempest*, Alonzo and Ferdinand, father and son, are returned to one another after each had thought the other drowned. Ariel is restored to freedom and Prospero to his dukedom. There is Miranda's recognition of the nature she shares with, and glorifies in others; "How beauteous mankind is! O brave new world that has such people in't." "In one voyage," says old Gonzalo, summing up, young Ferdinand found a wife—

> *Where he himself was lost; Prospero his dukedom*
> *In a poor isle; and all of us ourselves,*
> *When no man was his own.*

What I have in mind to convey by the words recognition, restoration and return in Shakespeare's last plays is independent of the turns the stories take. It is an element of present and lyrical experience which is of Shakespeare himself. It is felt as constantly moulding the stories to its own likeness: and it shows otherwise in the quality of Shakespeare's response to life, centering on his heroines the quality of thrilling tenderness—of wonder and surprise intermingled with tenderest recognition. This element of present experience in Shakespeare's last plays has been distilled by a modern poet from *Pericles*, the one play among them which foreshadows all the elements of the others. T. S. Eliot's rhythms will convey it better than any analysis which I can find words for:

What seas what shores what grey rocks and what islands
What water lapping the bow
And scent of pine and the woodthrush singing through the fog
What images return
O my daughter . . .

What is this face, less clear and clearer
The pulse in the arm, less strong and stronger—
Given or lent? more distant than stars and nearer than the eye . .

This form, this face, this life
Living to live in a world of time beyond me; let me
Resign my life for this life, my speech for that unspoken,
The awakened, lips parted, the hope, the new ships.

What seas what shores what granite islands towards my timbers
And woodthrush calling through the fog
My daughter.

The final and ever so poignant flowering of Herman Melville, which is the element of present lyrical experience in *Billy Budd*, is the same essentially as Shakespeare's in his last play. The hero was drawn from Melville's friend, Jack Chase, the Jack Chase of *White Jacket*, but in essence he derives from still earlier and less trammeled sources. In *Omoo*, Melville had described Tahiti. "Such enchantment," he had written, "breathes over the whole, that it seems a fairy world, all fresh and blooming from the hand of the Creator." Almost half a century after Melville had been in the South Seas, writing his last book, he described his hero as like a Tahitian, but as the Tahitians were before civilization had got its dirty paws on them. The story, he remarked, was "not unwarranted by what happens in this incongruous world of ours." What happens in the book apart from the story was warranted by Melville's final insight into the nature of life. In *Billy Budd*, in the person of his hero, of whom he wrote, "the bonfire in his heart made luminous the rose-tan in his cheek," who combined a maidenly grace with great masculine strength, to whom song was more native than speech, in whom there is the same pristine quality, the same immediacy to meadows and gardens and the cycle of the seasons as there is in Shakespeare's last heroines—in *Billy Budd* Melville returned to the contemplation of life as he had painted it in *Typee*. This much is obvious. It is obvious on second sight that there was more to this than wilful or sentimental retrospection. The same enchantment of life which he had thrilled to in his first book, he has returned to by force of insight in his last, and recognized it anew. Now, however, it is not localized; it is not identified as lying afar off,

Where Eden, isled, empurpled glows
In old Mendanna's sea.

Such is the force of Melville's final insight that the innocence and loveliness and joy of life is represented on board a man-of-war, Melville's own symbol for the world in its most opposite aspects to life as he had identified it with Typee valley. True, this innocence suffers a shameful death at the hands of this man-of-war world. Yet, in Billy's life there is more promise of salvation for the world than there is of damnation in his death. And Melville has partaken of its salvation. His intellectual passion spent, and illuminated by his insight of a mind which by accepting its limitations has transcended them and has found within itself, at its own mysterious centre, a calm not to be found elsewhere, Melville has been restored to the radiant visage of life, whose shining secret is, it has its salvation in its own keeping.

Index